Income Tax – Trading and Property Income 2003/2004

The CCH Practitioner's Guidance Tax Pack

Capital Gains Tax 2003/2004 by Michelle Gilbert
Corporation Tax 2003/2004 by Sue Whiting
Income Tax 2003/2004 by Roger Barnard
Income Tax – Employment and Related Income 2003/2004 by Roger Barnard
Income Tax – Trading and Property Income 2003/2004 by Roger Barnard
National Insurance Contributions 2003/2004 by David Heaton
Value Added Tax 2003/2004 by Mark Mckaig

Income Tax – Trading and Property Income 2003/2004

Roger Barnard LLB, LLM, FCA, FTII

TENON

145 London Road
Kingston upon Thames
Surrey
KT2 6SR
Tel: +44(0) 870 241 5719
Fax: +44(0) 870 247 1184
E-mail: customerservices@cch.co.uk
Website: www.cch.co.uk

British Library Cataloguing-in-Publication Data

A catalogue record for this book is available from the British Library.

Typeset in the United Kingdom by RefineCatch Ltd, Bungay, Suffolk
Printed by Clays Ltd, St Ives plc

Preface

This book is part of a set of companion volumes. In previous years, there was one work on income tax but for this and future years income tax has been divided into the topic covered here and a separate book on employment and related income.

Roger Barnard, the author has worked for over 30 years as a tax practitioner in a medium-sized firm. He is a chartered accountant and also a Fellow of The Chartered Institute of Taxation. He also has been involved for many years with the examinations of the Chartered Institute of Taxation including the setting of examination papers and marking scripts. He also holds the Advanced Financial Planning Certificate.

As before the text is designed to explain the principles involved, particularly aiming at the general practitioner. The text is deliberately selective, covering those topics that are most likely to be of interest to the busy practitioner. Where appropriate, reference has been made to less common areas where detailed knowledge can be obtained in more specialised works. Based on experience, though, the author firmly believes that there is no real substitute for reading the source material such as statutes and cases.

Unlike employment taxation, there were relatively few changes applying to this book, although generally there is no let up in the ever-changing nature of taxation. The topics here are in the rewrite pipeline, other than capital allowances, which were the subject of the first rewrite legislation. The practitioner must also be clear on the growing differences in the treatment of trading income between income tax and corporation tax, such as intangible assets and research and development expenditure.

The text is written for the tax year 2003/2004 and so it must be borne in mind that for earlier years different rules may have applied, to which reference should be made where appropriate. The statute law is based as at 1 September 2003 after the granting of Royal Assent to the Finance Act 2003. Case law is also stated as at the same date.

Roger Barnard LLB, LLM, FCA, FTII
September 2003

Contents

Abbreviations

ACT	advance corporation tax
AVC	additional voluntary contribution
CAA 1990	Capital Allowances Act 1990
EC	European Community
EIS	Enterprise Investment Scheme
ESC	Extra-Statutory Concession
EU	European Union
F(No2) A 1997	Finance (No2) Act 1997
FA 1997	Finance Act 1997
FSAVC	free standing additional voluntary contribution
FRSSE	Financial Reporting Standard for Smaller Entities
FURBS	funded unapproved retirement benefit scheme
ICTA 1988	Income and Corporation Taxes Act 1988
IR	Inland Revenue
ISA	individual savings account
MIRAS	mortgage interest relief at source
PAYE	pay as you earn
PEP	personal equity plan
PSO	Pensions Scheme Office
QBD	Queen's Bench Division
SCD	Special Commissioners' Decisions
SCO	Special Compliance Office
SP	Statement of Practice
SSAP	Statement of Standard Accounting Practice
STC	Simon's Tax Cases
TC	Tax Cases
TCGA 1992	Taxation of Chargeable Gains Act 1992
TESSA	tax-exempt special savings account
TMA 1970	Tax Management Act 1970
VCT	venture capital trust

Table of cases

(References are to paragraph)

Table of statutes

(Statutes are in chronological order. References are to paragraph)

Table of statutory instruments

1 Introduction

1.1 Scope of this book

The scope of this book is to explain the taxation of income from trades, professions and vocations. It also deals with income from property, particularly given that the determination of income assessable under Schedule A (or Schedule D Case V relating to overseas property) follows largely the same rules as Schedule D Cases I and II for trades, professions and vocations. There is also some link with Schedule D Case VI and so that is also dealt with in this book, including the complex anti-avoidance provisions in relation to land in s776 ICTA 1988.

The Income and Corporation Taxes Act 1988 remains the primary statutory source for income covered in this book, although many of these rules were added by subsequent Finance Acts, particularly with the introduction of self-assessment in 1996/97. As most practitioners will be aware our tax law is currently being rewritten. The first Act covered by this was the Capital Allowances Act 2001, which is dealt with in Chapter 5. CAA 2001 is primarily concerned with trades, professions and vocations but also gives relief for allowances against property income and employment income. Eventually, all our tax law will have been rewritten. A rewrite is as far it goes as no attempt has been made to rethink the entire structure of the tax system. This could perhaps have been achieved by a simple consolidation, to bring all the law together in one place and in a more organised way, but the idea is to make the law simpler to read by rewriting it. Experience so far suggests that the law is no simpler. Indeed, in one or two instances the old law is clearer. It is difficult to see how the complexities can be made crystal clear by what appear to be stylistic changes.

The remainder of this chapter sets out a summary of the basic principles with particular regard to the interpretation of tax statutes. Those principles continue to apply notwithstanding the rewrite although hopefully with fewer semantic difficulties. Nevertheless, as the cases before the courts demonstrate, many of the problems relate to the complications of the law to a given set of facts. A rewrite can do nothing about that, which could only be achieved by a fundamental review of the tax system to produce greater consistency.

1.2   Sources of tax law

1.2.1   Primary sources

Many areas of law have been created by judges and then later supplemented and altered by statute. Tax law has no existence other than through the authority of Parliament expressed in one of its statutes. It is the language of an Act of Parliament that must be interpreted by judges in the application to the facts of a given situation. The interpretation of statutes is dealt with in more detail below but essentially the courts do not have any discretion. If the words of a statute are clear beyond doubt they must be applied by a court, subject to the possibility nowadays of not contravening European law (but rarely so in income tax matters). The Human Rights Act 1998 is now in operation and is being used to challenge tax legislation. In *King* v *Walden* [2001] STC 822, the High Court held that the imposition of penalties for fraudulent or negligent conduct is criminal for the purposes of human rights law.

As mentioned above the main statute dealing with the subject matter of this book is the Income and Corporation Taxes Act 1988. This is the consolidation of previous Acts. There is a presumption that mere consolidation does not alter the law if there is some other interpretation that can be placed on the words used by the drafter. Since 1988, there has been the usual procession of Finance Acts, and not necessarily confined to one a year. Every year there is at least one budget, currently in the spring, and the Finance Act is usually enacted towards the end of July.

The Finance Acts have become very long and even then there is a modern trend to delegate the drafting of detailed rules. A statutory instrument cannot go beyond the powers of the enabling legislation, otherwise it would offend the *ultra vires* principle. A statutory instrument is as much a source of law as a statute. In practice, statutory instruments do not usually come under the same level of scrutiny as a statute, but that does not have any bearing on their effectiveness if not *ultra vires*.

Our law is also now subject to the EC Treaty and Directives and Regulations made thereunder. There are no treaty provisions having a direct impact on income tax at the present time. Indirectly, though, taxation laws could be affected by other principles. Examples are Article 6 of the Treaty, which prevents discrimination on grounds of nationality, and Article 52, which provides for the abolition by progressive stages of any restriction of the freedom of the establishment of nationals of one Member State in the territory of another Member State.

1.2.2 Secondary sources

Income tax is under the overall supervision of the Inland Revenue. The Revenue must act according to law but it is firmly decided that in doing so they can exercise discretion. One particular example is the issue of extra-statutory concessions. These are published, subject to the caveat that they are not likely to be available to the taxpayer in a case of tax avoidance. They recognise the imperfections that can arise in the tax system, where particular circumstances were not in the mind of the draftsman in preparing the legislation.

Having published a concession, the Revenue must act fairly and be even-handed between taxpayers. They must not, on a whim, withhold the application of a concession, otherwise there could be a legal challenge.

In addition to concessions, the Revenue also publish statements of practice. These seek to set down the Revenue's interpretation of the law. Again, the Revenue should not deviate from their published interpretation, although the application to the facts of a case is a different matter. In *R v IRC ex parte Kaye* [1992] STC 581, the taxpayer argued that the Revenue's views set out in a statement of practice should be applied to a transaction carried out before publication, as if it had been dealt with in such a way to produce a smaller liability to tax. The suggestion that the Revenue were in breach of their obligation of fairness was firmly rejected by the Court. There had been no abuse of power and the consequence of accepting the taxpayer's argument could have prevented the Revenue issuing any statements of practice in the future, for fear of similar action.

Other materials include the regular *Tax Bulletins*, in which the Revenue set out their views on particular matters, including the application of tax law to circumstances that have actually arisen in practice. These are very helpful and relevant extracts are referred to in various chapters. The Revenue have published their manuals, although parts have been excluded where not appropriate for publication. These all help in understanding how the Revenue interpret and apply the law, but are always subject in turn to challenge in the courts. In most cases, the tax at stake is not sufficient to challenge the official view of the Revenue if that view is persisted in. Helpful as these publications are, they have also added in many ways to the burden of the practitioner in identifying all the relevant material in advising clients. Without doubt, information technology aids research but only, perhaps, if used as a tool rather than the decision-making process itself.

Ultimately, the practitioner must advise a client based on the facts in a case, with knowledge of the relevant law and practice. Added to that must be an understanding of the particular client, general business knowledge and a touch of common sense.

1.3   Challenging the Inland Revenue

Inevitably, an inspector of taxes or some other officer of the Revenue will challenge the approach taken in deciding how much, or when, tax should be charged. In most cases, agreement is reached, usually after protracted correspondence. Ultimately, a dispute may be compromised without either side conceding the principle. The client may wonder why this could not have been achieved much earlier, and at less cost, except that early capitulation often results in a higher tax liability.

If neither side can agree, the first stop is either the Special or General Commissioners. The Commissioners are the judges of fact. They hear the evidence of the taxpayer and the Revenue. The law is argued and it is then left to the Commissioners to determine what the law is and apply it to the facts in hand. Either side is entitled to appeal to the High Court. Under ss56 and 56A TMA 1970 the appeal to the High Court must be on a point of law. The Court cannot rehear the matter but must accept the facts found by the Commissioners. The Special Commissioners set out their findings of fact in their written decision. Where the appeal is from the General Commissioners the aggrieved party can, within 30 days of the final determination, require the Commissioners to set out the facts and determination under the case stated procedure (reg 20 General Commissioners (Jurisdiction and Procedure) Regulations 1994 SI 1994/1812). If the case stated is deficient the Court has the power to send the matter back to the General Commissioners for a further finding of fact or amendment if required. The Court can only allow an appeal against the Commissioners' decision if there is an error of law on its face or if the decision is such that no reasonable body of Commissioners could have come to the conclusion based on the evidence. The House of Lords' decision in *Edwards* v *Bairstow and Harrison* (1955) 36 TC 207 is the clear authority that a judge cannot simply substitute his own view if the conclusion of the Commissioners is a possible one based on the facts. For example, in the case of a sale of land, one person might see this as trading and another as a capital transaction. If both views are tenable, the decision of the Commissioners could not be reversed by the courts. There are many instances where a judge has indicated that, had he been a Commissioner, he may not have come to the same conclusion, but at the same time recognises that he did not hear the evidence. The Court of Appeal restored the Special Commissioners' decision that the receipt of sub-underwriting commissions did not amount to trading in *Clarke* v *British Telecom Pension Scheme Trustees* [2000] STC 222. As Robert Walker LJ put it, the case fell within 'no man's land'. In that situation the courts cannot interfere with the Commissioners' decision. In turn, either side can appeal to the Court of Appeal and ultimately to the House of Lords. However, leave must be given for an appeal to the House of Lords under s1 Administration of Justice (Appeals) Act 1934. There is a leap-frog procedure to circumvent the Court of Appeal, but rarely used in taxation law.

The procedure described above should normally be the only way in which an appeal can be made to the courts. In some cases, applications are made for judicial review, which avoids the initial hearing before the Commissioners. This procedure is appropriate where, for example, there is a challenge along the lines of the *Kaye* case, where there is an alleged abuse of power. An attempt to circumvent the Commissioners by an application for judicial review was rejected in *R* v *IRC ex parte Caglar* [1995] STC 741. An application for judicial review should only be used in exceptional circumstances and not where there is an appropriate statutory appeal procedure.

Taxpayers can complain to the Adjudicator if the Revenue have mis-handled their affairs. Complainants dissatisfied with the Adjudicator's decision can ask a Member of Parliament to refer their complaint to the Parliamentary Ombudsman.

1.4   Interpretation of tax statutes

1.4.1   General principles

There are no principles of common law or equity in taxation, simply the need to interpret the tax statutes. Decisions of the courts are binding in the same way as other decisions. Thus, all lower courts and tribunals must follow decisions of the House of Lords and the High

Court and Commissioners the decisions of the Court of Appeal. However, the Court of Appeal is not bound by its own decisions if there are conflicting decisions, or an important matter was clearly overlooked. The High Court is not bound by other High Court decisions and neither do the Commissioners need to take account of other decisions of either the General or Special Commissioners. Indeed, not all of the decisions of the Special Commissioners are published. There is no means of publishing General Commissioners' decisions. There has recently been an instance of two bodies of Special Commissioners coming to the opposite conclusion on similar facts, until the matter was ultimately resolved by the courts.

In interpreting statutes and statutory instruments, tax is no different to other areas of law. There is a substantial body of tax law of some complexity, and its interpretation is often up for consideration by the courts. Historically, there are three 'rules' adopted by the courts; being the literal, golden and mischief rules. The literal rule holds simply that the words used should be given their ordinary and natural meaning. If there is more than one meaning, the golden rule states that a literal construction should be sacrificed in favour of avoiding an absurdity. If neither of these rules helps, the court can consider the mischief behind the statute. The Interpretation Act 1978 must also be referred to on detailed matters of interpretation. For example, this requires gender to be read as both masculine and feminine unless the context clearly means otherwise and that the singular includes the plural. Schedule 1 to that Act also defines certain expressions such as 'land', so as to include buildings on land unless the contrary intention appears. Another example, particularly relevant in deciding whether the Revenue have met time limits in serving enquiry notices into a self-assessment return, is s7, which applies where any Act of Parliament authorises or requires any document to be served by post.

Whatever the rules of interpretation developed by the courts over the years, in the end all a court is trying to do is determine the intention of Parliament from the words that have been used. Simply interpreting particular words is not sufficient. As has been said, a word is known by the company it keeps and so it is necessary to consider the surrounding provisions and the principles that can be established. However, if there is really only one interpretation, that must prevail even though the result may appear arbitrary. In practice, judges nowadays apply a more purposeful approach to the interpretation of statutes, particularly with the influence of European law. They seek wherever possible to make sense of the statutory provisions, to the extent, sometimes, that they appear to add words. As mentioned, our tax law is currently the subject of a major re-write to try and make it clearer but it will be some time before this project is completed. The proof of the pudding must await the practical application of the new style. So far, the only rewrite affecting this book is the Capital Allowances Act 2001, apart from consequential changes caused by the Income Tax (Earnings and Pensions) Act 2003.

One particular issue that was resolved recently on statutory interpretation is the extent to which external materials can be used in determining the intention of Parliament. The tax case of *Pepper* v *Hart* (1992) 65 TC 421 made a major change to the then practice. The House of Lords held that in appropriate cases resort could be had to *Hansard*, where a statement in Parliament can, with relative ease, put a matter beyond doubt. The use of *Hansard*, though, is circumscribed. In his speech, Lord Browne-Wilkinson said that the relaxation should only be permitted where:

'a   Legislation is ambiguous or obscure, or leads to an absurdity;

b   The material relied on consists of one of more statements by a minister or other promoter of the Bill together if necessary with such other Parliamentary material as is necessary to understand such statements and their effect;

c   The statements relied upon are clear.'

There is concern that the use of *Hansard* should not become the rule in every case but only when the words used are obscure or ambiguous. This begs the question as to when something is obscure. In practice, the use of *Hansard* is likely to be of help in construing anti-avoidance legislation where a particular scheme or arrangement is under attack. There have certainly been past instances where a clear statement has been made by a Minister but, without access to *Hansard*, a court has held that the words used could tax the very situation the Minister indicated was not under attack.

There are other more detailed rules that have been developed as an aid to interpretation, such as the *ejusdem generis* rule. This means that a general word following particular words should normally be construed as being of the same class as those specially mentioned. Another rule states that specifying a member of a particular class implicitly excludes others. These are not rigid rules and ultimately they are no more than practical aids to interpretation. Other principles relevant to taxation are that retrospective legislation requires particularly clear words and that in cases of doubt a taxing statute should be interpreted in favour of the taxpayer. There is nothing to stop Parliament making something retrospective by sufficiently clear words.

There is no magic in interpreting statutes, simply an understanding of the basic principles and the application of educated common sense.

1.4.2 The substance of transactions

The 1970s saw an expanding business in tax avoidance schemes. These were schemes constructed purely to avoid tax without any commercial purpose. Quite often, money went round in a circle and a claim made for some loss or deductible payment. These types of scheme were dealt a heavy blow by the important House of Lords' decision in *WT Ramsay Ltd* v *IRC* (1981) 55 TC 324. The approach in that case was supplemented by later decisions such as *Furniss* v *Dawson* [1984] STC 153 and the more recent House of Lords' decision in *IRC* v *McGuckian* (1997) 69 TC 1.

This approach has been labelled by the judges as no more than a principle of construing tax legislation. In applying the appropriate statutory provisions, the substance of the transaction should be identified, disregarding artificial steps in a composite transaction or series, or transactions inserted only for the purpose of seeking a tax advantage. This could perhaps be seen as little more than a judicial dislike of such schemes, at the other end of the spectrum to the Law Lords who found in favour of the taxpayer in the well-known case of *IRC* v *Duke of Westminster* (1936) 19 TC 490. As Lord Steyn states in his speech in the *McGuckian* case:

> 'During the last 30 years there has been a shift away from literalist to purposive methods of construction. Where there is no obvious meaning of a statutory provision the modern emphasis is on a contextual approach designed to identify the purpose of a statute and to give effect to it.'

In the *McGuckian* case, the Revenue, under what is now s739 ICTA 1988, attacked a transaction attempting to convert a dividend into a capital sum. There was in fact a specific anti-avoidance provision which would have caught the transaction in any event, but the Revenue were not fully aware of the facts until too late. It was held that the *Ramsay* principle applied nevertheless. In applying this principle, the assignment of the right to the dividend was disregarded, as it had no purpose other than as part of the avoidance scheme. Having ignored the assignment, the dividend retained its character as such and therefore became income assessable under s739. The following extract from the speech of Lord Brightman in *Furniss* v *Dawson* was approved as setting out the classic requirements for the application of this principle:

> 'First, there must be a pre-ordained series of transactions; or, if one likes, one single composite transaction. This composite transaction may or may not include the achievement of a legitimate commercial (ie business) end ... Secondly, there must be steps inserted which have no commercial (business) purpose apart from the avoidance of a liability to tax – not 'no business effect'. If those two ingredients exist, the inserted steps are to be disregarded for fiscal purposes. The court must then look at the end result. Precisely how the end result will be taxed will depend on the terms of the taxing statute sought to be applied.'

Other extracts from speeches in the *McGuckian* case demonstrate how far the courts have moved in the interpretation of tax statutes. In commenting on the principle derived from the line of cases beginning with *Ramsay*, Lord Cooke of Thorndon said:

> 'Perhaps more helpfully, however, it may be recognised as an application to taxing Acts of the general approach to statutory interpretation whereby, in determining the natural meaning of particular expressions in their context, weight is given to the purpose and spirit of the legislation.'

The most recent case in this area is the House of Lords' decision in *MacNiven* v *Westmoreland Investments Ltd* [2001] STC 237, in which the Revenue argued that the *Ramsay* line of cases should apply to treat interest as not paid for corporation tax purposes, because there was an arrangement involving a borrowing from the recipient of that interest (which was an exempt pension scheme). The basis of the House of Lords' decision is that the *Ramsay* type of cases are simply examples of instances where the courts have interpreted the views of a particular word or phrase in a taxing statute, applying a purposive construction. On the facts, the word 'paid' for the purposes of the particular provision in hand was to be interpreted by applying its normal legal meaning and in that sense the interest had been paid. If anything, this decision muddies the water. A case by case approach is required and it is quite clear that the Revenue cannot simply apply the *Ramsay* principle where there is tax avoidance. Matters before a court are decided by judges, who cannot in practice disregard their own background and personality. The constitution of the House of Lords in the cases mentioned has been quite different throughout and will inevitably change again as these principles are worked out case by case.

For practical purposes, this might be summarised simply as requiring that there should always be some commercial, financial (other than tax saving) or personal purpose in a transaction, such that it might have been carried out irrespective of a tax benefit. A very broad distinction has been drawn between tax mitigation and unacceptable tax avoidance schemes. These terms are not defined. Tax mitigation is usually seen as something which is contemplated by Parliament in enacting a statute, whereas an outright avoidance scheme is seeking an advantage which was clearly not intended. The identification of these elephantine qualities is not quite so easy in practice. It might also be observed that most clients are not well served by over complicated and uncertain arrangements. Some clients, certainly in the minority, are attracted by the high risk strategy of aggressive avoidance arrangements. For most, the fear of a long, drawn out argument, with the potential for a detailed investigation, far outweighs any possible saving in taxation.

1.5   Inland Revenue rulings

There are certain statutory provisions under which a taxpayer can force the Revenue to come to a decision on whether or not the taxpayer is subject to tax. An example is s707 ICTA 1988 in connection with transactions in securities. However, there are relatively few formal clearance procedures. The Revenue, in accordance with Code of Practice 10, will give post-transaction rulings.

The Revenue are not bound to express a view on any pre-transaction circumstances put to them. They could simply decline to answer, although in practice they may be prepared to give an opinion. This could be a response to a general enquiry on the application of the law to circumstances or on particular facts when a clear ruling is required. A formalised procedure for advance rulings was dropped after consultation.

Where the Revenue are prepared to give a ruling, anyone wishing to rely upon that must bear in mind the House of Lords' decision in *Matrix-Securities Ltd* v *IRC* [1994] STC 272. In that case, the Revenue withdrew an advance clearance of an arrangement. On an application for judicial review, it was held that this did not amount to an abuse of power. In withdrawing the clearance, the Revenue then proceeded to act on their interpretation of the strict law. The initial clearance had been given by an inspector of taxes without reference to a specialist division of the Revenue. This was a tax avoidance scheme and clearance was withdrawn before acted upon. It was made clear that, in order to rely upon an advance clearance, the taxpayer must make a full disclosure of the relevant circumstances. If the taxpayer is aware that a clearance must be obtained in a particular way, such as by reference to head office, then this cannot be ignored. Although the case dealt with a complex avoidance scheme, the principle of full disclosure applies to rulings at any level from the Revenue, if reliance is to be had at a later date.

1.6 The taxpayer, the practitioner and the Revenue

1.6.1 Relationship between practitioner and taxpayer

The practitioner is a professional person in relation to his client, the taxpayer, but at the same time there is a business relationship. The practitioner is the agent of the client in dealing with taxation matters, which among other things means that the client, as principal, has a right to call for any correspondence with the Revenue.

The practitioner and his client enter into a contractual relationship and in the event of a dispute it may be essential to establish the terms of that contract. Even if it did nothing else, the Financial Services Act 1986 caused letters of engagement to be issued, which set out in writing the terms agreed. Care must be taken in preparing model letters and in altering them to meet particular circumstances. Specific tax advice may require a separate letter of engagement, as a general one is unlikely to cover the relevant aspects. If a practitioner fails to do something which is either explicitly or implicitly within the contractual terms, he could be liable for breach of contract.

If a practitioner fails to carry out his instructions, in not meeting the required standard of care, he could be liable in negligence if not for breach of contract. It may be possible to exclude liability or cap it to an agreed figure, although the Unfair Contract Terms Act 1977 might nullify such exempting or limiting provisions unless considered reasonable. A practitioner may agree to carry out professional services but does not possess the relevant skills. If everything is left to implication, there is a great danger that, if something goes wrong, the client will argue that those special skills were part of the arrangement. Solicitors in *Hurlingham Estates Ltd* v *Wilde & Partners* [1997] STC 627 were sued for breach of their contractual duty of care and the tort of negligence. A property transaction was carried out in such a way that a tax charge arose on part of a premium under s34 ICTA 1988. This charge could have been avoided if the transaction had been structured differently. The conveyancing solicitor had minimal knowledge of tax law and argued that there was a limit on his duties, to exclude taxation advice. The firm was held liable for damages. Any agreement to exclude liability for taxation matters should have been clear and unambiguous. Had the client known he could have sought specialist tax advice or instructed other solicitors for the entire transaction.

1.6.2 Relationship with the Revenue

As mentioned above, the practitioner is the agent of his client in dealing with taxation matters. Depending upon the precise terms of engagement, the practitioner will assist clients in meeting their tax obligations and advise on particular matters from time to time. The practitioner can only advise on the basis of the relevant law, giving sufficient caveats where a matter is not certain. There may be a need to take the opinion of tax counsel and practitioners have, for some years now, had direct access to counsel, without the need to instruct through a solicitor. Where the amounts involved are sufficiently large, this should give some protection to the practitioner, not only against an action by his client but also if the Revenue should suggest that insufficient tax has been paid and the practitioner has been at fault somewhere. To get the best out of counsel, the instructions should be drafted carefully. The full facts must be given together with copies of supporting documents. It is also helpful if the practitioner can, as far as possible, give his provisional views on the relevant law and raise particular questions with counsel for consideration. A conference is often the most productive means of dealing with the matter, followed by either a full opinion of counsel or a note that counsel settles. Simply throwing a file at counsel is not good value for money.

Guidelines have been produced by the Institute of Chartered Accountants in England and Wales in conjunction with the Chartered Institute of Taxation on *Professional Conduct in Relation to Taxation*. These contain useful information, having been reviewed by the Revenue.

A not uncommon situation is the potential for difference of opinion between a practitioner and his client on what should be disclosed to the Revenue. This applies not only to the information in a tax return, for example, but also the procedure if an error is discovered after submission. The last thing a practitioner wants is any suggestion from the Revenue that he has been implicated in something fraudulent. A relatively simple example is where a client receives an over repayment of tax and this is known both by him and the practitioner. Unless the difference is so trivial that it can be disregarded, the client should be encouraged to advise the Revenue of the error. If consent is not forthcoming, the practitioner should consider carefully his position and take separate legal advice as appropriate.

Tax tip

The guidelines make particular mention of engagement letters. A statement on the following lines is recommended for inclusion in a letter of engagement:

'We will observe the ethical guidelines of our professional Institute and accept instructions to act for you on the basis that we will act in accordance with those guidelines. In particular you give us authority to correct Inland Revenue errors.'

The inclusion of this simple paragraph may resolve many practical issues. It is a fact that the Revenue do consider prosecutions and particularly so when professional advisers are involved. The Theft Act 1968 contains many offences potentially relevant to taxation, such as dishonestly retaining an over repayment of tax. There is also the common law offence of cheating the Revenue. This was the basis behind criminal charges in *R* v *Charlton and others* [1996] STC 1418. The Revenue were successful in prosecuting four professional individuals who had been involved with the implementation of a dishonest tax scheme or in concealing it from the Revenue. The arrangements involved interposing an off-shore company to purchase goods from the real supplier and resell them to the UK at a higher price. Schemes to evade UK tax were also the basis for a successful Revenue prosecution in *R* v *Dimsey* [2001] STC 1520 and *R* v *Allen* [2001] STC 1537. The sophistication of what appear to be tax avoidance (i.e., legal) schemes may be lost on a judge trained in criminal law and in directing a jury of lay people.

2 Trades, professions and vocations – meaning and related matters

2.1 The basic charging provisions

2.1.1 The main statutory provisions

Section 18(1) ICTA 1988 provides generally that tax is charged under Schedule D in respect of:

'(a) the annual profits or gains arising or accruing –
   (ii) to any person residing in the United Kingdom from any trade, profession or vocation, whether carried on in the United Kingdom or elsewhere.'

Section 18(3) then provides that Schedule D Case I applies to tax in respect of any trade carried on in the United Kingdom or elsewhere but not contained in Schedule A. Schedule D Case II applies to tax in respect of any profession or vocation not contained in any other Schedule.

There is one further important definition, contained in s832(1). This defines 'trade' as including 'every trade, manufacture, adventure or concern in the nature of trade'. This particular definition has been the subject of considerable litigation over many years. It is dealt with in more detail below.

2.1.2 Distinction between trades, professions and vocations

The distinction is largely historical but still remains. In most cases the distinction has no practical consequences. The FA 1998 removed one practical distinction, taking professions and vocations off the cash basis.

A remaining distinction is that the wide definition of trade is not extended to professions or vocations. Thus, there is no such thing as an adventure in the nature of a profession or vocation. If an individual is carrying on a profession, he is taxed under Case II. If he simply receives occasional receipts then strictly he should be assessed under Schedule D Case VI.

2.1.3   Trade as opposed to business

There is an important distinction between a trade and a business. The word 'business' is a global one, encompassing trading activities. It could also include other economic activities, such as property letting. As can be seen from Chapter 8, property letting is treated as a Schedule A business for income tax purposes. It is not, though, a trade in most circumstances.

The word 'trade' is of narrower meaning than 'business'. Every trade is a business but not every business is a trade.

2.1.4   Territorial limitations

The basic Schedule D Case I charging provision applies to a trade carried on in the UK or elsewhere. On the face of the matter, therefore, a trade carried on wholly outside the UK is also within the Case I charge.

However, in *Colquhoun* v *Brooks* (1889) 2 TC 490, the House of Lords placed limitations on the apparently wide meaning of these words. In that case, the taxpayer was UK resident and a partner in a firm carrying on a trade entirely in Australia. It was held that his share of the profit was properly assessable under Case V as a foreign possession and not Case I. At the time, this was particularly relevant because the remittance basis applied irrespective of domicile. As Lord Herschell put it:

> 'The Income Tax Acts . . . themselves impose a territorial limit, either that from which the taxable income is derived must be situated in the United Kingdom or the person whose income is to be taxed must be resident there.'

In a later case, *Ogilvie* v *Kitton* (1908) 5 TC 338, a UK sole trader owned a business in Canada, run by managers there. As a matter of fact, it was found that the taxpayer had the sole right of management and control. It was held that he could be assessed under Schedule D Case I rather than Case V, because he had the ability to control the trade, whether or not in practice he actually did so. An individual in that situation may have no need to interfere, but he has the right to do so if it moves off course. Indeed, the judge regarded it as impossible for a sole trader resident in this country to carry on a business wholly abroad, where he has exclusive power of control over it.

The distinction between Schedule D Cases I and V is particularly relevant where losses have been incurred. Losses arising from a Case V trade are more restricted in their use. Section 65(3) ICTA 1988 provides that the Schedule D Case I and II rules apply in determining the results of a Case V trade, profession or vocation, including the basis period rules.

2.2 Meaning of 'trade'

2.2.1 The badges of trade

Apart from the extended meaning of trade in s832, there is no further statutory guidance on what is a trade in given circumstances. It has been left to the Commissioners and the courts, on appeal, to determine whether a trade exists on given facts. Some of the cases are difficult to reconcile. This is an area where it is more difficult for either the taxpayer or the Revenue to appeal on a question of law. The Commissioners are the judges of fact and they have heard the evidence in particular circumstances. The evidence will produce an impression in their mind. Provided their conclusion is not inconsistent with the facts, it should be unassailable. In reading any of the cases, this point must be borne in mind. There may well have been nuances in a given case which influenced the Commissioners, but are not wholly apparent from the case stated.

A few of the many cases are mentioned below. A useful starting point is the report of the Royal Commission in 1955. Having reviewed the cases to date, it listed six 'badges of trade'. These badges of trade are helpful in reviewing the cases and sifting the relevant facts. However, they cannot be used simply as a checklist to decide whether or not a trade does exist. They are no more than guidance to be used with common sense. It is the overall impression which will usually decide a dispute.

There clearly does not need to be a continuing trade in the normal sense, as the extended definition can include something which has the characteristics of a trading venture. Moreover, anything of a commercial character can amount to a trade whether or not it involves the buying or selling of goods. In *Clarke* v *British Telecom Pension Scheme Trustees* [2000] STC 222 the Court of Appeal indicated that subunderwriting commissions were capable of being trading income, even though they restored the Special Commissioners' finding that on the facts of this particular case they were not trading receipts.

The six badges identified by the Royal Commission were:

- the subject matter of the realisation;
- the length of period of ownership;
- the frequency or number of similar transactions by the same person;
- supplementary work on or in connection with the property realised;
- the circumstances that were responsible for the realisation; and
- motive.

2.2.2   The badges in more detail

Subject matter

An asset may be purchased for the income it produces, its practical use or aesthetic value. Thus, land and stock market investments are often purchased to derive rents or dividends, as the case may be. An individual may purchase a motor car to transport him and a work of art to hang on his wall. The selling of such assets would not amount to trading, in the absence of other factors.

Equally, a garage business or fine arts dealer may purchase the car or work of art simply to sell at a profit. That profit is clearly of a trading nature. These examples are beyond doubt but in the middle ground there could be a situation where there is no established trade in the normal sense of the word. In that case, the frequency of the transactions (see below) would be particularly relevant.

On the other hand, there could be situations where the asset purchased is such that the only real inference from the facts is one of trading. For example, in *CIR* v *Fraser* (1942) 24 TC 498, a woodcutter bought whisky in bond for resale, which was sold two or three years later at a profit, owing to the scarcity of whisky on the outbreak of the Second World War. He did not take delivery and neither did he blend the whisky nor advertise it. He had no special knowledge of the whisky trade and the sales were through agents. The following extract from the judgment of the Lord President is a useful guide in this type of situation: ·

> 'But the purchaser of a large quantity of a commodity like whisky, greatly in excess of what could be used by himself, his family and

friends, a commodity which yields no pride of possession, which cannot be turned to account except by process of realisation, I can scarcely consider to be other than an adventurer in a transaction in the nature of a trade . . . an excursion into the sphere of trading for profit . . .'.

On the other hand, in the more recent case of *Salt* v *Chamberlain* (1979) 53 TC 143 the taxpayer claimed that he was trading on the stockmarket. Using his expertise in computer technology to forecast share movements, he carried out some 200 purchases and sales of stock in just over four years. He made a loss in one year and claimed to set this against his other income. Oliver J rejected his appeal against the Commissioners' decision that he was not trading. Stock Exchange transactions are, for an individual, usually an investment matter. This seemed to be behind the decision of the General Commissioners. Oliver J commented as follows:

'. . . given the totality of the background facts proved or admitted – the frequency of the transactions, the size of the operation and the supporting organisation – the issue was whether the Appellant in dealing against that background in stocks and shares (rather than for instance, sardines, real property or second hand cars) was carrying on a trade. And that, as it seems to me, is pre-eminently a question of fact.'

This illustrates again the importance of establishing all the relevant facts before the commissioners. Their decision can only be challenged on a question of law or if their conclusion cannot be justified on the facts they have found. This is highlighted further by the following extract from Oliver J's judgment:

'In particular, I doubt whether the question whether in any given case a person is or is not carrying on a trade is capable of solution by the application of a logical progression of propositions culled from decided cases. The question is, I think, one of overall impression.'

A type of asset which has frequently been before the courts is land, and its development. Land is worthy of separate consideration and so is dealt with in more detail later in this chapter.

Length of period of ownership

The general nature of a trading transaction is such that there is a relatively short interval between buying and selling an asset. The longer an asset is held the greater the chance that it is held as an investment, or at least not for trading purposes. However, in a given situation there may be particular reasons why an asset is sold. Thus, this can only be one factor and much may depend upon the subject matter, as certain types of investments tend to be bought and sold over a shorter period than others.

Frequency of similar transactions

There is no bar to a one off transaction constituting a trading transaction. This is the very essence of the definition of trade, which is an adventure or concern in the nature of trade. This is clearly capable of covering a single transaction. For example, in *CIR* v *Livingston* (1927) 11 TC 538 three individuals bought between them a cargo vessel with a view to converting it to a steam drifter. Extensive work was carried out and after three months it was sold at a profit. This was held to be a trading venture. In *Wisdom* v *Chamberlain* (1969) 45 TC 92, the purchase of gold bullion and its sale in the short term following a sudden increase in price, was held to amount to trading. In *Leach* v *Pogson* (1962) 40 TC 585, the taxpayer was held to be trading in driving schools, having started them up and transferred to companies at a profit. Harman J indicated that doing this once would probably not have been trading, but when done three or four times usually is.

More recently, in the *Clarke* v *British Telecom Pension Scheme* case mentioned in **2.2.1** above, the regular nature of the sub-underwriting arrangements did not of itself turn the activities into a trade. In that case Robert Walker LJ indicated that frequency cannot itself be decisive. An investor may change his investments frequently without the investments losing their character.

Supplementary work

The case of *CIR* v *Livingston* mentioned above is also an example of a situation where the work on the boat influenced the decision of the court. Thus, where an asset is purchased in such a state that it can only realistically be sold after carrying out work, and is sold on completion of those works, there is a clear inference of trading. However, if the initial intention had been to retain the asset on completion of the works, but intervening circumstances caused the sale, then those facts could rebut such an inference. Carrying out relatively minor operations in relation to an asset, simply to make it more saleable or to realise its best value, would not of itself amount to trading. The case of *Taylor* v *Good* under **2.3** on land illustrates this.

Circumstances of the realisation

A person could be compelled to sell an asset by a change in circumstances, such as a worsening financial position. The asset could well have been acquired to be held in the longer term but is sold after a short interval to pay debts which are unconnected with that transaction. If, though, monies are borrowed on a short-term basis to help purchase or improve the asset, this itself could be indicative of trading. In that situation, the evidence might suggest that the finance was only available for the short term on the assumption that the asset is sold to clear those borrowings. There could also be an outside influence, such as in *Taylor* v *Good*, where the taxpayer's wife's opinion of the property purchased was a determining factor on the disposal.

Motive

Most of the facts in any one case are either wholly objective or partly objective. The commissioners can form their own view as to whether or not there is a trade based on the facts as presented to them, such as the subject matter, the frequency and the time interval. However, in a finely balanced case, the subjective nature of the taxpayer's motive could be the critical point. A person's motive itself is a question of fact, best judged by the evidence of the taxpayer. However, if the external factors suggest trading, then the motive is not likely to be a defence. For example, in *British Legion* v *CIR* (1953) 35 TC 509, public dances were held with a view to building a local war memorial, and the balance to provide club rooms for ex-members of the armed forces. This was held to be trading, being run on reasonably commercial lines. It is suggested that at best, motive is a tiebreaker. There is recent support for this approach in *Clarke* v *British Telecom Pension Scheme Trustees*. Robert Walker LJ stated in his judgment that if the legal or commercial characteristics of a transaction point unequivocally to trading, the trader's subjective purpose or motive cannot change the character of the transactions. However, the character of the transaction may be ambiguous, to be resolved by reference to purpose or motivation.

2.3 Land

2.3.1 General comments

As mentioned above, there are many decided cases involving land. The very subject matter of land is wide ranging, covering not only bare land itself but land already developed, or about to be developed or redeveloped. Some acquire land to derive an income, such as rents, whereas others, such as a builder, might buy land to build houses on and then sell at a profit. The first case is clearly one of investment and the second is clearly one of trading.

It should also be borne in mind that until 1965 there was no capital gains tax, only an income tax charge on short-term gains. If a profit on the sale of land was not trading then it may not have been subject to any tax. This fact might just have influenced commissioners or a court, in marginal cases.

Nowadays, it is not obvious that a finding of investment is beneficial to a person. The rates of tax tend to be the same, whether income or capital gain but with an annual exemption and indexation up to April 1998. Following the changes to taper relief in FA 2000 and 2002, the capital gains tax treatment of business assets is now very favourable, especially where the two-year qualifying period of ownership test is used. A trading profit is, though, eligible as a basis for pension contributions. Moreover, it might be possible to deduct certain expenses which cannot be allowed for capital gains tax purposes, such as interest on the purchase or improvement of land. If a loss arises, a commercial trading loss can be set against other income whereas a capital loss can only be set against other capital gains. The practitioner is not infrequently in the position of arguing the opposite on not too dissimilar facts. Inspectors of taxes do likewise, as there are no conclusive ways of arriving at a clear decision in these situations.

2.3.2　Section 776 ICTA 1988

Even if a transaction in land is not trading under Schedule D Case I, it may nevertheless be treated as of an income nature under Schedule D Case VI, if s776 can apply. This is an anti-avoidance provision designed to protect the Revenue against convoluted land transactions. However, as business taper relief kicks in, there will be more of an incentive for the Revenue to raise a s776 argument if a Schedule D Case I attack cannot be sustained. This is dealt with in more detail in Chapter 7.

2.3.3　Illustrations from decided cases

Taylor v *Good* [1974] STC 148 has been mentioned above. In that case, a retailer, who lived in a council flat over one of his shops, bid successfully for a large house where his wife had worked in her school holidays. He had in mind living there but, on viewing the house, his wife rejected it as impracticable. As a result, he sought and obtained planning consent to redevelop the land for 90 dwellings. About four years after purchase he sold the property to developers, making a substantial gain. It was held by the Court of Appeal that this was not an adventure in the nature of trade. The purchase had not been made for the purpose of resale, on the evidence. Merely obtaining planning consent was not sufficient work in connection with the land to turn it from investment into trading stock. It was acknowledged that the degree of post-acquisition improvements can amount to trading in appropriate circumstances. On the facts in this particular case, though, there was no intervening trade. This illustrates the importance of examining the facts surrounding the purchase.

A borderline case is *CIR* v *Reinhold* (1953) 34 TC 389, where the director of a warehouse company bought four houses which he resold at a profit nearly three years later. He admitted to instructing agents to sell when a suitable opportunity arose and that the houses had been bought with the intention of resale, having received rents in the meantime. The four-man body of General Commissioners had divided equally, giving the benefit of the doubt to the taxpayer. The Court refused to upset their decision. Lord Russell rationalised this as follows:

'It was prima facie a form of investment capable of yielding an income: it was retained for three years and then sold; and the transaction was an isolated case, and not in the line of business in which the Respondent was engaged.'

Based on this, the taxpayer in *Page* v *Pogson* (1954) 35 TC 545 might have felt aggrieved. He built one house, in which he lived with his wife, and sold it at a profit a few months later. He then built another in which he also lived. Having been unemployed, he sold the house on taking up a new appointment. The General Commissioners held that he was trading in reselling the second house (not the first) and although the judge was not totally convinced, he felt unable to disturb the decision, as a finding of fact.

A more recent case is the House of Lords' decision in *Simmons* v *CIR* (1980) 53 TC 461. An individual and associates formed a number of companies, which acquired properties for development. As a fact, the Commissioners found that the properties were acquired with a view to creating permanent investments, although it was contemplated that one development might have to be realised before completion to conserve funds for other developments. The Special Commissioners made a finding of trading in the case of certain developments which were neither completed nor fully let when the decision to liquidate was made, after encountering difficulties. The following extract from the speech of Lord Wilberforce contains useful principles:

> 'Trading requires an intention to trade: normally the question to be asked is whether this intention existed at the time of the acquisition of the asset. Was it acquired with the intention of disposing of it at a profit, or was it acquired as a permanent investment? Often it is necessary to ask further questions: a permanent investment may be sold in order to acquire another investment thought to be more satisfactory; that does not involve an operation of trade, whether the first investment is to be sold at a profit or at a loss. Intentions may be changed. What was first an investment may be put into the trading stock, and – I suppose, vice versa. If findings of this kind are to be made precision is required, since a shift of an asset from one category to another will involve changes in the company's accounts, and, possibly, a liability to tax. What I think is not possible is for an asset to be both trading stock and permanent investment at the same time, nor to possess an indeterminate status – neither trading stock nor permanent asset.'

2.4   Commencement and cessation of trade

2.4.1   Commencement of trade

It is important to establish the date on which a trade commences, or, indeed, whether a trade has in fact commenced at all. Establishing a date is clearly relevant in computing the profits or losses in the commencement years. A loss can only be deducted if trading has actually commenced. If a trade never starts then none of the expenditure incurred could be allowable in any form whatsoever for income tax purposes.

However, where there is pre-trading expenditure, s401 ICTA 1988 deems expenditure incurred not more than seven years before commencement as having been incurred on the first day of trading, provided the expenditure would have been allowable under Schedule D Case I or II. However, if an individual incurs the expenditure and the trade is eventually carried on by a company, no relief will be available (*Tax Bulletin* November 1992).

The date of commencement is a question of fact and is not always easy to determine. Operations which are preparatory to trading would not ordinarily be trading as such. The actual circumstances of a given case need to be considered. The essential point, perhaps, is whether or not the individual is in a position to provide the goods or services which are his trade or profession. For example, a solicitor could spend several weeks finding office premises, taking on staff and meeting various regulatory requirements. He completes all these and one day sits in his office available to meet anyone who may happen to ring or call in. His profession must have commenced at the latest on that day, even though his first professional work may not arrive until a later time. There are relatively few cases on this. An old case is *Birmingham and District Cattle By-Products Co Ltd* v *CIR* (1919) 12 TC 92. Over approximately four months the directors of a company arranged for the erection of works and purchase of plant and machinery. Agreements for the purchase of products and sale of the finished products were entered into. It was held that trading commenced on the day the plant, etc., was installed completely, which was also the day on which raw materials were received.

The main part of the taxpayer's business might involve the creation of a structure, but operations of an ancillary nature are carried out before completion, from which income is obtained. On the facts, trading could well have commenced at the earlier date and not when the main project is completed. A case in support of such a conclusion is *Cannop Coal Co Ltd* v *CIR* (1922) 12 TC 31.

2.4.2 Cessation of trade

This is the converse case and again is subject to the facts. Simply ceasing to take on new client work or purchase goods does not of itself amount to cessation of trading. Trading will continue as long as goods are to be sold or existing projects completed. Another old case is the House of Lords' decision in *J & R O'Kane* v *CIR* 12 TC 303, where wine merchants announced their decision to retire from business. Over the next few months practically the whole of the stock was sold, mainly to existing customers. It was held that trading had continued while stocks were being run down.

There are special rules to tax amounts received after the date of cessation of trading, after deducting any expenses incurred which would otherwise be allowable had the trade continued. These provisions are contained in ss103 to 109 ICTA 1988. Section 109A ICTA 1988 also provides limited relief for post cessation expenditure, where there is no or insufficient income arising after cessation to cover that expenditure. The relief only applies for seven years after cessation and even then only to payments made wholly and exclusively under the following broad headings:

- remedying defective work, goods supplied or services rendered;
- legal and other professional expenses in connection with claims for defective work;
- insuring against claims or professional expenses;
- collecting debts; and
- debts which prove to be bad or released as part of a voluntary arrangement, etc.

Any amount falling within this section for a year of assessment within the seven-year period can be set against other income. If there is insufficient income, s90(4) FA 1995 treats the excess as a capital loss on making a claim. There are no provisions for carry back or carry forward. If expenses accrued when trading remain unpaid at the end of a tax year, that amount is deducted from the allowable post-cessation expenditure and reinstated if actually paid (s109(5) ICTA 1988).

2.4.3   Changes in the trade

The question posed here is whether or not changes to the trade are such as to either cause a cessation of one trade and the commencement of another, or possibly the continuation of one trade and the creation of a new and distinct trade. For example, an individual runs a newsagent and then starts in business as a carpenter. In the absence of exceptional circumstances, the newsagency trade would continue and he will be regarded as setting up a new trade of carpentry. At the other end of the spectrum, if his newsagency business expands into the sale of cigarettes and similar items, this is likely to be regarded as an extension of the existing trade. In that example, the activities would be from the same premises, supported by the same staff and the customers would be very similar.

In *Spiers & Son Ltd* v *Ogden* (1932) 17 TC 117, a building company confined itself to contracting work for customers. Subsequently, it developed land on its own account, either selling or letting the property. It was held that there was one trade throughout. As Finlay J said:

> 'Throughout, the business was one business carried on by the company with the same staff, the same accounts, the same everything.'

Again, this is largely a question of fact and a good deal depends upon the circumstances. For example, the geographical location of the activities could be relevant, the type of goods or services, the trading name and the general administration of the business. If an existing business is acquired and tacked on to an existing business, this is likely to be seen as simply an expansion of the existing business. A case supporting this is *Maidment* v *Kibby* [1993] STC 494 in which it was held that the acquisition of a fish and chip business, to add as another outlet of their existing business, did not amount to a succession, merely adding to what was simply part of the same trade. It was relevant that the shop acquired was absorbed into the existing trade in their own style, rather than carried on quite separately.

The Revenue have given guidance on this in *Tax Bulletin* of February 1996. This reiterates their view that if there is a succession, and single accounts are prepared for all branches of a business, the profits have to be apportioned for the early years (so that the commencement rules can apply to the business acquired, until such time as the normal continuing basis applies to all outlets). It is also made clear that, whatever the circumstances, an individual cannot succeed to part of an existing trade. It is all or nothing.

In *Edmunds* v *Coleman* [1997] STC 1406 the High Court, in reversing the decision of the General Commissioners, held that a freelance producer continued the same trade when he moved from working part-time to full-time.

2.4.4 Suspension of trading

If an individual in trade ceases to manufacture goods, for example, does he then cease to trade? If at a later date he recommences manufacturing, is that a new trade or simply the continuation of the existing trade? The facts are all important, as can be seen from two cases decided in different ways.

In *Kirk & Randall Ltd* v *Dunn* (1924) 8 TC 663, the taxpayer company looked for contracts over a six-year period (around the First World War) but could not obtain any. It was held that there was no discontinuance on determination of existing contracts. Looking for contracts is trading.

In *J.G. Ingram & Son Ltd* v *Callaghan* (1968) 45 TC 151, the Court of Appeal came to the opposite conclusion, supporting the decision of the Special Commissioner. The facts were different in that owing to the appointment of a receiver the factory was sold, and for a few months plastic goods were sold instead of the previous rubber goods. Later, following a chain of changes in ownership of the shares in the company, the same type of goods were manufactured as previously, albeit in a different type of material. It was held that there had been a cessation of trade and that a new trade commenced at the later date, even though very similar to the original trade. Vitally important were the facts set out by Harman LJ:

> 'I cannot see any evidence that, when the company's factory was closed and its machinery disposed of and its staff dismissed . . . there was any intention of merely keeping it in abeyance to resume at a favourable opportunity.'

2.4.5   Deemed cessation on change of residence

Section 110A ICTA 1988 contains a similar provision for sole traders as partnerships, where an individual either becomes or ceases to be resident in the UK. Where the trade is carried on wholly or partly outside the UK, any such change in residence is treated as the permanent discontinuance of the trade, etc., and a new commencement. The carried forward of losses under s385 ICTA 1988 is preserved.

2.4.6   Overseas implications

As indicated above, a UK resident individual who carries on trading activities outside the UK will almost certainly be treated as carrying on a trade assessed under Schedule D Case I, on all profits wherever arising.

The question addressed here is the reverse situation: whether a non-resident is trading in the UK. If so, an individual so trading will be subject to UK income tax under Schedule D Case I on the profits arising from the trade carried on in the UK. Some apportionment may have to be made and in practice the Revenue may have to look to the non-resident's UK representative, which will be the branch or agency in the UK through which the trade is carried on (s126 and Sch 23 FA 1995). The provisions of a relevant double tax treaty with the country of residence of the overseas trader should also be considered, and particularly the definition of 'permanent establishment'.

In practice most problems arise for the purposes of corporation tax, simply because commercially an overseas trade in this situation would typically be carried on through a corporate structure. However, there may be situations when an individual carries out transactions in the UK. There are several cases on this topic. There is a very broad distinction between trading in the UK and trading with the UK. If trading with the UK, this is simply an export market in the absence of any other connection.

A person is likely to be trading in the UK in the case of goods if contracts are made here. See, for example, *Maclaine & Co* v *Eccott* (1926) 10 TC 481. However, simply ensuring that contracts are made outside the UK is not necessarily conclusive. This can be seen from the House of Lords' decision in *Firestone Tyre & Rubber Co Ltd* v *Lewellin* (1957) 37 TC 111. The following comment from the judgment of Atkin LJ in *Smidth & Co* v *Greenwood* (1920) 8 TC 193 was approved:

> 'I think the question is, where do the operations take place from which the profits in substance arise?'

Incorporation triggers the cessation provisions for income tax. For a full discussion on incorporation tax see Tax Digest 189 *Considerations on Whether to Incorporate*.

2.5 Other matters

2.5.1 Illegal and tax-inspired activities

The decided cases indicate that simply because activities are illegal does not necessarily negate trading. In *Southern* v *AB Ltd* (1933) 18 TC 591 a bookmaking business was carried on, which involved offences for unlawful betting at the time. This was held to be a trade even though unlawful. A more recent case is *IRC* v *Aken* [1990] STC 497, in which a prostitute's income was held to be derived from trading.

If activities are carried out for tax avoidance purposes, these may not amount to trading. There are various cases involved with dividend stripping where trading losses were claimed as a deduction against dividends. See, for example, *Thomson* v *Gurneville Securities Ltd* (1971) 47 TC 633.

2.5.2 Farming trades

Section 53(1) ICTA 1988 provides that all farming and market gardening in the UK shall be treated as the carrying on of a trade, chargeable under Schedule D Case I. Section 53(2) then provides that:

> 'All the farming carried on by any particular person, partnership or body of persons shall be treated as one trade.'

Thus, even if two farms are in different parts of the country they will be treated as part of the same trade if carried on by the same individual or partnership. This much is made clear in *Bispham* v *Eardiston Farming Co [1919] Ltd* (1962) 40 TC 322. Losses on one farm can be carried forward against profits on another, and in that case there was a five-month gap between selling one farm and buying another.

Note that the cultivation of short rotation coppice is treated as farming and not forestry by s154 FA 1995. Short rotation coppice is defined as a perennial crop of tree species planted at high density, the stems of which are harvested above ground level at intervals of less than 10 years.

3 Trades, professions and vocations – basis periods and losses

3.1 Basis periods

3.1.1 General

The basic rule for assessing trades, professions and vocations is the current year basis as provided by s60 ICTA 1988. For an ongoing business, profits are ordinarily assessed based on the accounts ending in the relevant tax year. Thus, an individual drawing up accounts to 31 December will be assessed for 2003/04 on results for the year to 31 December 2003. If accounts for two or more periods end in the same tax year, the effect of s60(5) ICTA 1988 is to amalgamate the results into one account ending on the latest accounting date.

Complications arise in the following situations:

- commencement years;

- change of accounting date; and

- cessation of trade.

The statutory provisions, in ss60 to 63A ICTA 1988, are relatively compact, but the drafting is convoluted in part. The important point always to remember is this. Under the new basis of assessment, over the life of a person's trade, income tax will be assessed on the total profits, as adjusted for tax purposes. The only question is how those profits are allocated, particularly in the opening and closing years. If all the tax adjusted profits of the business are added up, they will equal exactly the profits assessed in the relevant years. If they do not, there will have been an error somewhere. This basic principle is a useful acid test to see whether or not the complications in the circumstances mentioned above have been dealt with correctly. Under the old preceding year basis of assessment, it was more by luck than judgement if this happened, giving rise to an element of arbitrariness.

Under the current year basis, this exactitude is provided by the concept of overlap relief, as set out in s63A ICTA 1988.

Example 3.1

An individual commenced trade 1 October 1997 and ceased 31 May 2002, with the following taxable profits:

	£	£
Year to 30 September 1998		8,000
Year to 30 September 1999		15,000
Year to 30 September 2000		29,000
Year to 30 September 2001		27,000
Eight months to 31 May 2002		20,000
		99,000

These profits are taxable as follows:		£
1997/98 6/12 × 8,000		4,000
1999/99 year to 30 September 1998		8,000
1999/00 year to 30 September 1999		15,000
2000/01 year to 30 September 2000		29,000
2001/02 year to 30 September 2001		27,000
2002/03 Eight months to 31 May 2002	20,000	
Less: overlap relief	(4,000)	16,000
		99,000

3.1.2   Overlap relief

An understanding of s63A ICTA 1988 is vital in appreciating the subtleties of the current year basis. A calculation of overlap profit is carried out whenever the same profits are brought into a calculation twice in arriving at taxable profits. In essence, where profits have been included in computations for two successive years of assessment, the amount of those profits and the period which is included twice should be identified. If there is a change of accounting date such that the basis period is more than one year, a sufficient part of the overlap relief pool should be deducted so that effectively 12 months' profits are assessed. Any balance of overlap relief will be carried forward until either another change of accounting date having that same result or on the cessation of the trade. In some cases, the change of accounting date can cause profits to be assessed more than once, in which case additional overlap relief will be created. As a rule of thumb, the period of overlap should be such that, if there is a cessation at a given date, the length of the final basis period to cessation, less the period of overlap, should equal the period of time from 6 April in the year of cessation to the date of cessation.

Example 3.2

Based on the previous example:

Length of final basis period	8 months
Less: overlap period	6 months
Period from 6 April 2002 to 31 May 2002	2 months

3.1.3 Opening years

Section 61 ICTA 1988 provides that the first year of trading is based on the profits arising in that year and so effectively this will be the date of commencement through to the following 5 April, in practice time apportioning the profits where the accounting year is not 5 April (or 31 March based on the Revenue practice). Unless there is a discontinuance within a very short space of time, the second year of assessment depends upon the period for which the first set of accounts is prepared. If those accounts are prepared for more than 12 months, the second year of assessment will be based on the 12 months ending with that accounting date, applying s60(3)(8) ICTA 1988. If, on the other hand, the first accounts are prepared for a period of less than 12 months, s61(2) ICTA 1988 provides that the basis period for this second year of assessment is the period of 12 months beginning with the date on which trade commenced.

The first set of accounts prepared for business could bridge a complete tax year, such as where trade commences 1 January 2003 and the first accounts are drawn up to 30 June 2004. In that case, the basis period for the second year is effectively the year to 5 April 2004, under s60(1) ICTA 1988.

The impact of ss60 and 61 ICTA 1988 is best illustrated by examples as set out below, and which make reference to the relevant statutory provision in question. These examples are computed by reference to months, which the Revenue will accept. Strictly, the computations should be made according to the exact number of days in each relevant period. A 31 March accounting year can be treated as if ending on 5 April and up to the first five days of a business commencing between 1 April and 5 April can be ignored (see Help Sheet IR 222).

Example 3.3

First accounting date less than 12 months.

Sole trader commences in business on 1 August 2002, preparing accounts as follows:

	£	£
9 months to 30 April 2003	18,000	
12 months to 30 April 2004	30,000	
Assessable profits are:		
2002/03 (period to 5 April 2003 – s61(1) ICTA 1988) 8/9 × 18,000		16,000
2003/04 (first 12 months – s61(2) ICTA 1988)	18,000	
+ 3/12 × 30,000	7,500	25,500
2004/05 (12 months to 30 April 2004 – s60(3)(a) ICTA 1988)		30,000
Overlap relief 16,000 + 7,500 (11 months in total being 1 August 2002 to 5 April 2003 and 1 May 2003 to 31 July 2003)		23,500

Example 3.4

First accounting date 12 months or more.

Sole trader commences on 1 August 2002 and accounts are prepared for:

	£	£
15 months to 31 October 2003	27,000	
12 months to 31 October 2004	36,000	
Assessable profits are:		
2002/03 (period to 5 April 2003) 8/15 × 27,000		14,400
2003/04 (12 months to 31 October 2003 – s60(3)(a) ICTA 1988) 12/15 × 27,000		21,600
2004/05 (12 months to 31 October 2004 – s60(3)(b) ICTA 1988)		36,000
Overlap relief 5/15 × 27,000 (five months being 1 November 2002 to 5 April 2003)		9,000

Example 3.5

No accounting date ending until third year.

Same basic facts as previous two examples, but with accounts prepared for:

	£	£
22 months to 31 May 2004	49,500	
12 months to 31 May 2005	33,000	
Assessable profits are:		
2002/03 (period to 5 April 2003) 8/22 × 49,500		18,000
2003/04 (12 months to 5 April 2004 – s60(1) ICTA 1988) 12/22 × 49,500		27,000
2004/05 (12 months to 31 May 2004 – s60(3) (a) ICTA 1988)12/22 × 49,500		27,000
2005/06 (12 months to 31 May 2005 – s60(3)(b) ICTA 1988)		33,000
Overlap relief 10/22 × 49,500 (10 months from 1 June 2003 to 5 April 2004)		22,500

3.1.4 Change of accounting date

If a valid accounting date change is made, complying with s62A ICTA 1988, it is necessary to apply s62(2) ICTA 1988. A change is valid if the following conditions in s62A are met or the change is in the second or third year of assessment.

- The first accounting period ending with the new date must not exceed 18 months.

- Notice of the change of accounting date must be given to the Revenue in a s8 TMA 1970 return by the date the tax return has to be filed (or in the equivalent partnership tax return).

- There has been no change of accounting date in any of the five years immediately preceding the year of assessment in which a change first takes place.

- If that five-year test cannot be met, the relevant tax return should set out the reasons for the change. The Revenue must be satisfied that this is for bona fide commercial reasons (not obtaining a tax advantage). If the inspector does not dissent within 60 days he is deemed to have agreed the change.

Example 3.6

Assume a trader has carried on a business for many years, preparing annual accounts to 31 October. Overlap relief on commencement is £25,000 (for five months).

Accounts are drawn up showing profits as follows:

	£	£
12 months to 31 October 2001	42,000	
16 months to 28 February 2003	72,000	
12 months to 28 February 2004	50,000	

Assessed as follows:		
2001/02 (12 months to 31 October 2001)		42,000
2002/03 (s62(2)(b) ICTA 1998)		
16 months to 28 February 2003	72,000	
Less: overlap relief 4/5 × 25,000	(20,000)	
		52,000
2003/04 (12 months to 28 February 2004 – s60(3)(b) ICTA 1988)		50,000
Overlap relief (now reduced to 1 month)		5,000

Example 3.7

Assume instead, the change had been to 30 June 2002, with profits as follows:

	£	£
12 months to 31 October 2001	42,000	
8 months to 30 June 2002	30,000	
12 months to 30 June 2003	52,000	

Then, assessable profits are:	
2001/02 – as above, no change	42,000
2002/03 (12 months to 30 June 2002 – s62(2)(a) ICTA 1988) 4/12 × 42,000 + 30,000	44,000
2003/04 (12 months to 30 June 2003 – s60(3)(b) ICTA 1988)	52,000
Additional overlap relief of 4 months 4/12 × 42,000 (£14,000) and total increased to	39,000

This is now a total period of nine months, representing what would be the difference in time between 1 July and 5 April in the penultimate year.

If the conditions in s62A are not met, the trade will be assessed as if the change had not been made, apportioning profits when necessary. At some point the five-year test will be met, in which case s62(2) can then be applied.

Example 3.6 opposite illustrates the situation where the first accounting date produces a period of more than 12 months and example 3.7 where the resulting period is less than 12 months. The net effect of these computations is that, after any overlap relief, the effective period charged is always 12 months.

If there is a change and the next period of account bridges a complete tax year, the change is treated by s62(5) ICTA 1988 as made in the first year to which accounts would have been drawn up but for the change. This is illustrated by the following example:

Example 3.8

X has the following results having traded for many years using the same accounting date. He has no overlap relief given his old accounting date.

		£
Year to 31 March 2003		60,000
13 months to 30 April 2004		91,000

The assessments are:

2002/03 Year to 31 March 2003		60,000
2003/04 Year to 30 April 2003		
11/12 × 60,000	55,000	
1/13 × 91,000	7,000	
		62,000
2004/05 Year to 30 April 2004 12/13 × 91,000		84,000

Overlap relief is created of £55,000, being the 11 months to 31 March 2003.

3.1.5 Optimum accounting date

Is there an optimum accounting date? There is no universal date and in many instances the choice makes little difference. Commercial reasons must be considered carefully, especially in seasonal trades. Predicting trading results is always difficult and there are likely to be some costs involved in a change. Generally, if profits are increasing, an accounting date ending early in the tax year (such as 30 April) is better than one ending later. The advantage of 31 March tends to be one of simplicity, particularly on a cessation, as there is no need to consider overlap relief.

There may occasionally be circumstances when a change might produce an advantage, subject to the detailed figures.

Tax tip

A trader started on 1 July 1998 and has always prepared accounts to 30 June each year. Profits to date have been in the region of £20,000 p.a. and overlap relief is £15,000 (nine months).

Owing to an exceptional contract the taxable profit for the year to 30 June 2003 is £45,000. However, a downturn in work is affecting profits and as a result the year to 30 June 2004 is expected to breakeven. Thereafter, profits should return to the £25,000 p.a. level.

If no action is taken the Schedule D Case I profits for 2003/04 will be £45,000.

By changing the accounting date to 31 December 2003 the assessable profit becomes:

	£
Profit – 18 months to 31 December 2003	45,000
Less: overlap relief for 6 months 6/9 × £15,000	(10,000)
Schedule D Case I 2003/04	35,000

Overlap relief can only be used once. However, by triggering part now not obly is there a cash flow advantage but £10,000 of the relief attracts an income tax reduction at 40%. If profits continue as expected, relief at only basic rate is likely. The added advantage is that if there are no profits for the year to 30 June 2004 the personal reliefs will be wasted, assuming the trader has no other income.

Detailed computations must be made in each case, based on assumptions that may not prove to be accurate. No further accounting date change can be made for five years.

3.1.6 Cessation of trading

Applying s63 ICTA 1988, the basis period for the year in which a trade, etc., is discontinued runs from the end of the basis period for the preceding year of assessment to the date of discontinuance. The profit for that period is reduced by overlap relief, as set out in **3.1.2** above. This is illustrated by the examples in **3.1.1** and **9.2.4** for partners.

For VAT considerations, see *Value Added Tax 2002/2003*, chapter **15**.

3.2 Farming trades

3.2.1 Averaging

The profits from farming or market gardening trades in the UK can be averaged over two consecutive years of assessment, under s96 ICTA 1988. The profits finally assessable for the year, not the basis period, are averaged. Losses are not averaged and are simply treated as nil profits.

Full averaging is only available if the profits for one of the two years being averaged does not exceed 70 per cent of the profits for the other year or are nil. There is marginal relief if profits are between 70 per cent and 75 per cent of the profits for the other year, under s96(3) ICTA 1988. There is no reason in principle why a year, if averaged once, should not in turn be averaged with the next year.

A claim for averaging must be made within 12 months of the 31 January next following the second of the two years of assessment, with an extension permitted if profits are adjusted. In the case of a partnership, it is up to each partner to decide whether or not averaging should apply to his share.

Tax tip

A farmer has a profit of £50,000 assessable for 2001/02, based on his accounts to 30 September 2001. In the year to 30 September 2002 he incurs a loss of £10,000. An averaging claim reduces his overall income tax liability. The profits for the year 2002/03 are treated as nil and if this year is averaged with 2001/02 the resulting assessable profits are as follows:

2001/02 1/2 × £50,000 + nil	£25,000
2002/03 1/2 × £50,000 + nil	£25,000

The loss of £10,000 in 2002/03 can be claimed separately, including a s380 claim against either 2002/03 or 2001/02.

3.2.2 Treatment of animals

The general rule under Schedule 5 ICTA 1988 para 1(1) is that animals kept by a farmer for the purposes of his farming are treated as trading stock. Normal principles apply to value them at the end of each period of account at the lower of cost and realisable value. However, if an animal is kept wholly or mainly for work on the farm, it is not to be treated as trading stock (Sch 5 para 7). Although working animals are no doubt rare these days, there seems to be no reason in principle why a working animal should not be treated as plant for capital allowance purposes.

A major tax feature for farmers holding production herds is the availability of the herd basis. A production herd is one kept for its produce, such as milk in the case of a dairy herd, as opposed to beef cattle which are reared for sale. An election for the herd basis must be made under Schedule 5, specifying the relevant class of herds, within 12 months from 31 January next following the year of assessment (other than the commencement year) in which the herd is first kept. In the case of a partnership, the election must be made on behalf of the partnership in accordance with s42(6) TMA 1970 and remade each time there is a change in partners. An election is irrevocable.

The detailed computational matters are quite complex and reference should be made, in particular, to the *Inspectors Manual* (paragraph 2300 onwards) on this topic. Broadly, the tax advantage of the herd basis is that on either selling an entire herd or a substantial part the gain arising is not subject to income tax. However, if within five years of the sale the farmer acquires another production herd of the same class or animals to replace a part of the herd sold the tax-free status of the disposal can be prejudiced. None of the animals in the herd or any additions thereto are treated as trading stock but more like a capital asset. However, if animals are replaced the sale proceeds of the animals sold are treated as a trading receipt and the cost of the replacement animal as an expense (except where bred by the farmer and the cost treated as a Schedule D Case I expense in the normal way). If a farmer transfers an additional animal to the herd, the cost of breeding and rearing that animal to maturity is treated as a trading receipt.

3.2.3 Other matters

The treatment of grants and subsidies is relevant to farmers, particularly as to when such receipts should be recognised. Reference should be made to the *Business Economic Note* 19, which explains this in detail. *Tax Bulletin* December 1994 comments on particular animal grants, accepting that such grants can be recognised either at the end of the retention period or on receipt, if applied consistently.

For dairy farmers, milk quota is a complex area. Compensation for permanent cuts is treated as a capital gain (*Tax Bulletin* May 1994) and *Tax Bulletin* of August 1994 confirms that superlevy is an allowable deduction. Acquiring quota is treated as a capital cost, even where bought to avoid the superlevy.

The treatment of grants and subsidies is dealt with in detail in the *Inspectors Manual* at paragraph 2266 and quotas at paragraph 2286.

For a fuller discussion of farming see Tax Digest 205 *Taxation of Farmers in the UK and Farming IAAG* (published by ABG Publications).

3.3   Sub-contractors in the construction industry

For many years there has been a requirement for payments made to sub-contractors in the construction industry to be paid under deduction of income tax where paid by a contractor or another sub-contractor, or certain other specified bodies. Deduction of tax can be avoided if the recipient holds a valid certificate. The statutory rules are contained in ss559 to 567 ICTA 1988 and the Income Tax (Sub-contractors in the Construction Industry) Regulations 1993 SI 1993/743. These provisions were amended substantially in 1995 and 1998, the changes taking effect from 1 August 1999.

These rules were enacted to prevent the evasion of income tax in respect of labour payments in the construction industry. Broadly, whenever there is a contract relating to 'construction operations', other than under an employment contract, the person making the payment must do one of the following:

(a) Deduct income tax at 18 per cent from the payment, after deducting the amount shown to represent the direct cost of materials used, and account for that tax to the Inland Revenue as required by the regulations. A deduction certificate (taxed payment voucher) must be given to the sub-contractor each month. This procedure is appropriate where the recipient does not hold a valid gross payment certificate. Even so, the recipient should hold a registration card issued by the Inland Revenue, which the contractor must inspect and record relevant information.

(b) If the recipient holds a valid gross payment certificate, the payer must inspect this and record the relevant information. Payment can then be made gross without any tax deductions.

Ordinarily, both the payer and recipient will be involved in 'construction operations'. The meaning of this is set out in s567 ICTA 1988 and in general only applies to operations carried out in the UK. Otherwise, the expression applies to virtually any work in connection with the construction industry, whether new work or repair, but excluding the manufacture of building components, professional services, sign writing, etc., and the installation of security systems. The responsibility is on the payer to ensure that the rules are met, and that payer could be a main contractor or a sub-contractor himself. The rules do not apply to payments made where the payer is not in business in the construction industry, such as a private house owner. However, s560 ICTA 1988 widens the scope to include local authorities and any person in business, even though not in the construction industry, whose average annual expenditure on construction operations exceeds £1m, usually averaged over a three-year period.

Until the rules changed with effect from 1 August 1999, it was possible for most individuals in the construction industry to obtain a certificate, to avoid deduction of tax, even though the recent purge by the Revenue on the construction industry has probably meant that there are relatively few labour only individuals remaining self-employed. The following are the main requirements that must be met by an individual in order to obtain a valid gross payment certificate.

- The business must be carried on in the UK involving construction operations.

- The business must be carried on to a substantial extent by means of a bank account.

- Proper records must be kept, especially with a view to meeting income tax and National Insurance contributions obligations.

- The business must be carried on from proper premises and with proper equipment, stock and other facilities.

- There must have been compliance with income tax and National Insurance obligations in the three years ending with the date of the application for the certificate (unless the Revenue accept that any failure was minor and technical), and an expectation of compliance in the future.

- The turnover threshold must be satisfied, which means that annual turnover, excluding the cost of materials, must exceed £30,000 per annum, applying either the six-month or the main three-year test.

- In the case of partnerships, similar rules must be met as far as the business requirements are concerned and each of the partners must meet the income tax and National Insurance compliance requirements. A turnover threshold is also applied to partnerships, the limit being either £30,000 p.a. multiplied by the number of partners or exceed £200,000 p.a.

3.4 Lloyd's Underwriters

This is a specialist area and only brief mention is made here. The provisions were changed substantially by FA 1993 to fit in with self-assessment.

Broadly, profits are assessed by reference to the underwriting year, which is 31 December. No other accounting date can be used. The assessment is under Schedule D Case I to include the syndicate results declared in the underwriting year and profits or losses arising from assets forming part of a premiums trust fund. A member can also deduct personal expenses paid in the same year. Investment income on ancillary funds is also included in the Schedule D Case I results. Capital gains on ancillary trust funds, such as investments forming part of the member's deposit, are dealt with in the same way as any other gains for capital tax gains tax purposes. Payments can be made to a special reserve fund established under s175 FA 1993, being amounts set aside to be withdrawn if losses are made. The limit under Schedule 20 para 3 FA 1993 is the lower of 50 per cent of the syndicate profit for a year and an amount to bring the value of the fund up to 50 per cent of the member's overall premium limit.

Special rules apply on cessation, including death, under ss179 and 179A FA 1993. On cessation other than death, the final year of assessment is that in which the member's deposit is paid over. On death, the member's personal representatives are treated as carrying on the business until the deposit is paid over. The personal representatives are assessed on the whole underwriting year in which the member dies.

Underwriting profits are treated as earned income under s180 FA 1993 and as a result can be the basis for making personal pension contributions.

3.5   Creative artists' averaging

FA 2001 added a new Schedule 4A ICTA 1988 as replacement relief for creative artists whose profits fluctuate from one year to another. The relief only applies where the profits are derived wholly or mainly from qualifying creative works, which means literary, dramatic, musical, artistic works or designs created by the individual person or by one or more of the partners personally, in the case of a partnership.

The relief is similar to farmers averaging to allow the assessable profits for two successive years to be averaged, including the results of a year that has already been subject to an averaging claim. As with farmers, the profits for one year must be less than 75 per cent of the profits for the other (or one of those years being nil profits). If the profits from one of the years is 70 per cent or less of the other (or is nil) then the adjustment is a simple averaging with a more complex adjustment where the profits for one year are between 70 per cent and 75 per cent of the other year. The first pair of years that can be averaged is 2000/01 and 2001/02 and a claim cannot be made in relation to years of commencement and cessation. The time limit for a claim is 12 months from 31 January next following the end of the later of the two years to which the claim relates.

4 Trades, professions and vocations – computational matters

4.1 Overview

The previous chapter sets out the basis periods and relief for losses. This chapter deals with the approaches to establishing those profits or losses. Tax legislation does not contain a comprehensive set of rules as such to determine how accounts for tax purposes should be drawn up. There are statutory rules to which regard must be had, usually prohibiting the deduction of a type of expense for tax purposes. The starting point is the accounts drawn up in accordance with established principles of commercial accountancy.

Class 4 NIC is also charged on profits, see *National Insurance Contributions 2002/2003* **7.2.**

4.2 Commercial accounting principles

For much of the last century, accountancy as a profession was still developing, whereas the legal profession was well established. As a result, many of the early cases on deductibility followed a legalistic approach, analysing the legal form of relevant transactions. It was rare, if ever, for accounting evidence to be heard. Gradually, the courts have taken on board commercial accounting principles, to the point where they take precedence in the absence of any clear statutory guidelines to the contrary. Indeed, s44 FA 1998, referred to in **4.6** below, is drafted in very wide terms, beyond the initial aim of taxing professions on the accruals basis. Section 42 FA 1998, as amended, now refers to generally accepted accounting practice and there is a statutory definition of this expression in a new s836A ICTA 1988. This means the generally accepted accounting practice with respect to the accounts of UK companies that are intended to give a true and fair view has the same meaning in relation to individuals as it has in relation to UK companies.

A case leading the way is the House of Lords' decision in *Southern Railway of Peru Ltd* v *Owen* (1956) 36 TC 602 and in particular the speech of Lord Radcliffe. A claim to deduct a contingent accruing liability for employee retirement benefits was held not to be allowable, but only because the quantification of that liability was not accurate enough. That case was decided in 1956. Since then, accounting techniques and principles have become more sophisticated, particularly with the introduction of Statements of Standard Accounting Practice. Three recent cases illustrate clearly the development of the law in this area.

The first is the Court of Appeal decision in *Gallagher* v *Jones* (1993) 66 TC 77. The taxpayer hired out narrowboats on short-term arrangements, which he leased in on finance leases. Rent was paid for a primary period of 24 months at a substantial figure, and thereafter for a secondary period of 20 years at a nominal rent. The taxpayer claimed to deduct the payments when made, thereby weighting the leasing costs in the first two years. This treatment conflicted with the Revenue view in SP 3/91. It also disregarded SSAP 2 and SSAP 21 on finance leases. It was held that the strict legal analysis, under which the payments actually fell due in the first two years, was inappropriate, being at variance with the accounting evidence. Sir Thomas Bingham MR put it this way in the conclusion to his long judgment:

> 'The object is to determine, as accurately as possible, the profits or losses of the taxpayers' businesses for the accounting periods in question. Subject to any express or implied statutory rule, of which there is none here, the ordinary way to ascertain the profits or losses of a business is to apply accepted principles of commercial accountancy. That is the very purpose for which such principles are formulated. As has often been pointed out, such principles are not static: they may be modified, refined and elaborated over time as circumstances change and accounting insights sharpen. But so long as such principles remain current and generally accepted they provide the surest answer to the question which the legislation requires to be answered.'

In the following year, Knox J rejected the Revenue's appeal against the Special Commissioners' decision in *Johnston* v *Britannia Airways Ltd* (1994) 67 TC 99. The company operated an airline and following the purchase of an aircraft began making provision for the major overhaul of each engine, which was likely to be required every three or four years. This was calculated accurately by reference to the average cost of overhaul per hour flown. Knox J clearly indicated the importance of accounting evidence when he said:

> 'The court is slow to accept that accounts prepared in accordance with accepted principles of commercial accountancy are not adequate

for tax purposes as a true statement of the taxpayer's profits for the relevant period. In particular, it is slow to find that there is a judge-made rule of law which prevents accounts prepared in accordance with the ordinary principles of commercial accountancy from complying with the requirements of the tax legislation.'

In *Herbert Smith* v *Honour* [1999] STC 173, the taxpayer firm of solicitors ceased to occupy premises but were committed for the remainder of the lease. They claimed a deduction for the amounts to be paid for future rents, following a move to new premises. The High Court held that there had been sufficient accounting evidence produced to the Special Commissioners in support of the deduction for tax purposes, reversing the Commissioners' decision.

The Revenue argued that the future rents should not be deductible for tax purposes because the approach involved an anticipation of liabilities. Lloyd J in his judgment preferred the taxpayer's submission that the commissioners' position was wrong, not being capable of being justified by the evidence before them. He rejected counsel for the Revenue's alternative argument that the decision was supported by a supposed independent rule against anticipation of liabilities. Such a rule would be inconsistent with resort to generally accepted principles of commercial accounting. If correct, it would disallow any provision made in accordance with the concept of prudence. In *Gallagher* v *Jones* the Court took the view that generally accepted commercial accounting principles, as applied in that case, themselves operated so as to preclude illegitimate anticipation. Furthermore, although he would not say that the judge-made rule as to the relevance of account prepared in accordance with generally accepted principles of commercial accounting does not permit non-statutory exceptions beyond those already recognised in decided cases, he was not able to hold that the relevance of such accounts is subject to a general exception prohibiting the deduction provisions made in accordance with the prudence concept in SSAP2.

Sir Thomas Bingham's comment above that accounting principles are not static is illustrated by FRS 12, dealing with provisions, contingent liabilities and assets. The provision made in the British Airways case would now be affected by FRS12. Smaller businesses applying the FRSSE are not currently subject to FRS 12 but nevertheless it does illustrate sound accounting principles. Broadly, for a provision to be recognised in accounts there must be a present obligation as result of a past event; a probability that there will be a transfer of economic benefits to settle the obligation; and a reliable estimate made to quantify that obligation. An obligation can include the restructuring of a business, but as a rule only where either a plan has been implemented before the balance sheet date or the main features have been announced in sufficient detail for those affected to have a valid expectation that the restructuring will be carried out.

It can be seen that this rule can work both ways: against the taxpayer in the *Gallagher* case and for the taxpayer in the *Britannia Airways* and *Herbert Smith* cases. Accounting principles are developed all the time. Not only are there SSAPs but also Financial Reporting Standards and Urgent Issue Task Force Abstracts. Not every standard applies to all businesses. Some specifically apply only to companies. Moreover, there has recently been a relaxation for most small businesses, which can apply the less exacting rules set out in Financial Reporting Standard for Smaller Entities (FRSSE). In *Tax Bulletin* December 1997 the Revenue indicate that on the assumption the rules in the FRSSE become generally accepted practice, they should be acceptable for tax purposes and should prevail over the more precise rules for larger entities contained in other standards. Nevertheless, the rules contained in all standards and abstracts demonstrate clearly the correct principles, even where not mandatory as such.

An important publication of the Accounting Standards Board is the Statement of Principles for Financial Reporting which sets out the principles that the Board believes should underlie the preparation and presentation of general purpose financial statements. In particular, information provided by the financial statements should be relevant and reliable. Reliability should not involve overuse of the old concept of prudence. Prudence is not appropriate where there is no uncertainty and should not be used to create hidden reserves or excessive provisions. Nevertheless, a degree of caution in exercising judgement is required in making the necessary estimates where there are conditions of uncertainty. More confirmatory evidence is required for the existence and measurement of assets than for liabilities. An asset or liability should not be recognised unless there is sufficient evidence of its existence and it can be measured in monetary terms with sufficient reliability. The statement is appropriate for all entities, both large and small, although it recognises that the application of the principles, can be different for smaller entities. Generally speaking, though, the fundamental accounting concepts prescribed by SSAP 2 remain so that accounts should be prepared by taking into account, where appropriate, the going concern concept on an accruals basis and applying a consistent approach.

The following are the main accounting standards likely to be relevant to income tax. The Statement of Principles for Financial Reporting is mentioned above and also the FRSSE. A business applying FRSSE is exempt from many of the following standards but, as mentioned, they do illustrate good accounting practice. Moreover, the FRSSE in many instances effectively applies the more detailed standard but in précis form. Where relevant, financial statements should state that they have been prepared in accordance with the FRSSE.

1. Statements of Standard Accounting Practice
    *   SSAP 4   Accounting for government grants
    *   SSAP 5   Accounting for value added tax
    *   SSAP 9   Stocks and long-term contracts
    *   SSAP 17   Accounting for post balance sheet events
    *   SSAP 20   Foreign currency translation
    *   SSAP 21   Accounting for leases and hire purchase contracts
2. Financial Reporting Standards
    *   FRS 5   Reporting for substance of transactions
    *   FRS 8   Related party disclosures
    *   FRS 12   Provisions, contingent liabilities and contingent assets
    *   FRS 18   Accounting policies
3. UITF Abstracts
    *   UITF Abstract 4   Transfers from current assets to fixed assets
    *   UITF Abstract 24   Accounting for start-up costs
    *   UITF Abstract 26   Barter transactions for advertising
    *   UITF Abstract 28   Operating lease incentives
    *   UITF Abstract 29   Web site development costs

4.3   Statutory intervention

4.3.1   Section 74 ICTA 1988

This is a most important provision, as it is of general application. It contains the wholly and exclusively rule considered in more detail below. There is no substitute for setting out the section in detail. The language is somewhat archaic and at times illustrates confusion in the draftsman's mind of accounting principles. Many of the rules overlap.

'74(1) Subject to the provisions of the Tax Acts, in computing the amount of profits to be charged under Case I or Case II of Schedule D, no sum shall be deducted in respect of:

(a) any disbursements or expenses, not being money wholly and exclusively laid out or expended for the purposes of the trade, profession or vocation;

(b) any disbursements or expenses of maintenance of the parties, their families or establishments, or any sums expended for any other domestic or private purposes distinct from the purpose of the trade, profession or vocation;

(c) the rent of the whole or any part of any dwelling-house or domestic offices, except any such part as is used for the purposes of the trade, profession or vocation, and where any such part is so used, the sum so deducted shall not, unless in any particular case it appears that having regard to all the circumstances some greater sum ought to be deducted, exceed two-thirds of the rent bona fide paid for that dwelling-house or those offices;

(d) any sum expended for repairs of premises occupied, or for the supply, repairs or alterations of any implements, utensils or articles employed, for the purposes of the trade, profession or vocation, beyond the sum actually expended for those purposes;

(e) any loss not connected with or arising out of the trade, profession or vocation;

(f) any capital withdrawn from, or any sum employed or intended to be employed as capital in, the trade, profession or vocation, but so that this paragraph shall not be treated as disallowing the deduction of any interest;

(g) any capital employed in improvements of premises occupied for the purposes of the trade, profession or vocation;

(h) any interest which might have been made if any such sums as aforesaid had been laid out at interest;

(j) any debts except:
    (i) a bad debt;
    (ii) a debt or part of a debt released by the creditor wholly and exclusively for the purposes of his trade, profession or vocation as part of a relevant arrangement or any compromise; and
    (iii) a doubtful debt to the extent estimated to be bad, meaning, in the case of the bankruptcy or insolvency of the debtor, the debt except to the extent that any amount may reasonably be expected to be received on the debt;

(k) any average loss beyond the actual amount of loss after adjustment;

(l) any sum recoverable under an insurance or contract of indemnity;

(m) any annuity or other annual payment (other than interest) payable out of the profits;

(n) any interest paid to a person not resident in the United Kingdom if and so far as it is interest at more than a reasonable commercial rate;

(o) any interest in so far as the payment of that interest is or would be, otherwise than by virtue of section 375(2), either:
   (i)   a payment of interest to which section 369 applies, or
   (ii) a payment of interest to which that section would apply but for section 373(5);

(p) any royalty or other sum paid in respect of the user of a patent.'

4.3.2 Comments on aspects of section 74

Later sections of this chapter consider in more detail certain of the above prohibitions. The following are comments on other parts of s74:

* Paragraph (b) requires little comment as it seems almost impossible that any private expense would not fall foul of the wholly and exclusively rule. Similarly, any expenditure falling within paragraph (c) is also likely to fall in paragraph (a). In *Caillebotte* v *Quinn* [1975] STC 265, it was held that the lunch costs of a carpenter were not allowable, not being incurred wholly and exclusively for his trade. The Revenue had also argued that paragraph (b) applied but the judge did not need to form a view on this.

* For many years, the Revenue contended that paragraph (d) prevents any provision for repairs, where the cost has not actually been incurred. This view has been rejected, in the taxpayers' favour, by the Special Commissioners in *Jenners Princes Street Edinburgh Ltd* v *IRC* [1998] STC (SCD) 196. The meaning of this provision has been considerably narrowed by this case. The Revenue did not appeal against this decision. Accounting principles will determine whether a provision for repairs is deductible in a given period of account.

* Paragraph (e), debarring any loss not connected with or arising out of the trade, etc. also seems to overlap with paragraph (a). It has been the reasoning behind the non-deductibility in certain cases such as irrecoverable loans made by a solicitor in *CIR* v *Hagart & Burn-Murdoch* (1929) 14 TC 433, where it was found that lending money was not an essential and necessary part of a solicitor's profession. A loss arising on guaranteeing loans made by third parties to clients, where there was evidence that such guarantees were part of the practice of a solicitor, has been held to be allowable in *Jennings* v *Barfield and Barfield* (1962) 40 TC 365. This paragraph may also be the preferred reasoning why criminal penalties

incurred as a result of trading are not deductible, although in truth public policy must be a factor behind this. A case in point is *CIR* v *Alexander von Glehn Ltd* (1920) 12 TC 232.

Paragraphs (h) and (k) prevent the deduction of notional sums and paragraph (1) ensures that an expense cannot be deducted where it is recovered under insurance etc. A case where paragraph (1) was applied is *Bolton* v *Halpern & Woolf* [1979] STC 761.

Paragraphs (o) and (p) prevent deductions because of the entitlement to deduct tax at source under the MIRAS provisions and royalty, etc. payments subject to deduction of tax at source.

4.4 The wholly and exclusively rule

This is the so-called 'dual purpose' rule given by s74(1)(a) ICTA 1988.

The cases on this are many and varied. The facts in any given situation may well determine the outcome but differences of opinion between judges in cited cases illustrate the conceptual difficulties. A small selection of cases is considered below.

One consequence of this rule is that there can be no apportionment of expenditure that is not wholly and exclusively for the purposes of the trade. Thus, if there is duality of purpose none of the expenditure can be deducted, even though a common-sense method of apportionment could be applied. Having said that, in practice the Revenue will agree apportionments which, on their face, fall foul of s74(1)(a). For example, modest claims for use of home as an office are usually accepted, despite the inclusion of fixed costs. In *Gazelle* v *Seivini* [1995] STC (SCD) 324 the taxpayer practised from home as an accountant. His claim to deduct 50 per cent of the total running costs was rejected in favour of the Revenue's suggested 20 per cent.

Even though at first glance expenditure has a non-business element, the decision in *Copeman* v *Flood & Sons* (1941) 24 TC 53 may allow an apportionment without breaching the rule, where a payment can be dissected. It was held that although excessive director's fees were paid, part of that expenditure could have been justified as being wholly and exclusively for the purposes of the trade. Thus, if £10,000 is paid to a sole trader's wife as an employee but only £3,000 is appropriate based on the work involved, it can be said that the whole of that sum of £3,000 is incurred wholly and exclusively for the purposes of the business. This is a very fine but important distinction.

The distinction can also be illustrated by the costs of foreign travel. A sole trader might visit Europe for business purposes, perhaps to meet suppliers or customers. When over there, he incurs expense in travelling from his base to meet friends. The overall cost of the trip can be broken down because the travel to and from the destination is clearly incurred wholly and exclusively for trading purposes. Provided the visit to friends is incidental to that purpose, it is only that internal cost which will be disallowable as having some duality of purpose. No part of that cost is allowable even if, on the same visit, the trader took the opportunity to look at local manufacturing methods. Broadly, an expense which has some private element is likely to be disallowed, unless that part is so small as to be a necessary incident to the main purpose. Under SP A16 the Revenue allow living expenses when abroad on business, including both accommodation and subsistence.

Apart from this, the strict position is that expenditure on meals is not a deductible expense for tax purposes. Mr Stephen Oliver QC, in his decision as Special Commissioner in *GS & F Marsden v Eadie* [1999] STC (SCD) 334, made it clear that expenditure of traders in keeping themselves fed is not deductible. The expenditure is not incurred wholly and exclusively for the purposes of a trade. There is a dual motive in providing food; to keep the individual alive as well as to defray the extra cost of eating away from home in the course of a trading activity. This principle he regarded as established in *Caillebotte v Quinn* [1975] STC 265.

Where there is a clear personal benefit, the motive for incurring the expense does not make it allowable. Thus, in *Spofforth & Prince v Golder* 26 TC 310, costs incurred in successfully defending a criminal charge, to prevent damage to the individual's reputation as an accountant, were held not to be allowable as it was as likely to avoid the personal as well as professional consequences. However, in *McKnight v Sheppard* [1999] STC 669 the House of Lords confirmed the decision of the Special Commissioner and Court of Appeal that legal fees in defending alleged breaches of Stock Exchange rules were deductible. On the evidence, the taxpayer's objective had been to protect his business, any personal benefit being incidental to this. The taxpayer had not appealed against the High Court's decision that the fines imposed by the Stock Exchange were not deductible.

Claims for clothing have almost consistently been rejected, except where the expenditure is on a uniform. This was the basis of the decision in *Mallalieu* v *Drummond* [1983] STC 665 where, ultimately, the majority view of the House of Lords prevailed on a claim by a barrister to deduct dark clothing bought for court appearances. There was evidence to the effect that the barrister would not have bought such sober clothing had it not been a Bar Council requirement. However, there was duality of purpose because at least in part the purpose was to preserve warmth and decency.

In *MacKinlay* v *Arthur Young McClelland Moores & Co* (1989) 62 TC 704 the House of Lords rejected a claim for removal costs of partners of a large accountancy practice, where moves were required by the firm's executive committee for the benefit of the practice. It had been admitted that a sole trader could not have claimed such a deduction. There was no reason in principle why a partner, who is party to carrying on the business, should be in any different position. The following extract from the speech of Lord Oliver draws the distinction between purpose and motive:

> 'Nobody could say with any colour of conviction that in purchasing new curtains he or his wife was acting upon partnership business. In my judgment once one escapes from what I regard as the fallacy of confusing the purpose of the expenditure with the motives of the members of the executive committee (and inferentially, of the other partners) in resolving to reimburse the expenditure, the case presents very little difficulty and is, indeed, a much clearer and easier case than *Mallalieu* v *Drummond*.'

Travelling expenses have been a cause of disagreement. The taxpayer was successful in *Horton* v *Young* (1971) 47 TC 60, on the grounds that his home was also his base of operations. Travelling to building sites was, therefore, allowable. This is essentially, though, a question of fact, as the barrister in *Newsom* v *Robertson* (1952) 33 TC 452 had his claim to deduct travelling expenses between his chambers and home rejected by the Court of Appeal, even though he worked several hours each night at home. His base was at his chambers and not his home. In *Sargent* v *Barnes* [1978] STC 322 the taxpayer failed in his claim to deduct the cost of travelling between a dental laboratory he visited most days to collect dental supplies and his surgery. The laboratory was between his home and the surgery. The expenditure was incurred, at least in part, in getting from his house to his surgery and could not, therefore, have been incurred wholly and exclusively in carrying on his profession. In the case of foreign trades, ss80 and 81 ICTA 1988 deem expenditure in appropriate cases to have been incurred wholly and exclusively for the purposes of the trade.

The Revenue will accept the authorised mileage allowance rates for Schedule D Case I or II purposes if, at the time the car is acquired, the turnover of the business does not exceed the VAT registration threshold. No other expenses can be claimed. The basis must be applied consistently. A change of basis can be made when one car is replaced by another (*Tax Bulletin* April 1996).

In suitable cases, the Revenue can argue that expenditure is of benefit not only to the trade in question but also an associated business. In practice this is more likely perhaps to apply to companies, but could arise where an individual is concurrently a sole trader and in partnership. Care needs to be taken in apportioning expenses, but the wholly and exclusively rule should not be taken to extremes. Otherwise, the consequence could be that an expense, which is wholly incurred for some business purposes, is not allowable because two different trades actually benefit. The decision of the Court of Appeal in *Vodafone Cellular Ltd* v *Shaw* [1997] STC 734 is helpful in resisting any such arguments by the Revenue where a liability has been incurred by one business, but another might also receive some benefit from the expenditure. It is important to determine the particular object of the taxpayer when he incurred the expense.

The treatment of interest paid is also often regarded as problematical. In principle, provided the wholly and exclusively test is met, interest payable will be deductible on an accruals basis. Difficulties arise if the proprietor's capital account is overdrawn as in that situation the Revenue will seek a disallowance. Moreover, they do not accept that the proprietor's account can be put into credit simply by revaluing assets (*Tax Bulletin* November 1991). A detailed example of the Revenue approach is set out in the *Inspector's Manual* at paragraph 780. Further guidance to the approach to be taken is provided by the Special Commissioner's decision in *Silk* v *Fletcher* [1999] STC (SCD) 220. This emphasises the need to consider the underlying reality, by looking in particular at the cash flow movements. Adjustments may, therefore, be necessary for cumulative depreciation. Moreover, simply because an individual's capital account is not overdrawn does not mean that an interest adjustment cannot be made. The essential question is whether or not interest charged in the accounts is incurred wholly and exclusively for the purposes of the trade.

> **Tax tip**
>
> If the Revenue argue that there is duality of purpose, it is worth examining the facts in detail. Any personal benefit could be no more than incidental to the essential business purpose. Even if that is not the case, it may be possible to dissect expenditure into separate components.

4.5 Capital expenditure

4.5.1 Capital versus revenue expenditure

In many instances, expenditure is categorised as being of a capital nature. In principle, capital expenditure is not deductible, in the absence of a statutory rule to the contrary. Thus, depreciation is not allowable or the writing off of capital expenditure on intangible property. The main statutory exception is the capital allowances regime, which is considered in detail in Chapter 5. Whether or not expenditure is capital or revenue is essentially a question of law, notwithstanding the accounting treatment. Commercial accounting principles do not determine the question, although they may be persuasive.

The result of this general rule is that capital expenditure may not be allowable in any circumstances, whatever the depreciation borne by the trader, although such expenditure may be deductible in arriving at a chargeable gain for the purposes of capital gains tax. Examples are the acquisition of goodwill and the consideration paid for the assignment of a lease. Relief is now given by FA 2002 for goodwill and other intangible assets acquired from 1 April 2002, but only for companies. The main element of the value of a lease may well be the right to pay a lower market rent until the next rent review, but the expenditure is nevertheless capital. An exception to this rule is s87 ICTA 1988 where a trader has paid a premium to a landlord and the landlord is assessable on that premium to some extent under the Schedule A rules. The tenant is allowed to treat the Schedule A part as if it were rent paid by him on a time basis over the duration of the lease. Indeed, this deemed rent deduction will pass to an assignee, based though on the original premium paid and not the purchase price.

Other examples of capital costs specifically permitted by statute are:

(a) Section 77 ICTA 1988 allows the incidental costs of obtaining loan finance as a deduction. These costs are defined as fees, commissions, advertising, printing and other incidental matters (not including stamp duty), provided the expenditure was incurred wholly and exclusively for the purpose of obtaining the finance, providing security or repaying it. Protection against foreign currency movement or premiums on repayment of a loan are not allowable. The Revenue also take the view that life assurance premiums, even where required by a lender, are not incidental costs (*Tax Bulletin* February 1992). In practice, the author has agreed with the Revenue that redemption sums, such as where calculated according to interest rates, are allowable. As for timing, the section is silent and accounting principles should be followed (*Tax Bulletin* April 1996).

(b) Expenditure in obtaining patents, trade marks and any other intellectual property rights are deductible (s83 ICTA 1988).

(c) For taxpayers in the waste disposal business, there are special rules for site restoration costs in sections 91A, B, BA and C ICTA 1988.

4.5.2 Repairs and improvements to premises

In practice, a common disagreement between an inspector of taxes and an adviser arises in connection with work on property. Compromises in grey areas are usually reached by negotiation. There are several cases which can be cited by both sides in support of their argument. A case which an inspector might cite is *Wm P Lawrie* v *CIR* (1952) 34 TC 20. A factory roof had fallen into a state of disrepair and was no longer watertight. After advice from an architect it was decided to reconstruct the whole roof and, in conjunction with this, lengthen and heighten the building. The taxpayer claimed a deduction based on the ratio of the old floorage to the new floorage area. This was rejected and is authority against any concept of notional repairs. The roof costs had been incurred on the reconstruction of the building as a whole and there were no grounds for attributing any part of the expense to a hypothetical repair. However, had the roof simply been replaced without any other work the expenditure could well have been allowed. In many of the cases the courts have sought to identify what is the entirety in a given case. Usually it is the building as a whole, which was the finding of the Court in this case, and not the roof. See also the comments at **8.2.3** based on *Tax Bulletin* of June 2002 as similar principles should apply to trades.

The taxpayer won in *Conn* v *Robins Bros Ltd* (1966) 43 TC 266. The lease of premises had three years to run, but the company was certain that it would be able to continue in occupation thereafter. Substantial costs were incurred on the building without creating additional space, part of which had been agreed as capital. The building was very old and any incidental improvements were an essential part of the repair.

When premises are acquired and work carried out shortly thereafter, the Revenue will examine the work to see if in truth if it is of a capital nature. If the premises were in such a poor state that they could not be used, or if the value was reduced on account of the state of disrepair, the expenditure could well be capital. *Odeon Associated Theatres Ltd* v *Jones* (1972) 48 TC 257 is clear authority for this, distinguishing the old case of *The Law Shipping Co Ltd* v *CIR* (1924) 12 TC 621. The Court of Appeal in the *Odeon* case also regarded accounting evidence as relevant in holding that on the facts the expenditure was deductible.

Most leases require the lessee to carry out repairs from time to time and particularly at the end of the lease, usually referred to as dilapidations. If the lessee carries out the necessary works to discharge the dilapidation's burden, the cost will usually be allowable as an expense of a revenue nature. However, making a payment to the assignee of a lease to represent the estimated dilapidations is likely to be treated as a capital expense, particularly following the Revenue's success before the Special Commissioner in *Southern Counties Agricultural Trading Society Limited* v *Blackler* [1999] STC (SCD) 200. A payment to a landlord as compensation in lieu of carrying out the repairs at the end of a lease, especially where part of the overall terms for the early surrender of a lease, could be treated as capital. A tenant must balance the overall commercial costs of doing a deal with a landlord to bring an end to the financial obligations with the tax treatment.

4.5.3 Other capital expenditure

Many cases have been heard by the courts and the decisions are not easy to reconcile, as has been acknowledged by judges. There have been one or two recent cases which summarise the old cases and bring the law up to date.

The classic starting point is the speech of Viscount Cave in *Atherton* v *British Insulated and Helsby Cables Ltd* (1926) 10 TC 155, where he said:

> 'But when expenditure is made, not only once and for all, but with a view to bringing into existence an asset or advantage for the endur-

ing benefit of a trade, I think that there is good reason (in the absence of special circumstances leading to an opposite conclusion) for treating such an expenditure as properly attributable not to revenue but to capital.'

In that case, it was held by a majority in the House of Lords that the initial contribution to an employee pension scheme was capital. In *Tucker* v *Granada Motorway Services Ltd* (1979) 53 TC 92 the House of Lords held that a lump sum payment to vary the method of computing rent under a lease was capital expenditure. In summarising the cases, Lord Wilberforce made the following comment, which was cited in the *Johnson Matthey* case referred to below:

'I think that the key to the present case is to be found in those cases which have sought to identify an asset. In them it seems reasonably logical to start with the assumption that money spent on the acquisition of the asset should be regarded as capital expenditure. Extensions from this are, first, to regard money spent on getting rid of a disadvantageous asset as capital expenditure and, secondly, to regard money spent on improving the asset, or making it more advantageous, as capital expenditure. In the latter type of case it will have to be considered whether the expenditure has the result stated or whether it should be regarded as expenditure on maintenance or upkeep, and some cases may pose difficult problems.'

In the later case of *Lawson* v *Johnson Matthey Plc* [1992] STC 466 the House of Lords disagreed with all four judges in the lower courts by accepting that on the facts a payment of £50m was of a revenue nature. It had been paid into an insolvent subsidiary company and at the same time the shares were sold for £1, under arrangements agreed with the Bank of England. The expenditure was not part of getting rid of an onerous asset (the shares) but to prevent the collapse of the subsidiary company. The resulting loss of confidence in the taxpayer company would have affected its banking business.

Getting rid of an onerous asset, such as a lease, is capital expenditure, as was held in *Mallett* v *Staveley Coal and Iron Co Ltd* (1928) 13 TC 772. However, where there is no identifiable asset as such, but simply a trading contract, expenditure to get rid of that contract is likely to be of a revenue nature. Cases supporting this are *Anglo-Persian Oil Co Ltd* v *Dale* (1932) 16 TC 253 and the *Vodafone* case mentioned above.

The Revenue take the view that expenditure on training courses to give proprietors new expertise, knowledge or skills is of a capital nature, bringing into existence an intangible asset. There is some authority for this in *Sargent* v *Eayrs* [1973] STC 50. Courses to update knowledge are normally revenue (*Tax Bulletin* November 1991). Initial franchise fees are usually treated as capital, even where paid by instalments. However, if part can be allocated to revenue matters, including staff training, then to that extent the sum will be treated as allowable (*Tax Bulletin* June 1995).

Expenditure on abortive capital projects is still disallowable. An example is the cost of applying for planning consent to extend a building used as a fixed asset where the application is rejected by the planning authorities.

4.6 Debts

Section 74(1)(j) prevents the deduction of debts except where provided by that paragraph as set out above. Normal trading debts which are either bad or doubtful can be deducted. A general provision is not allowable. Any provision must be specific. In practice, it is rare for there to be a general provision, as it is usually possible to allocate a provision against specific debts, sometimes based on an age analysis. The Revenue have given some guidance on the extent to which post balance sheet knowledge can be taken into account (see *Tax Bulletin* August 1994). In essence, if the information simply establishes that facts existed at the balance sheet date, the provision is allowable. The mere fact of slow payment is not a ground for a provision. There must be some other factor.

Releasing a debt is only allowable if incurred wholly and exclusively as part of a voluntary arrangement or compromise or arrangement under s425 Companies Act 1985.

A bad debt arising on transactions between connected parties is likely to be examined carefully by the inspector, as the circumstances could well indicate that the wholly and exclusively rule has been breached.

Until recently, it was possible for professions or vocations to prepare accounts on the so-called cash basis. There were various methods of this, but essentially the accounts would not recognise outstanding debts and/or work in progress. Section 42 FA 1998 (as amended by s101 FA 2002) now provides that:

'For the purposes of Case I or II of Schedule D the profits of a trade, profession or vocation must be computed in accordance with generally accepted accounting principles, subject to any adjustments required or authorised by law in computing profits for those purposes.'

This very generally worded provision is perhaps wider than the initial intention, which was to ensure the ending of the cash basis. This new rule applies to periods of account beginning after 6 April 1999. There are transitional rules for professions and vocations to bring into account the debts etc., not taxed previously, over a 10-year period. The detailed rules are contained in Schedule 6 FA 1998.

Finally, if a debt is released in favour of a taxpayer, s94 ICTA 1988 provides that the amount released (otherwise than as part of a voluntary arrangement or compromise etc.,) is to be treated as a trading receipt in the period in which the release is effected. This only applies where the debt has been allowed for trade, etc. purposes. The simple release of money lent to a trader would not fall within this provision for income tax purposes.

4.7   Stock and work in progress

4.7.1   Basis of valuation

The Revenue accept that parts of SP 3/90 dealing with stocks and long-term contracts need to be withdrawn as a result of the *Jenner Princes Street, Edinburgh Ltd* and *Herbert Smith* cases. Any method of valuing stock and work in progress should now be acceptable for tax purposes, provided it conforms with the principles of commercial accountancy. A change in basis, where both the old and new basis are valid, is dealt with in **4.8** below. If the change is from a non-valid basis the Revenue will review earlier years. Provided there is neither fraud nor neglect they will not seek tax for past years on an amount greater than the resulting uplift.

The previous Revenue view that a provision for an expected future loss is not allowable does not survive the recent decisions of the courts mentioned above. The relevant test is whether or not proper accounting principles have been applied. According to *Tax Bulletin* of December 1994, the Revenue will accept formulae for stock provisions and write-downs.

4.7.2 Professions

As mentioned above, s44 FA 1998 required a true and fair view approach, and so for the first time many professions had to consider the valuation of work in progress (or at least refine existing methods where appropriate).

In valuing work in progress, the time spent by partners must not be included, as their cost is an appropriation of profit. The direct costs of fee earners should be included together with an appropriate addition for overheads. Guidance has recently been issued by the Institute of Chartered Accountants in England and Wales (ICAEW) in TAX 30/98 to the effect that:

- The direct cost of fee earners should be included in a valuation, in all cases.

- Overheads can be ignored for a sole practitioner and up to four partner firms (unless there is an unusually high ratio of fee earners to partners).

- For medium-size firms, some recognition of overheads should be taken in the valuation. The Revenue will accept a fairly rough and ready approach.

- For a larger firm, a fair proportion of overheads should be brought into account, applying SSAP 9.

- Adjustments may be required to reduce cost to net realisable value, including cases where a client may be unable to pay for the work.

- In the case of contingent fees, work in progress should only be brought into account if it is known, when the accounts are prepared, that the case has been won.

- Once an assignment has become billable the full fee should be recognised, whether or not actually billed by the end of the period of account.

4.7.3 Appropriations to and from trading stock

In *Sharkey* v *Wernher* (1955) 36 TC 275, the House of Lords held that when the taxpayer, who carried on a stud farm, transferred horses to a racing establishment also carried on by her, she should treat the horses so transferred as if sold at market value (and not cost). The consequence of this is that any trader who transfers stock for his own benefit should effectively credit his accounts for own consumption based on market value. In practice, an inspector of taxes will take a reasonable line in applying this rule (SP A32). This basic principle is also relevant where an asset moves from trading stock to fixed asset.

Example 4.1

A builder constructs a house on land with the intention of selling it in the course of his trade. The land cost £50,000 and the house £100,000 to build. It appears as stock in his accounts at £150,000 (assuming this to be less than market value). The housing market is depressed on completion of the house and so he decides to hold it for the time being, obtaining a rent in the meantime.

The house will remain as trading stock even though rents are received, because there remains an intention to sell it. If the builder decides not to sell the house after all but keep it for the long term as an investment, and the accounts in particular reflect this, he is treated as if he had sold the house at its market value. Thus, if the market value at that time is £200,000, his accounts for that year will show an additional profit of £50,000.

Facts are rarely this clear cut in practice but the accounting treatment would be conclusive if they show the asset as an investment or as a charge to drawings.

The principle in *Sharkey* v *Wernher* also applies in reverse. If a trader brings into trading stock an asset which he has held privately then he should introduce that asset at market value. For example, an individual who has bought antiques over many years for his own enjoyment decides to set up in business as an antique dealer. He introduces certain items to his shop as stock. He should be treated as if he had acquired those items at market value, which would also be a disposal for capital gains tax purposes (see the *Capital Gains Tax* volume).

This principle only applies to trading stock. It does not require a person carrying on a profession or vocation to bring in at market value the services he renders for nil or less than market value. If costs have been incurred directly on a matter this should be excluded as an expense, but not general overhead expenses. A case in point is *Mason* v *Innes* (1967) 44 TC 326 where it was held that an author, having assigned as a gift to his father the copyright in a book he had written did not have to bring in the value of that copyright as part of his professional receipts. Up to two years previously, he had deducted the expenses in writing the book and which had been allowed at the time.

4.7.4   Stock and work in progress on cessation of a business

There are statutory rules on this in ss100 to 102 ICTA 1988. In summary, if stock is sold to another trader who can deduct the cost of the stock, the amount to be brought into the accounts of the discontinuing trader is the consideration received. If the persons are connected, then an equivalent price should be substituted for the actual price paid, if different. Otherwise, stock is to be valued at the date of cessation on the basis of its market value. A joint election can be made under s100(IC) to use the acquisition value, if not less than the actual sale price, where the transfer is between connected persons (such as on the incorporation of the business of a sole trader or partnership).

Similar rules apply to work in progress where a profession or vocation ceases, except that an election can be made under s101(2) ICTA 1988 for the excess over the actual cost to be taxed under s103 as a post-cessation receipt as and when realised. This could affect the year of assessment and consideration needs to be given to the likely tax rates applying in the relevant years.

4.8   Change of accounting basis

A statutory procedure dealing with adjustments arising from a change of accounting basis was first introduced by s44 and Schedule 6 FA 1998. Those provisions have now been replaced by s63 and Schedule 22 FA 2002 where the change of basis takes effect in a period of account ending after 31 July 2001. The change of basis is treated as taking effect in the first period of account in which the new basis is adopted.

These rules only apply if the old basis and the new basis accord with the law and practice applicable in relation to the period of account both before and after the change. A change of basis means either a change of accounting principle or practice in accordance with generally accepted accounting practice or an adjustment required or authorised by law in computing profits for tax purposes (but excluding amending legislation that does not apply to the previous period).

Where the effect of the change is that profits were understated on the old basis, the adjustment is chargeable to tax under Schedule D Case VI as income arising on the last day of the period of account for which the new basis is adopted. Where profits were overstated on the old basis, the adjustment is allowed as a deduction in computing profits as an expense arising on the last day of the first period of account for which the new basis is adopted.

There are special rules for barristers in the early years of practice where, under s43 FA 1998, they are allowed to apply the cash basis on those years.

There are also special rules applying where, as a result of a change of basis, the expenses brought into account on the old basis would, under the new basis, be brought into account over more than one period after the change. In this case, no adjustment is made and it is specifically provided that there can be no deduction by applying the new basis (to avoid giving relief more than once). That rule is contained in para 6 of Schedule 22 and para 7 deals with how adjustments are made that result from a tax adjustment affecting the calculation of stock or work in progress and depreciation.

4.9 Receipts

4.9.1 Voluntary receipts

The fact that payment is not received under a contractual or quasi-contractual basis does not mean it cannot be assessed. If a voluntary payment is made to assist a trader in meeting expenses or in recognition of particular services then it is taxable. For cases supporting this see *CIR* v *Falkirk Ice Rink Ltd* [1975] STC 434 and *Rolfe* v *Nagel* [1982] STC 53. On the other hand, in *Murray* v *Goodhews* [1978] STC 207 an *ex gratia* sum paid by a brewery on terminating a tied tenancy agreement was held not to be a trading receipt. There had been no negotiation and the payment was calculated by reference to rateable values rather than trading results.

If an amount owed is not claimed by the creditor and is written back by the debtor, the Special Commissioners' decision in *Anise Limited* v *Hammond* [2003] STC (SCD) 258 suggests that the amount so credited in the accounts is not taxable.

4.9.2 Compensation payments

The main rule established is that a payment made to compensate a trader for receipts which would have formed part of his trading profit are also taxable. This was put by Diplock LJ in *London and Thames Haven Oil Wharves* v *Atwool* (1967) 43 TC 491 as follows:

> 'I will start by formulating what I believe to be the relevant rule. Where, pursuant to a legal right, a trader receives from another person compensation for the trader's failure to receive a sum of money which, if it had been received, would have been credited to the amount of profits, if any, arising in any year from the trade run by him at the time when the compensation was so received, the compensation is to be treated for tax purposes in the same way as that sum of money would have been treated if it had been received, instead of compensation.'

This principle was applied in *Donald Fisher (Ealing) Ltd* v *Spencer* [1989] STC 256. The company had claimed damages from an estate agent who had failed to serve a counter notice against a proposed rent increase. As a result, more rent was paid for a period of years than would have been the case but for the negligence. It was held that the compensation payment of £14,000 was a trading receipt. The lease itself had not been altered in any way, only the application of the rent review clause until the next review.

However, where a contract is so fundamental to the business as to be part of its structure, then compensation for loss of that right is likely to be treated as capital receipt. This was the situation in *Van den Berghs Ltd* v *Clark* (1935) 19 TC 390. The question of capital gains tax should be considered, as there could well be a disposal for the purposes of that tax. However, in other cases, such as *Kelsall Parsons & Co* v *CIR* (1938) 21 TC 608, compensation payments for the loss of agency agreements were held to be trading receipts. Contracts have been regarded as merely incidental to the normal course of a business even where comprising over 80 per cent of total business, as in *Fleming* v *Bellow Machine Co Ltd* (1965) 42 TC 308.

4.9.3 Intellectual property rights

The treatment of the sale proceeds of know-how interacts with capital allowances and is dealt with in Chapter 5. Essentially, the sale of know-how (as defined) is treated as a trading receipt in one way or another. However, where a trade or part of a trade is also sold at the same time, it is treated as goodwill, unless the parties to the transaction make a joint election to the contrary (s531(3) ICTA 1988).

Lump sums received by authors for the grant of copyright or sale of manuscripts are revenue receipts (see the recent case of *Wain* v *Cameron* [1995] STC 555 as an illustration of this).

4.9.4 Reverse premiums

Section 54 and Schedule 6 FA 1999 deem reverse premiums in relation to land to be of a revenue nature, where received after 8 March 1999. Where the land transaction relates to a trade, profession or vocation carried on by the recipient, the amount will be taxable under Schedule D Case I or II, according to the appropriate commercial accounting treatment. Guidance on this is given by UITF abstract 28.

To be a taxable reverse premium, there must be a payment or other benefit by way of inducement in a transaction whereby the recipient, or a connected person, becomes entitled to an estate or interest in land (usually a leasehold interest). The payment etc must be made by the person granting the interest or a nominee or connected person, so a payment by an assignor of an existing lease to the person taking over that interest would not normally be a reverse premium.

Payments to fit out premises, for example, are not taken into account for this purpose to the extent that the expenditure for capital allowances purposes is reduced by such payments (Sch 6 para 6).

Schedule 6 does not apply to an individual where the transaction relates to premises occupied or to be occupied by him as his only or main residence.

4.9.5 Adopters and foster carers

Section 327A ICTA 1988, added by FA 2003, provides that various payments to a person who has adopted or intends to adopt a child are not treated as income payments for tax purposes, with effect from 2003/04 onwards.

Schedule 36 FA 2003 also provides relief for income tax purposes to individuals who provide foster care, again from 2003/04 and later years. To qualify for the relief, the following conditions must be met:

- The individual has foster care receipts, which otherwise would be fully chargeable under Schedule D Case I, II or VI. Foster care means providing accommodation and maintenance for a child under the stipulated statutory provisions. Moreover, the individual providing the care must not be a parent of the child or have parental responsibility.

- The only taxable income from the trade etc in relation to which the foster care receipts arise is from that activity.

If the total foster care receipts for a year of assessment do not exceed the individual's limit for that year, the profits are exempt from income tax. An individual's limit is the aggregate of a fixed amount of £10,000 (adjusted if the period in question is not exactly one year) and a weekly amount for each foster child. That weekly amount is £200 where a child is under 11 years of age throughout the week and £250 in other cases (counting part of a week as a whole week). Where more than one individual having foster care receipts provides the care in the same residence, the fixed amount is divided between those individuals on an equal basis. Where, in the case of a trade etc., the period of account is other than 5 April, the test as to whether or not the individual's limit is exceeded for the year of assessment is determined by reference to the period of account ending in the year.

If the limit is exceeded for a year of assessment, the individual can elect for the alternative method, which is only beneficial if the resulting profit is less than that calculated on a conventional basis. The effect of the election, which must be made by 31 January in the year but one following the year of assessment, is .to deem the profits of the year to be the difference between the foster care receipts for that year and the individual's limit. This is very similar to the rent a room scheme for Schedule A purposes. Again, the calculation is made by reference to the period of account ending in the year of assessment where other than 5 April. The practical benefit of making the election is that there is no need to compute the profit by reference to expenses and the like although a broad calculation would have to be made by an individual to test whether or not the tax difference is significant.

There are special rules for capital allowances to ensure that these are not given in a year when the foster care receipts are either below the limit or the election has been made, but without giving rise to a balancing adjustment. If in a subsequent year the individual becomes chargeable in the normal way, he is deemed to have incurred capital expenditure on plant and machinery that was held previously and is still owned. Effectively, that plant or machinery will be brought in at its market value but not exceeding cost. Any capital expenditure incurred in a period when the foster care receipts are below the individual's limit or election is made do not count either but again can be brought in on the same basis if he becomes chargeable in the normal way in a later period.

4.10 Other statutory provisions

4.10.1 Entertaining

Section 577 ICTA 1988 prevents a deduction for expenditure on business entertainment, which includes hospitality of any kind. It does not include, though, anything provided for bona fide members of a trader's staff unless incidental to the provision for others (such as an employee joining a lunch with customers). The disallowance also extends to gifts, other than small items containing a conspicuous advertisement not exceeding £50 in cost (but excluding food, drink, tobacco or vouchers exchangeable for such goods).

The disallowance applies irrespective of whether or not the customer is in the UK or overseas. If plant or machinery is used for entertaining purposes, that use is treated as for a non-trade purpose. Thus, in considering capital allowances apportionment is required if an asset is used partly for entertaining purposes (s269 CAA 2001).

4.10.2 Redundancies

Section 579 makes it clear that statutory redundancy payments are deductible. Section 90 ICTA 1988 extends this to additional redundancy payments. These are payments which would otherwise not be allowable provided they do not exceed three times the s579 payment. A provision for redundancy payments made after the year end will be accepted by the Revenue if a definite decision was made in the period and payment is made within nine months of the end of the period of account (*Tax Bulletin* February 1995).

Until recently, the Revenue took the view that severance payments on cessation of trade were not allowable unless falling with the statutory provisions mentioned above. Following the Privy Council decision in *CIR* v *'Cosmotron Manufacturing Co Ltd* (1997) 70 TC 292, the Revenue now accept that such payments made to employees can be deductible where there is a legal liability (but not to ex gratia payments which exceed those allowable under s90 ICTA 1988).

4.10.3 Expenditure involving crime

Section 577A ICTA 1988 prevents the deduction of any expenditure which constitutes the commission of a criminal offence or expenditure of a trader who has succumbed to blackmail. Section 67 FA 2002 extends this to expenditure incurred after 31 March 2002 to payments made outside the UK and which would have constituted a criminal offence had they been made in the UK.

4.10.4 Employment payments and pensions

Section 43 FA 1989 provides that a payment of employee's remuneration is not allowable unless paid within nine months of the end of the relevant period of account. For this purpose, the meaning of paid is the same as for Income Tax (Earnings and Pensions) Act 2003, with its wide definition of payment.

Pension payments for the benefit of employees can only be deducted when paid and not on an accruals basis (s592(4) ICTA 1988).

4.10.5 Car hire and leasing

Section 578A ICTA 1998 restricts the expenditure eligible for relief on the hiring of a motor car, if the retail price of the car when new exceeds £12,000. The allowable element is the following fraction:

$$\frac{(£12,000 + \text{Retail price})}{2 \times \text{Retail price}}$$

Example 4.2

A motor car with a retail price of £20,000 is provided to a trader on an operating lease. The monthly payments are £450 including maintenance element of £50 (excluding VAT).

The maintenance charge is treated as any other motor expense provided it is identified separately. The balance of the payment is restricted, for income tax purposes, by the following percentage:

$$\frac{12,000 + 20,000}{2 \times 20,000} = 80\%$$

Thus, only 80 per cent is allowable and this is also subject to any private use restriction.

Rebates of rental are similarly reduced by the same fraction (s578A(4)). The section does not apply to hire-purchase arrangements, unless the purchase option payment exceeds 1 per cent of the retail price (s578B). According to *Tax Bulletin* April 2000, where the lessee knows the actual price paid by the lessor for the car when new, that can be used as the retail price.

This restriction does not apply to low emission and electrically-propelled cars eligible for a first-year allowance (see **5.3.2**)

4.10.6   Sundry provisions

There are also provisions covering the following:

- expenses concerned with foreign trades – ss80 and 81 ICTA 1988;

- contributions to local enterprise agencies, etc. – ss79 and 79A ICTA 1988;

- gifts to educational establishments – s84 ICTA 1988;

- interest paid to non-residents – s82 ICTA 1988;

- exemption for regional development grants under s92 ICTA 1988;

- payments and expenses for charitable purposes as specified in ss86 and 86A ICTA 1988 and s47 FA 1998; and

- VAT penalties, interest and surcharges are not allowable – s827 ICTA 1988;

- deductibility of payments for restrictive undertakings, where taxed on the employee under s313 ICTA 1988 – s73 FA 1988; and

- expenditure on research and development related to a trade is allowable even though technically it might fall foul of s74 ICTA 1988 (s82A ICTA 1988). It should also be noted that the enhanced tax relief deductions for 'R & D expenditure' apply only to companies (see Schedule 20 FA 2000).

5 Trades, professions and vocations – capital allowances

5.1 Scope of chapter and general points

5.1.1 Scope

The basic unfairness in not allowing the depreciation of fixed assets is recognised by the capital allowances system in CAA 2001. This Act came into force on 6 April 2001 and was the first enactment of the new style in which tax legislation is being restated. No changes to the law are intended though. This chapter is concerned only with trades, professions and vocations. Allowances in relation to property income are set out in Chapter 8.

5.1.2 Method of giving relief

The method of giving relief is much simpler under self-assessment. Section 247 CAA 2001 for trades provides that allowances for plant and machinery, as an example, are to be given effect to as follows:

> 'If the qualifying activity of a person who is entitled or liable to an allowance or charge for a chargeable period is a trade, the allowance or charge is to be given effect in calculating the profits of that person's trade, by treating –
> (a)   the allowance as an expense of the trade, and
> (b)   the charge as a receipt of the trade.'

Section 251 CAA 2001 contains a similarly worded rule for professions and vocations and s352 CAA 2001 applies to buildings. Section 6 CAA 2001 defines 'chargeable period' as being a period of account, and then goes on to define 'period of account'. Normally, this is the period for which accounts are made up for the purposes of the trade, etc. In the rare example where two periods of account overlap, the period common to both is deemed to fall in the first period only. Where there is an interval between two periods of account, the interval is also deemed to be part of the first period. Another refinement is that for capital allowance purposes, a period of more than 18 months is divided into separate periods of account to ensure that none is more than 12 months. Given that on a change of accounting date a period should not exceed 18 months, this provision is more likely to apply on a commencement.

Example 5.1

A taxpayer commenced trading on 1 February 2001 and the first accounts are for the 23 months to 31 December 2002.

Capital allowances are calculated by reference to the following periods:

12 months to 31 January 2002

11 months to 31 December 2002

Thus, expenditure and disposals must be allocated between the two periods with writing-down allowances calculated by reference first to 12 months and then for 11 months. The total allowances for the 23 months period are then treated as a trading expense of the accounts for that period in applying ss60 and 61 ICTA 1988.

5.1.3   Value added tax

In the normal situation this is quite straightforward. If activities are wholly standard rated then any capital expenditure incurred for that purpose is net of VAT. In the case of an exempt business, the expenditure includes the appropriate VAT. For partially exempt businesses, the appropriate proportion of the VAT, which is not treated as input tax, should be added to the purchase price.

Difficulties arise, though, for partially exempt businesses where expenditure is within the capital items legislation. This is more likely to apply to construction work, although it can apply to substantial expenditure on plant. Under the capital items scheme, the initial amount of allowable input tax is effectively provisional. Calculations are carried out for up to 5 or 10 years and additional VAT may become deductible or payable, depending upon the changes in the use for partial exemption purposes. Sections 234 to 246 CAA 2001 for plant and machinery and ss345 to 351 for buildings contain special rules for determining the effect of any such additional VAT or rebate and s549 as to when adjustments arise. In the normal case where a VAT return has been submitted, the liability or rebate is treated as incurred or made in the period of account which includes the last day of the period to which that return relates. If cessation of trade intervenes, the liability or rebate is dealt with on the last day of trading.

5.1.4 Time when capital expenditure is incurred

Subject to the special rule for additional VAT liabilities mentioned above, s5 CAA 2001 provides that:

'(1) For the purposes of this Act, the general rule is that an amount of capital expenditure is to be treated as incurred as soon as there is an unconditional obligation to pay it.

(2) The general rule applies even if the whole or a part of the expenditure is not required to be paid until a later date.'

This definition is particularly important to ensure that expenditure is in the correct period and in the application of any initial or first year allowances. Merely entering into a contract does not cause expenditure to be incurred, but the contractual terms could well be relevant in determining the question. Where plant or machinery is acquired, commonly the relevant date is delivery, and not the date when the purchase price is to be paid. Revenue guidance is given in *Tax Bulletin* of November 1993.

Section 5 contains the following refinements:

(a) If under an agreement an asset becomes the property of, or is attributed to, a person before the obligation to pay becomes unconditional, in a period of account, and the date of becoming unconditional is within one month from the end of that period the expenditure is deemed to be incurred at the end of that period of account.

(b) If the whole or any part of capital expenditure is payable on a date more than four months after the date of becoming unconditional, the expenditure is deemed to be incurred at the latest date when the payment is required to be paid.

(c) To counter avoidance, if an obligation to pay becomes unconditional on a date earlier than that which accords with normal commercial usage and the sole or main benefit is the acceleration of allowances, the relevant date becomes the latest due date for payment.

> ### *Example 5.2*
>
> A trader draws up his accounts to 30 September 2002. In September two machines are delivered, both becoming his property on delivery. However, for one machine the contract provides for installation and payment is conditional upon that. Installation occurs on 20 October 2002. For the other machine, the trader does not have to pay until 31 March 2003. In the case of the first machine, the expenditure is incurred in the year to 30 September 2002 under s5(4) CAA 2001. The machine became the trader's property in that year and the obligation to pay arose within one month of the year end.
>
> In the case of the second machine, s5(5) CAA 2001 applies to treat the expenditure as incurred on the date it becomes payable (31 March 2003) as this is more than four months after delivery, when the obligation to pay became unconditional.

5.1.5   Apportionment of consideration

On a sale of a business, for example, the parties cannot simply apportion the proceeds to the best tax advantage. Section 562 CAA 2001 requires a just apportionment to be made, even if separate prices have been agreed.

5.2   Plant and machinery – meaning

5.2.1   The general meaning

Difficulty can arise in identifying whether expenditure is incurred on 'plant'. The identification of machinery is much simpler, as a machine is a device for the conversion of direction or motion. Motor vehicles and computers are regarded as machinery.

The well-known definition of plant, commonly cited by the courts, is from the non-tax case of *Yarmouth* v *France* (1887) 19 QBD 647 where Lindley LJ said:

> 'In its ordinary sense, it includes whatever apparatus is used by a businessman in carrying on his business, not his stock-in-trade which he buys or makes for sale; but all goods and chattels, fixed or moveable, live or dead, which he keeps for permanent employment in his business.'

This clearly excludes the premises or place in which a business is carried on (the setting). The treatment of expenditure on buildings and structures is more complex and is dealt with separately below. A case not involving a building is *Benson* v *Yard Arm Club Ltd* [1979] STC 266, in which the Court of Appeal held that a ship, which had been converted into a floating restaurant, was not plant. The ship, being moored permanently, was the structure within which the business was carried on, not part of the business apparatus. It remained a chattel but this did not affect its role in the particular business. In similar vein, a caravan fixed to a site for the sale of take away food would not be plant but a caravan on wheels, which moves from site to site, would qualify.

A barrister's library was held to be plant in *Munby* v *Furlong* [1977] STC 232. There is also a reference in Lindley LJ's judgment to live goods. Live goods would usually be part of a farmer's stock. However, a riding school which acquires horses and ponies on which to provide riding tuition should, in principle, be plant. They are no different to the motor cars of a driving school.

As a rule of thumb, plant has a life of at least two years. The House of Lords' decision in *Hinton* v *Maden & Ireland Ltd* (1959) 38 TC 391 gives some authority for this. In that case lives and lasts used in machines for shoe manufacturing, having a life of three years, were held to be plant. In the later case of *Rose & Co (Wallpaper & Paints) Ltd* v *Campbell* (1967) 44 TC 500, sample pattern books provided by a wallpaper retailer, and with a useful life of approximately two years, were held to be neither plant nor capital expenditure. The expense was allowable as revenue. The treatment of video tapes bought for rental is dealt with by the Revenue in *Tax Bulletin* of October 1995.

For a discussion of the definition of plant and machinery see Tax Digest 206 *Plant and Machinery*.

5.2.2 Statutory plant

CAA 2001 contains certain provisions deeming expenditure to be plant, even though it might not be so categorised in the normal sense of the word. These provisions include:

(a) Under s25 CAA 2001, expenditure on alterations to an existing building incidental to the installation of machinery or plant is treated as part of the cost of machinery itself. See also s26 CAA 2001 for the treatment of demolition costs.

(b) Under s28 CAA 2001, expenditure in adding insulation against loss of heat to an industrial building or structure is treated as plant. If a building is sold, the disposal value of this expenditure is deemed to be nil.

(c) Under s71 CAA 2001, capital expenditure on acquiring rights to use or deal with computer software or in creating such software is treated as machinery or plant. *Tax Bulletin* of November 1993 sets out the Revenue view on computer software expenditure generally. This repeats the view that software with a useful economic life of less than two years would normally be treated as revenue expenditure. Where both hardware and software are bought as a package, the expenditure can be apportioned, to treat as a revenue expense the amount allocated to software with a life of less than two years. Software costs to solve the year 2000 problem are accepted as revenue costs in *Tax Bulletin* of April 1998.

(d) There are special rules for films, tapes and discs which can, subject to the detailed provisions, be treated as revenue expenditure.

Fire safety expenditure to comply with a notice served by the fire authority under s5(4) Fire Precautions Act 1971 or in carrying out steps specified in writing under that Act on the application for a fire certificate, is treated as expenditure on plant, etc., under s29 CAA 2001. The disposal value is also deemed to be nil. Sections 30, 31, 32 and 33 CAA 2001 deal respectively with expenditure on safety at sports grounds and security.

5.2.3 Expenditure on buildings and structures

In *CIR* v *Barclay Curle & Co Ltd* (1969) 45 TC 221, the House of Lords held by a majority that expenditure on the construction of a dry dock, which acted like a hydraulic chamber to raise and lower ships for inspection and repair, was plant. The anticipated life of the dry dock was over 80 years. The reasoning is that the dry dock, notwithstanding its solid and fixed construction, was a piece of apparatus which functioned as plant in the company's trade. This decision encouraged more and more claims in relation to expenditure on buildings, some of which were successful before the courts, but many were not.

The Revenue were concerned that the courts could gradually extend the meaning of plant and wished to limit this. As a result FA 1994 added what is now in ss21 to 24 CAA 2001. The purpose of this is not to restrict the right to capital allowances but rather to codify the rules, based on judicial decisions up to that point. There will, no doubt, remain areas of disagreement but these are likely to be far fewer than previously.

The general rule is that expenditure on the provision of a building cannot be treated as plant or machinery. For this purpose, s21 CAA 2001 defines a building as including an asset which is incorporated in the building or, if not so incorporated, is of a kind normally incorporated in a building, whether moveable or not. Section 21 then goes on to specify other expenditure which is treated as expenditure on a building, where contained in list A, as follows:

- walls, floors, ceilings, doors, gates, shutters, windows and stairs;

- mains services, and systems, for water, electricity and gas;

- waste disposal systems;

- sewerage and drainage systems;

- shafts or other structures in which lifts, hoist, escalators and moving walkways are installed; and

- fire safety systems.

There is a similar system for structures, assets and works in s22 CAA 2001, which treats the following expenditure as set out in list B in that section as not being eligible as plant and machinery:

- a tunnel, bridge, viaduct, aqueduct, abatement or cutting;

- a way, hard standing (such as a pavement), road, railway, tramway, a park for vehicles or containers, or an airstrip or runway;

- an inland navigation, including a canal, basin or a navigable river;

- a dam, reservoir or barrage, including any sluices, gates, generators and other associated equipment;

- a dock, harbour, wharf, pier, marina or jetty or any other structure in or at which vessels can be kept, or merchandise or passengers may be shipped or unshipped;

- a dike, sea wall, weir or drainage ditch; and

- any other structure apart from relatively specialist items mentioned in item 7 of list B.

Lists A and B are very comprehensive and could exclude items that have always been treated as plant. List C in s23 CAA 2001 then sets out many items that are unaffected by ss21 and 22 but do not include any asset whose principal purpose is to insulate or enclose the interior of a building or to provide an interior wall, floor or ceiling which is intended to remain permanently in place. This means that as a rule false ceilings will not qualify as plant. The items in list C are as follows:

- machinery (including devices for providing motive power) not within any other item in this list;

- electrical systems (including lighting systems) and cold water, gas and sewerage systems provided mainly –
  - (a) to meet the particular requirements of the qualifying activity, or
  - (b) to serve particular plant or machinery used for the purposes of the qualifying activity;

- space or water heating systems; powered systems of ventilation, air cooling or air purification; and any floor or ceiling comprised in such systems;

- manufacturing or processing equipment; storage equipment (including cold rooms); display equipment; and counters, check-outs and similar equipment;

- cookers, washing machines, dishwashers, refrigerators and similar equipment; washbasins, sinks, baths, showers, sanitary ware and similar equipment; and furniture and furnishings;

- lifts, hoists, escalators and moving walkways;

- sound insulation provided mainly to meet the particular require-ments of the qualifying activity;

- computer, telecommunications and surveillance systems (including their wiring or other links);

- refrigeration or cooling equipment;

- fire alarm systems; sprinkler and other equipment for extinguishing or containing fires;

- burglar alarm systems;

- strong rooms in bank or building society premises; safes;

- partition walls, where moveable and intended to be moved in the course of the qualifying activity;

- decorative assets provided for the enjoyment of the public in hotel, restaurant or similar trades;

- advertising hoardings; signs, displays and similar assets;

- swimming pools (including diving boards, slides and structures on which such boards or slides are mounted);

- any glasshouse constructed so that the required environment (namely, air, heat, light, irrigation and temperature) for the growing of plants is provided automatically by means of devices forming an integral part of its structure;

- cold stores;

- caravans provided mainly for holiday lettings;

- buildings provided for testing aircraft engines run within the buildings;

- moveable buildings intended to be moved in the course of the qualifying activity;

- the alteration of land for the purpose only of installing plant or machinery;

- the provision of dry docks;

- the provision of any jetty or similar structure provided mainly to carry plant or machinery;

- the provision of pipelines or underground ducts or tunnels with a primary purpose of carrying utility conduits;

- the provision of towers to support floodlights;

- the provision of –
  (a) any reservoir incorporated into a water treatment works, or
  (b) any service reservoir of treated water for supply within any housing estate or other particular locality;

- the provision of –
  (a) silos provided for temporary storage, or
  (b) storage tanks;

- the provision of slurry pits or silage clamps;

- the provision of fish tanks or fish ponds;

- the provision of rails, sleepers and ballast for a railway or tramway;

- the provision of structures and other assets for providing the setting for any ride at an amusement park or exhibition; and

- the provision of fixed zoo cages.

For the avoidance of doubt, it is stated clearly that the acquisition of any interest in land cannot be treated as part of the cost of machinery or plant (other than expenditure which in law becomes fixtures and therefore part of the land under general English land law).

Recent cases, where the expenditure was not affected by ss 21 to 24 but which demonstrate the approach of the courts, include *Bradley* v *London Electricity* [1996] STC 1054, in which it was held that expenditure in constructing an underground substation was not plant. The structure and the equipment within could not be treated as a single functioning entity, distinguishing it from the dry dock in the *Barclay Curle* case. The fact that the structure was purpose-built and carefully designed to accommodate the equipment did not make it plant. In *Gray* v *Seymours Garden Centre (Horticulture)* [1995] STC 706 expenditure in constructing a 'planteria' (a glass house to store and lay out ornamental plants for sale) failed the test. However, had the structure been more sophisticated, with automatic opening of vents, etc., it might have moved into the category of plant, as being a single functioning structure (see *Tax Bulletin* of November 1992). In *Attwood* v *Anduff Car Wash Ltd* [1997] STC 1167, expenditure on the creation of a structure for a car washing site was held not to be plant. The washing equipment could operate without its surround, even though the structure facilitated the actual car washing. That was not sufficient to make it a single unit of plant.

Mezzanine floors are often a cause of disagreement. Claims were unsuccessful for raised restaurant floors in *Wimpy International Ltd* v *Warland* [1992] STC 273 but successful for movable storage platforms in *Hunt* v *Henry Quick Limited* [1992] STC 633. The *Capital Allowances Manual* sets out the Revenue view, accepting the principle only where the floor has not become part of the premises and is used only for storage.

The High Court recently considered whether an artificial all weather race track installed at Lingfield Park Racecourse was plant. Reversing the General Commissioners, Hart J in *Shove* v *Lingfield Park 1991 Ltd* STC [2003] 1003, held that the track was not plant. It could not be said to be apparatus separate from the premises, merely functioning as part of the premises on which the company conducted its business of staging horse-racing.

5.3 Plant and machinery – computational and related matters

5.3.1 The basic rules

The rules for most machinery or plant are set out here. There are, though, special provisions which may apply to the following and which are dealt with later in this section:

- motor cars;

- short-life assets;

- long-life assets;

- assets used partly for non-trade purposes;

- fixtures; and

- machinery or plant acquired on hire purchase, etc.

There are two main types of allowances available: a first-year allowance and a writing-down allowance. First-year allowances are given at a greater rate than normal, usually to encourage expenditure. A so-called small or medium-sized enterprise could claim a first-year allowance of 50 per cent for expenditure in the year to 1 July 1998 and 40 per cent from 2 July 1998 (s70 FA 2000 extended this indefinitely). First-year allowances cannot be claimed on motor cars, long-life assets and plant, etc., for leasing (s46 CAA 2001). Leasing is defined widely by s46 to include the hiring of an asset. The Revenue now accept that in most cases the supply of both plant and operator is not merely the hiring of an asset but the provision of a service. Thus, providing JCB's for digging under the control of an operator engaged by the supplier is not hiring for this purpose. For expenditure incurred after 16 April 2002, this leasing restriction does not apply to qualifying expenditure under s45A, D or E CAA 2001.

Expenditure on information and communication technology incurred by a small enterprise is eligible for a first-year allowance of 100 per cent where the expenditure is incurred in the four years to 31 March 2004 (s45 CAA 2001 as extended by FA 2003). Expenditure on information and communication technology is defined to include computers and associated equipment; certain types of telephone and transmission devices; and software used for the purposes of any qualifying equipment. However, computerised control or management systems or other systems that are part of a larger system whose principal function is not processing or storing information, do not qualify for the 100 per cent first-year allowance.

Otherwise the written-down value of the pool brought forward is added to the total expenditure on plant and machinery in the relevant period of account where not claimed for a first-year allowance, irrespective of the actual date the expenditure is incurred. A writing-down allowance at the rate of 25 per cent per annum, adjusted for shorter or longer periods, is given on a reducing balance basis. The disposal receipts of plant and machinery are deducted before calculating a writing-down allowance (s55 CAA 2001).

Example 5.3

A taxpayer commenced in business on 1 August 2002 and prepares his first accounts to 31 December 2003. His purchases and sales are as follows:

	£
Purchases – machinery 1 August 2002	18,000
Purchases – computer 8 September 2003	4,000
Purchases – office furniture 17 December 2003	6,000
Sales – piece of machinery (original cost £3,000)	1,500

Capital allowances will be given as a deduction in arriving at profits for the first 17 months in business and that net profit will then be the basis for the first two years of assessment. The capital allowances have to be calculated, however, for the entire period, as follows, and assuming first-year allowances are not claimed:

	General pool
	£
Machinery	18,000
Computer	4,000
Office furniture	6,000
	28,000
Less: sale of machinery – limited to cost	(1,500)
	26,500
Writing-down allowance 25% × 17/12	(9,386)
Written down value 31 December 2003	17,114

As mentioned, first-year allowances at 40 per cent are only available to a 'small or medium-sized enterprise'. This is defined by s47(2) CAA 2001 according to whether, if the business had been a company, it would have qualified as small or medium-sized for the relevant period. Broadly, a company will qualify as small or medium-sized if, both for that and the preceding financial year, it meets any two of the following tests:

- turnover is not more than £11.2m;

- its balance sheet total is not more than £5.6m;

- the average number of employees calculated on a monthly basis does not exceed 250.

A small enterprise, for the purposes of the 100 per cent first year allowance on information and communication technology, is defined by s47(3) CAA 2001. The relevant provisions of the Companies Act 1985 are applied as if the unincorporated business were a company, which means that it will qualify as small if, both for that and the preceding year, it meets any two of the following tests:

- turnover is not more than £2.8m;

- its balance sheet total is not more than £1.4m;

- the average number of employees calculated on a monthly basis does not exceed 50.

In both cases a company would also qualify as small or medium-sized or small, as the case may be, if it qualified as such in relation to the previous financial year.

A writing-down allowance is based on the available 'qualifying expenditure' as defined by s55 CAA 2001, less the disposal receipts to be brought into account. Broadly, a disposal receipt is brought into account if the plant ceases to belong to the individual, such as on sale; cessation of the business; permanent loss or ceasing to exist as such; or beginning to be used wholly or partly for non-trading purposes. However, no disposal value is brought into account where the plant or machinery is the subject of a gift giving rise to an employment income charge (s63 CAA 2001). Generally, see the table in s61 CAA 2001. Special provision is made in s72 CAA 2001 for computer software to ensure that capital sums received are adjusted.

In most cases the disposal value will, quite simply, be the sale proceeds or insurance monies where there is permanent loss. If the plant, etc., is sold for less than its market value or in any other non-specified circumstance, the plant should be treated as having been disposed of at that open market value. However, the actual proceeds, even if less than market value, can be used if the buyer is entitled to capital allowances on the expenditure or there is an employment income charge. On cessation of trade, the sale proceeds or insurance monies realised after cessation will be used, but market value if the trader decides to retain the asset for some other use.

Ordinarily the expenditure eligible for a first-year allowance is not brought into the pool of qualifying expenditure until the next period of account. However, it is possible to restrict the expenditure eligible for a first-year allowance to the amount specified in the claim, under s52(4) CAA 2001. The balance of the expenditure can then be brought into the pool, which could avoid a balancing charge otherwise arising.

Tax tip

A trader draws up accounts to 30 June 2002. The pool of qualifying expenditure brought forward is £4,000 and sale proceeds are £9,000. The sales include an asset sold for £5,000 which had cost £3,500. The disposal value is therefore reduced to £7,500 (s62 CAA 2001). In the same year office equipment eligible for a first-year allowance of 40% is purchased for £8,000.

Optimum capital allowances can be achieved as follows:

		£
WDV 1 July 2001		4,000
Addition – part		3,500
		7,500
Sale proceeds – limited to cost		(7,500)
Office equipment	8,000	
Less: included in pool	(3,500)	
		4,500
First-year allowance – 40%		1,800
WDV 30 June 2002		2,700

If the expenditure eligible for the first-year allowance is not restricted, there is a net balancing charge of £300.

Expenditure is eligible for a 100 per cent first-year allowance if it falls within s45A to C CAA 2001. In broad terms, this applies to expenditure on energy-saving plant or machinery where the items are unused and the expenditure is incurred after 31 March 2001. To be eligible, the plant and machinery must be of a description specified in the Capital Allowances (Energy-saving Plant and Machinery) Order

2001 SI 2001/2541. Where the expenditure qualifies, the size of the enterprise is irrelevant. Expenditure falling within the general exclusions in s46 CAA 2001 apply, thereby excluding, as examples, long-life assets and items for leasing, but see above for certain expenditure after 16 April 2002.

The range of assets eligible for 100% first-year allowance has been extended further by ss45H to J CAA 2001, added by FA 2003 in relation to expenditure incurred after 31 March 2003. To be eligible the expenditure must be on unused environmentally beneficial plant, which is not a long life asset or within the s46 exclusions. The Treasury specify the description of items that fall within this category and whether a certificate of environmental benefit is a prerequisite to eligibility. The Capital Allowances (Environmentally Beneficial Plant and Machinery) Order 2003 SI 2003/2076 was made by the Treasury, coming into force on 1 September 2003. Broadly, to be eligible plant or machinery must fall within the Water Technology Criteria and Product Lists published by the Department for Environment Food and Rural Affairs on 30 July 2003.

First year allowances can also be claimed for cars with low CO_2 emissions as explained in the next section.

5.3.2 Motor cars

Section 74 CAA 2001 applies where the capital expenditure on a car exceeds £12,000. Each car in this category has its own single asset pool. The maximum writing-down allowance is at the rate of £3,000 p.a. A balancing adjustment will arise on the sale of the car. In arriving at the writing-down allowance, a just and reasonable adjustment is made for any non-business use (s77 CAA 2001). The disposal value rules for plant and machinery apply in the normal way, except that market value is used on any sales between connected parties or otherwise falling within Chapter 17 CAA 2001 (but not exceeding cost).

In the case of motor cars that cost £12,000 or less, where there is a restriction for private use (such as for a proprietor's car) each such car is also dealt with separately. Before the changes made by s74 FA 2000, other motor cars were put into a separate car pool. However, with effect from periods of account ending after 5 April 2000, these motor cars are now dealt with through the general pool of machinery or plant. The written down value of the separate car pool brought forward will simply be added to the general pool at the start of that period.

A motor car is defined by ss81 and 82 CAA 2001 so as to exclude vehicles constructed primarily for the conveyance of goods; vehicles of a type not commonly used as a private vehicle and unsuitable to be used; and vehicles provided wholly or mainly for short-term hire to the public in the normal course of a trade. In *Bourne* v *Auto School of Motoring (Norwich) Ltd* (1964) 42 TC 217 it was held that driving school cars with dual controls are not motor cars within this definition.

First year allowances of 100 per cent are now available for motor cars with low carbon dioxide emissions, where the expenditure is incurred within the period from 17 April 2002 to 31 March 2008. To qualify, a car must either be electrically-propelled or be certified as having CO_2 emissions not exceeding 120g/per km. The car must be new and registered after 16 April 2002. For this purpose, the definition of car has its usual meaning except that motor cycles are excluded and hackney carriages qualify for this allowance. The restriction in s74 CAA 2001 mentioned above does not apply and so a car that costs in excess of £12,000 does not have to be pooled separately. Thus the entire expenditure will qualify for a first-year allowance. The detailed rules are contained in Schedule 19 FA 2002, which added a new s45D CAA 2001.

5.3.3 Short-life assets

It is possible, within 12 months from 31 January next following the end of the year of assessment in which a period of account ends, to elect that an item of machinery or plant is to be a short-life asset for the purposes of s83 CAA 2001.

Each item subject to such an election is allocated to a single asset pool. The main benefit in this will be the creation of a balancing allowance on disposal, rather than simply forming part of a pool of qualifying expenditure eligible for 25 per cent writing-down allowances. A balancing allowance can only be claimed, though, if the asset is disposed of before the fourth anniversary after the end of the period of account in which the expenditure was incurred. If, in the event, a taxpayer receives more than expected for the plant, he could have created a balancing charge by making this election, which is irrevocable. He could defer disposing of the asset and continue to use it in the trade, because if on that fourth anniversary no disposal value has been brought into account, the written-down value is allocated to the main pool (s86(2) CAA 2001). A disposal will be treated as at the market value of the asset at the time, unless an employment income charge arises or an election between connected persons is made under s89(6) CAA 2001.

Tax tip

A trader purchases specialised machinery at a cost of £10,000, with an expected life of three years, in the year to 30 September 2002. The machinery is sold in June 2004 for £500. By making an election and specifying the asset in question, the expenditure will be dealt with separately as follows:

	Specialised machinery £
Cost (August 2002)	10,000
First-year allowance year to 30 September 2002	(4,000)
	6,000
Writing-down allowance year to 30 September 2003	(1,500)
	4,500
Sold June 2004	(500)
Balancing allowance year to 30 September 2004	4,000

Strictly, each short-life asset should be dealt with in a separate claim and specified, complying generally with s85 CAA 2001. In practice, the Revenue recognise that this may be difficult or impracticable where large numbers of assets are purchased. They have given guidance in SP 1/86 so that information can be provided by reference to batches of acquisitions. Where an inspector can be satisfied that the actual life of a distinct class of assets is likely to be less than five years before they are sold or scrapped, a computation in the form set out in the statement of practice will be accepted.

A short-life asset election cannot be made in relation to long-life assets (see below) or any other assets listed in s84 CAA 2001. In particular, s84 excludes the following:

- motor cars;
- assets brought into use after non-trade use;
- assets where there is partly non-trade use;
- certain plant, etc., involved in leasing.

5.3.4 Long-life assets

Where machinery or plant has a useful economic life of at least 25 years it must be treated as a long-life asset for the purposes of ss90 to 104 CAA 2001. In practice, most long-life assets are likely to be acquired by companies, but these provisions can, in certain cases, apply to sole traders or partnerships. If they do, expenditure on long-life assets is put into a separate class pool and the writing-down allowance is 6 per cent p.a. only.

Normal capital allowances remain available for sole traders and partners where the expenditure on long-life assets does not exceed £100,000 in the period, adjusted rateably where the period is other than 12 months. However, for this to apply, s98 CAA 2001 also requires a sole trader to devote substantially the whole of his time in that period to the carrying on of the relevant trade or profession or, in the case of partnership, at least half of the individual partners to so devote their time.

The provisions exclude motor cars and fixtures in a building used wholly or mainly as, or as ancillary to, a dwelling house, retail shop, showroom, hotel or office.

5.3.5 Assets used only partly for trading purposes

Sections 205 to 208 CAA 2001 govern the position where an asset is used only partly for trade purposes. Commonly, this applies to motor cars where there is private use. A first-year allowance is not prevented simply by non-business use (such as a van used privately). Allowances are restricted on a just and reasonable basis to the extent of the business use.

For the purposes of writing-down allowances, each asset subject to non-trade use is put into a single asset pool. Thus, any disposals should be dealt with separately and not as part of the main pool, thereby giving rise to balancing adjustments on disposal. A balancing adjustment will also be subject to the non-business use factor.

5.3.6 Fixtures

One of the requirements for capital allowances is that the plant or machinery belongs to the taxpayer in consequence of his incurring the expenditure. In *Stokes* v *Costain Property Investments Ltd* [1984] STC 204 it was held that where the person incurring the expenditure is not the freeholder but a leaseholder, even with a very long lease, the expenditure does not belong to him. This somewhat technical distinction defied both common practice and common sense. Hence, what are now ss172 to 204 CAA 2001 were enacted. In essence, where machinery or plant is a fixture, and therefore part of the land belonging to a freeholder, the person who has actually incurred the expenditure (such as the lessee) is treated as if the fixture belonged to him.

Section 181 CAA 2001 also gives corresponding treatment to the purchaser of an existing leasehold interest, so that he in turn is entitled to capital allowances. The outgoing lessee is treated as having disposed of the fixtures for the consideration received. If a freeholder, for example, incurs expenditure first and then grants a lease for a capital sum, then under s183 CAA 2001 the two can make a joint election (within two years after the date the lease takes effect) to treat the fixture as belonging to the lessee. An election cannot be made if lessor and lessee are connected persons within s839 ICTA 1988. If the lessor has never used the fixture for the purposes of a trade, then s184 CAA 2001 ensures that it is the lessee who is entitled to allowances on the capital sum he pays to the lessor, on the sum apportioned to the fixture.

Where an interest in land is sold the acquisition value to the purchaser cannot exceed the original cost for capital allowance purposes. Subject to that, the two parties can agree the allocation of the total consideration to fixtures under s198 CAA 2001, by making a joint election. Thus, on the sale of a freehold property, the seller could minimise a balancing adjustment on the fixtures element by agreeing with the purchaser to make the election and fixing a low value as part of the overall sale price. Clearly, the purchaser would be entitled to allowances on a lesser figure than otherwise and might even negotiate for a higher price up to the original cost. If nothing else, an election gives certainty to both parties although the detailed rules set out in s201 CAA 2001 must be met in making the election, including compliance with the time limit of two years after the date of acquisition. There are corresponding provisions in s199 CAA 2001 where an incoming lessee pays a capital sum and an election is made under s183.

5.3.7 Machinery and plant on hire purchase, etc.

Where the contract under which a trader incurs capital expenditure on machinery or plant provides that the trader shall or may become the owner on the performance of the contract, s67 CAA 2001 deems that:

- the machinery or plant is treated as belonging to the trader at any time when he is entitled to the benefit of the contract; and

- all capital expenditure to be incurred under the contract after the time when the machinery or plant is brought into use for trading purposes is to be treated as having been incurred at that time of bringing into use.

Section 69 excludes fixtures from s67, which will, therefore, be dealt with under the separate rules for fixtures mentioned above.

A common example is a hire purchase agreement although s67 is not confined to this. Indeed, in *Tax Bulletin* of February 1992 the Revenue accept that abortive capital expenditure could be eligible for allowances if the requirements are met. If in the event the trader never becomes the owner, the asset is then treated as ceasing to belong to him and any capital sum received becomes a disposal value to be brought into the computation. More generally, s67 can have the effect of treating a deposit paid as eligible for allowances, on the basis that the trader will not become the owner until delivery, when the contract is performed.

Generally, in the case of hire or lease purchase agreements, capital allowances on machinery or plant can be claimed on the entire capital cost at the time the asset is brought into use, the financing charges being dealt with separately as a revenue cost over the period of the agreement. This should be distinguished from any other form of agreement whereby the ownership of the machinery or plant passes immediately to the trader, but payment is due over a period of time. In that instance, s5(5) CAA 2001 becomes relevant to the extent that instalments are payable more than four months after delivery.

5.3.8 Other matters

(a) There are special rules where a trade involves the leasing of assets, especially where overseas (see ss107 to 126 CAA 2001). Section 220 CAA 2001 restricts the writing-down allowance available on machinery or plant leased under a finance lease in the period of acquisition.

(b) There is a separate regime for expenditure on ships in ss127 to 158 CAA 2001.

(c) Expenditure for which any grant or subsidies are available should be reduced by the amount received, under s532 CAA 2001. This applies generally to all capital allowances.

(d) Where there is a succession to trades between connected persons, they can make a joint election under s266 CAA 2001 so as to effectively transfer the written-down value for tax purposes. In practice this is relevant on the incorporation of a business by a sole trader or partnership. The choice is either to make this election or create a balancing adjustment under the normal disposal value rules. Section 268 CAA 2001 provides for a similar election where there is a cessation on death and a beneficiary succeeding to the trade makes that election.

(e) There is no longer a requirement to notify the Revenue of expenditure on plant and machinery under s118 FA 1994. Section 73 FA 2000 abolished the requirement for periods of account that end after 31 March 2000.

(f) If machinery or plant already owned is brought into use for the purposes of a trade, capital expenditure equal to the open market value is deemed to have been incurred for writing-down allowance purposes (s13 CAA 2001). For assets brought into use after 20 March 2000, the actual expenditure incurred previously by the trader in acquiring an asset is used if lower than the open market value.

(g) If a trader is given machinery or plant and then brings it into use for trading purposes, open market value is also brought in for writing-down allowance purposes under s14 CAA 2001. If the donor and donee are connected, as they are likely to be in these circumstances, the actual expenditure incurred by the donor is used if lower than the open market value, being the broad effect of s218 CAA 2001.

5.4 Industrial buildings

5.4.1 Meaning of industrial building or structure

Section 274 CAA 2001 provides that an industrial building or structure is a building or structure in use for a specified purpose, including any of the following:

(a) a trade consisting of manufacturing goods or materials;

(b) a trade consisting of subjecting goods or materials to a process;

(c) a trade consisting of storing goods or materials:
   (i)   which are to be used in the manufacture of other goods or materials,
   (ii) which are to be subjected, in the course of the trade, to a process,
   (iii) which, having been manufactured or produced or subjected, in the course of a trade, to a process, have not yet been delivered to any purchaser, or
   (iv) on their arrival in the UK from a place outside the UK;

(d) certain agricultural or contracting activities;

(e) working farm plantations;

(f) a trade consisting of catching or taking fish or shellfish;

(g) mineral extraction trades;

(h) various utility type undertakings;

(i) transport, highway, tunnel, dock and bridge undertakings.

Section 277 CAA 2001 provides that the definition does not include a building to the extent that it is used as a dwelling house, retail shop, showroom, hotel or office, or for any ancillary purpose. Section 571 CAA 2001 is a general authority for apportionment of expenditure on a building where part only is within the definition. If, though, not more than 25 per cent of the total expenditure is non-eligible, such as the office element, then under s283 CAA 2001 the entire building is treated as an industrial building. For this purpose, it is the expenditure which needs to be considered and not simply floor area. A road is treated as part of the building if the buildings qualify (s284 CAA 2001).

Under s271 CAA 2001, a qualifying sports pavilion for the welfare of workers employed in a trade is eligible for allowances. This applies to any trade, but dance halls, etc., do not qualify.

The interpretation of s274 in relation to processing and storage trades has been litigated several times. To qualify as subjecting goods to a process, it is important to identify whether or not the items processed are goods. The cases indicate that this is confined to the merchandising context, so as to exclude the handling of documents in *Girobank Plc* v *Clarke* [1998] STC 182 and the storage of cash and its subdivision into wage packets in *Buckingham* v *Securitas Properties Ltd* [1980] STC 166. However, ss274 and 276(3) provide that maintaining or repairing the goods and materials of another trader qualifies, but not own goods unless the trade itself is eligible. A process suggests a substantial measure of uniformity of treatment.

A building used for storage purposes but ancillary to a manufacturing process, for example, qualifies as an industrial building. Indeed, if a part of a building is used for storage of own manufactured goods and goods bought in, the entire building will qualify unless there is segregation (*Saxone Lilly & Skinner (Holdings) Ltd v CIR* (1967) 44 TC 122). Where a trade is one of storage, it can been seen that merely storing goods does not in itself treat a building as industrial. Moreover storage should be seen as a purpose and end in itself and not something merely incidental to another business, such as the wholesale supermarket in *Bestway (Holdings) Ltd v Luff* [1998] STC 357. In *Tax Bulletin* of December 1999, the Revenue state that they are changing their practice in the light of this case. As a result, certain wholesale trades previously accepted as qualifying will no longer be eligible for allowances.

In the case of goods received on arrival in the UK, this should be for goods in transit where stored temporarily. Thus, permanent quarantine kennels failed the test in *Carr v Sayer* [1992] STC 396, following the earlier decision in *Copol Clothing Limited v Hindmarch* [1984] STC 33, where a claim for allowances on a warehouse building failed, as this was based some way from the port of arrival.

The exclusion for retail shops and offices, etc., has been the subject of some litigation. The word 'office' is construed narrowly to mean something having administrative or managerial function (see in particular *Girobank Plc v Clarke*). In *CIR v Lambhill Ironworks Ltd* (1950) 31 TC 393 it was held that a drawing office is not an office for this purpose.

5.4.2 Allowances available

No initial allowances are currently available on industrial buildings except where in an enterprise zone (see below). Initial allowances were last given for expenditure incurred in the year to 31 October 1993. At the present time, only a writing-down allowance of four per cent p.a. (straight line) is available.

A writing-down allowance can be claimed if, at the end of the period of account, the individual is entitled to an interest in an industrial building and held the relevant interest. The definition of 'relevant interest' is important in the context of certain disposals, and is defined by s286 CAA 2001. It applies particularly to the distinction between freehold and leasehold interest, being the interest that person held at the time he incurred the expenditure in question.

If a building ceases to qualify as an industrial building then the written-down value is still reduced, but by notional allowances. If a building falls out of use temporarily then s285 CAA 2001 treats it as continuing as an industrial building if it was one previously.

On disposal of the relevant interest, a balancing adjustment can arise under s314 CAA 2001. This includes in particular the sale of the relevant interest, demolition of the building and receipt of insurance monies. If the building does not qualify over the entire period, the balancing adjustment is made in such a way to ensure that the allowances available overall do not exceed the time apportioned part, relating to the industrial use, of the difference between the cost and the proceeds of sale. There is no balancing adjustment where the sale or other event occurs more than 25 years after first use.

A purchaser, within 25 years, will in turn be entitled to industrial buildings allowances but limited to the original expenditure which was eligible for allowances and not the purchase price paid by him. Strictly, this is expressed in terms of the residue of expenditure after deducting all initial and writing-down allowances (whether actual or notional) and adding or deducting the balancing adjustment, as the case may be. The purchaser is then allowed to deduct the amount so calculated on a straight-line basis over the residue of the 25 years from first use. The allowance is, therefore, at a greater rate than four per cent p.a.

The following points are also relevant:

(a) Expenditure on land does not qualify but expenditure on ground works preparatory to a building would. Otherwise, all costs are potentially eligible including appropriate professional fees for architects and surveyors. Planning and legal fees cannot be included.

(b) If an industrial building is purchased from a property developer, it is the price paid to that developer which is eligible for allowances. The Revenue would expect the land element to be excluded. If the building is bought unused from another person, allowances are based on the lower of the actual cost of construction and the price paid by that purchaser (ss295 to 297 CAA 2001).

(c) If a lease exceeding 50 years is granted for a capital sum, such that the relevant interest is not sold, the lessor and lessee can jointly elect under s290 CAA 2001 to treat the transaction as if there had been a sale of the relevant interest. The lessor has a balancing adjustment and the lessee will be entitled to claim allowances in the same way as any purchaser of an industrial building.

(d) To prevent tax avoidance by creating a balancing allowance where a scheme or arrangement has the obtaining of a tax advantage as a main purpose, s570A CAA 2001 (added by FA 2003) denies a balancing allowance where the relevant event occurs after 26 November 2002. However, the residue of qualifying expenditure after the balancing event is not increased, being calculated as if the balancing allowance had been made.

5.5 Other commercial buildings

5.5.1 Enterprise zone commercial buildings

To encourage the development of enterprise zones, a special initial allowance of 100 per cent is available under s305 CAA 2001. Moreover, if relevant the writing-down allowance is 25 per cent instead of 4 per cent. This applies to any commercial building, whether industrial or not, at a time when the site is in an enterprise zone or within 10 years after first inclusion. In practice, many such buildings have been the subject of investment by non-traders, attracted by the favourable tax allowances, but occasionally a trader may incur capital expenditure for the purposes of his trade in an enterprise zone.

5.5.2 Hotels

The provisions relating to industrial buildings can also apply to a hotel treated as qualifying under s279 CAA 2001. Construction expenditure before 12 April 1978 is disregarded. To qualify, the building must be permanent and meet the following requirements:

- open for at least four months in the season from April to October inclusive;

- when open in the season have at least 10 letting bedrooms (available to the public generally and not normally in the same occupation for more than one month);

- the sleeping accommodation offered in the season must consist wholly or mainly of letting bedrooms; and

- also in the season, the services provided for guests must normally include breakfast, evening meal, the making of beds and the cleaning of rooms.

The above tests are applied in each relevant period of account and, in the case of new hotels, to the 12 months beginning with first use (s279(4)). Accommodation available to a sole trader or partner when open in the season for private purposes is excluded but any building or part used for the welfare of workers does qualify for allowances.

Meeting the above requirements does not of itself mean that a building is a hotel. The establishment must be held out by the proprietor to provide food, drink and sleeping accommodation to any proper traveller, which would, therefore, exclude self-catering holiday accommodation, nursing homes and conference centres (*Capital Allowances Manual* paragraph 32402).

If a hotel ceases to qualify, then at the end of the two-year non-qualifying period it is treated as if sold for its open market price (s317 CAA 2001).

5.6 Agricultural buildings

5.6.1 Meaning of agricultural buildings

Broadly, allowances are available for capital expenditure on construction of farmhouses, farm buildings, cottages, fences or other works. A retail shop is an agricultural building to the extent that it sells produce of the farm. Under s361 CAA 2001, the expenditure must be incurred for the purposes of husbandry on the agricultural land. Husbandry is defined by s362 to include:

'(a) any method of intensive rearing of livestock or fish on a commercial basis for the production of food for human consumption.

(b) the cultivation of short rotation coppice.'

The Revenue accept that husbandry includes horticulture and market garden use, whether for growing plants, flowers or the production of food. The *Capital Allowances Manual* at paragraph 40100 now refers to husbandry as the occupation of land where the business depends to a material extent on the fruits (natural or commercial) of the land.

There is no statutory definition of cottage although it cannot be the property from which a farm is run, as that will be a farmhouse. The Revenue view in their *Capital Allowances Manual* paragraph 40100 is that a cottage is a small dwelling house. What is small may be a matter of opinion, varying from one generation to another, but a large and expensive architect designed house for a family member is not likely to qualify as a cottage.

In the case of farmhouses, a maximum one-third of the expenditure is taken into account, but could be less depending upon the extent of the farmhouse and its use (s369 CAA 2001). A farmhouse is the building from which the farming operations are conducted and which could be the house occupied by the farm manager if on the facts he runs the farm. In appropriate cases there could be more than one farmhouse, such as where partners occupy separate houses and the operations are run from both.

5.6.2 Allowances available

These are now given in a similar way to industrial buildings allowances, being over a writing-down period of 25 years, beginning with the first day of the period of account in which expenditure is incurred. Initial allowances are not available currently, being last available for expenditure in the year to 31 October 1993.

To be entitled to any allowances, the farmer must have a 'relevant interest' in the land as defined by s364 CAA 2001. This means a freehold or leasehold interest, which would not include a mere licence to occupy.

One major difference with industrial buildings is that on the sale of land there is no automatic balancing adjustment. Instead, the purchaser becomes entitled to the same allowances as were available to the vendor for the remainder of the writing-down period (s375 CAA 2001). However, the two parties can make a joint election under s382 CAA 2001 within 12 months from 31 January next following the year of assessment in which the relevant period of account ends, so that a balancing of adjustment is made. If the balancing event is the demolition or destruction, etc., of a building or works, the election can be made by the former owner alone. There are provisions to restrict the exploitation of balancing allowances including s570A CAA 2001 mentioned in **5.4.2** above.

Another difference compared to industrial buildings is that it is the first use that determines whether allowances are due. Thus, if the first use is for husbandry purposes the expenditure will be eligible and will continue to do so even if the use changes. In contrast, an individual buying a farm including buildings that were never used for husbandry purposes could not claim allowances on changing the use to farming.

5.7   Other allowances

Capital expenditure on research and development can be deducted in full in the relevant period, under s441 CAA 2001. Until FA 2000, this was known as scientific research expenditure. Section 437 applies the definition of research and development in the new s837A ICTA 1988, being activities that fall to be treated as research and development in accordance with normal accounting practice. This is somewhat wider than the previous definition, although SSAP 13 requires an appreciable element of innovation for expenditure to be classified as research and development. To qualify, the expenditure must also fall within the 'Guidelines on the Meaning of Research and Development (R&D) for Tax Purposes', issued by the Department of Trade and Industry on 28 July 2000 (Research and Development (Prescribed Activities) Regulations 2000 SI 2000/2081).

The CAA 2001 also contains provisions for the following types of expenditure, which are somewhat specialist and are not dealt with in any more detail here.

- a house let on an assured tenancy (ss490 to 531);
- mineral extraction (ss394 to 436); and
- dredging (ss484 to 489).

5.8   Intellectual property

5.8.1   Patent rights

Section 464 CAA 2001 provides for allowances and balancing adjustment for capital expenditure on the purchase of patent rights. An allowance of 25 per cent p.a. reducing (adjusted for periods of less than one year) is allowed in arriving at a person's trading profits. The allowance is based on the capital expenditure incurred after deducting sums received for the sale of any patent rights, but not exceeding the capital expenditure incurred in the purchase of those rights. The excess of receipts over the purchase price is taxed under Schedule D Case VI (s524 ICTA 1988).

5.8.2 Know-how

There are similar provisions for expenditure (less sale proceeds) on know-how used for the purposes of a trade, except that any sale proceeds (not limited to the purchase price) are brought into the calculation of qualifying expenditure. Generally, if a person has not incurred expenditure on know-how, the sale receipts are still treated as of a trading receipt nature, under s531 ICTA 1988. Allowances are not available if the sale is between bodies (including partnerships) under common control.

Know-how is defined in s452(2) CAA 2001 in a restrictive way, as:

'Any industrial information or techniques likely to assist in manufacturing or processing goods or materials.'

The definition is widened to include certain mining works and agricultural, forestry or fishing operations. Clearly, expenditure on acquiring confidential information does not of itself make it eligible for allowances, unless concerned in the manufacture or processing of goods. In general terms commercial know-how is excluded (see *Tax Bulletin* of August 1993).

5.8.3 Other intellectual property

Basically, any other expenditure of a capital nature on intangibles, including intellectual property rights, is not eligible for allowances (apart from the provisions allowing expenditure on registering patents, etc., as noted in Chapter 4).

6 Losses

6.1 General

Losses are also far simpler than previously, particularly because the loss automatically includes capital allowances to arrive at one figure. A loss can be created by overlap relief.

Broadly, the options for trading losses are as follows:

- claim against total income of a year or years;
- claim against chargeable gains;
- carry forward against future profits of the same trade;
- carry back against profits of the same trade if a terminal loss.

For a loss to be set against total income or chargeable gains, the trade must be conducted on a commercial basis. The test for s380 ICTA 1988 is slightly different to that for s381. Section 384 ICTA 1988 applies for s380 purposes, requiring a trade to be carried on with a view to the realisation of profits in the trade, whereas s381(4) refers to the trade being carried on in such a way that profits could reasonably be expected to be realised in that period or within a reasonable time thereafter. The reason for the difference is that s381 applies to losses in the early years when losses are more likely in establishing a business, whereas s380 can give relief for a loss at any time in the life of a trade.

A recent case on commerciality is *Wannell v Rothwell* [1996] STC 450, where the individual's activities resulted in a loss from dealing in shares and commodity futures. The Special Commissioner regarded this as borderline on whether or not there was a trade, but the taxpayer's admission of some casualness and lack of self-discipline meant that he was bound to fail the commerciality test. In *Delion Enterprises v Ellis* [1999] STC (SCD) 103 the Special Commissioner accepted the taxpayer's argument that the partnership trade was commercial. On the facts the business had made a profit at various times, but suffered in the relevant period from the national recession and depressive illness of the main partner.

6.2   Losses against other income

6.2.1   General rule

Under s380 ICTA 1988 an individual incurring a loss can claim for it to be set against total income in either the year in which the loss arises or the preceding year. The time limit for making a claim is 12 months from 31 January next following the end of the year of assessment in which the loss arises. In deciding the year of loss, this follows the same basis period that would have applied had there been a profit (s382(3) ICTA 1988).

Example 6.1

For a continuing business, a loss in the year to 30 September 2002 will be treated wholly as a loss for the tax year 2002/03. Had that been the first year in business, the loss would be allocated between the period from 1 October 2001 to 5 April 2002 and the period from 6 April 2002 to 30 September 2002.

It is up to the taxpayer to claim relief against either the current year or the preceding year, provided not more than the total loss is claimed. The taxpayer can specify the order in which the claims are made (*Tax Bulletin* May 1992).

Example 6.2

Taxpayer incurs a trading loss of £15,000 in the year to 31 December 2003. The choices are to claim that loss against:

income for the year 2003/04; or
income for the year 2002/03.

It is not possible to claim, say, £10,000 loss in 2003/04 and the balance in 2002/03. The claim is all or nothing but he could specify which year comes first. The choice could be affected by differences in tax rates and availability of personal allowances, etc. The claim must be made by 31 January 2006.

6.2.2   Carry back of opening year losses

Section 381 ICTA 1988 extends relief for losses incurred in the first year of trading or any of the next three years. The time limit for making the claim is the same. Section 381(2) specifies the order of set off, by setting the loss against income for the three years of assessment immediately preceding the year of loss, taking income for an earlier year first.

Example 6.3

Assume a taxpayer incurs a loss in first year of trading to 30 June 2003 of £20,000. That loss is effectively divided into two years of assessment (s382(4) ICTA 1988) being:

2002/03 £15,000
2003/04 £5,000

The loss in 2002/03 could be set against income for that year under s380, or earlier years under s381 in the order set out below:

1999/00
2000/01
2001/02

The loss in the year 2003/04 could similarly be set off against income of the previous three years, being 2000/01, 2001/02 and 2002/03.

If an individual joins a partnership, relief can be claimed under s381 for any losses arising in the first year of partnership and the next three years. It does not matter that the actual trade or profession commenced many years previously. However, in the case of spouses living together, relief can only be given if the loss arises in the year in which the trade was first commenced by one of them or the next three years (s381(5)). If two individuals are engaged to be married when the trade is first carried on by one of them, this restriction would not apply even if they marry subsequently.

6.2.3 Farming and market gardening trades

In addition to the commerciality test mentioned above, for farming and market gardening trades there is a further hurdle. Under s397 ICTA 1988, if a loss has arisen in each of the five years prior to the year of assessment in which loss arises, then losses in that sixth (or any later) year cannot be included in a s380 claim. If the loss sequence is again broken, the five year period starts all over again. Section 397 also contains the following refinements:

(a) Capital allowances or balancing charges are ignored but depreciation is added back as usual. This is only to determine whether a loss arises and not the quantum of the loss if s397 does not apply.

(b) There is no restriction if the test in s397(3) is met, which broadly requires the reasonable expectation of the realisation of profits if they had been undertaken by a competent farmer or market gardener and that in similar circumstances such a person could not reasonably have expected the activities to become profitable until after the end of the relevant year.

(c) Under s397(10), husband and wife are treated as if the same person so that a new five-year period cannot be created simply by transferring a business between husband and wife. Similarly, if the farming business has been transferred from a company which either of them controlled, or together, the five-year period to be considered can include a time when the trade was carried on by the company.

ESC B55 granted temporary concessional relief for 2000/01 and 2001/02. The conditions set out must be met including a requirement for a profit to have been made in specified preceding periods.

6.2.4   Losses against chargeable gains

If a claim is made under s380 ICTA 1988 in respect of a trading loss and part is unrelieved owing to insufficient income, it is possible to treat the unused amount as if it were a capital loss for capital gains tax purposes. The claim is made under s72 FA 1991 and should strictly be made at the same time as the s380 claim. However, the Revenue have stated in *Tax Bulletin* of August 1993 that they will accept a separate claim after the s380 claim provided it is made within the time limits for that claim.

Given that a s380 claim can cover either the actual year of loss or the preceding year, the chargeable gains for either of those years could be affected by a claim under s72 FA 1991. Points to bear in mind are that the chargeable gains are computed by disregarding the annual exemption and so care should be taken to avoid wasting it. The tax value of a loss could also be diminished if it has to be set against a capital gain eligible for taper relief. The possibility of making deferral claims such as 'roll-over' relief should also be taken into account, particularly given that under s75(5) FA 1991 events occurring after the s380 claim is finally determined are to be ignored. It would be possible to effectively convert a trading loss into a carry forward capital loss. Under s72(6) FA 1991 a capital loss so created cannot be set against chargeable gains accruing in any year of assessment beginning after the cessation of the trade, etc., in which the trading loss was sustained.

6.2.5 Leasing trades

Section 384(6) ICTA 1988 provides a further restriction in determining the amount of the loss for ss380 and 381 purposes in the case of leasing trades. To the extent that a loss includes capital allowances in respect of plant or machinery for leasing, those allowances are ignored unless the individual:

- has carried on the trade (alone or in partnership) for a continuous period of at least six months in, or beginning or ending in, the year of assessment in which the loss was sustained; and

- he devotes essentially the whole of his time to carrying on the trade throughout that year. If the trade commenced or ceased in the year, this requirement must be met for a continuous period of at least six months beginning or ending in that year.

6.3 Other uses of losses

6.3.1 Carry forward of losses

Except to the extent that loss relief has been given elsewhere, such as s380 or s381, any person can make a claim to carry forward the loss against future profits from the same trade or profession in later years of assessment and so on until the loss is fully utilised. It is vital for relief under s385 that the trade continues. This is a question of fact as mentioned in Chapter 2. Interest payments relating to the trade, etc., under s353 ICTA 1988 can be carried forward as a s385 loss if there is insufficient income in the year of assessment (s390 ICTA 1988).

6.3.2 Terminal losses

On cessation of a trade or profession, whether as a sole trader or in partnership, a loss in the final 12 months can, by making a claim, be carried back against profits of the same trade for the year of assessment in which the cessation occurs and the preceding three years (in reverse chronological order).

Section 388(6) specifies how the loss is to be computed. It can be a combination of the loss sustained in the cessation year of assessment together with the loss sustained in the part of the preceding year beginning 12 months before cessation. If deductible payments have been made under deduction of tax, and paid out of the trading profits, then both the trading profits in the earlier years and the terminal loss itself are reduced by the gross payments.

Example 6.4

A trader has the following results until cessation of his business on 30 September 2002. Overlap relief is £5,000.

	£	£
9 months to 30 September 2002 loss		(12,000)
12 months to 31 December 2001 profit		8,000
Year to 31 December 2000 profit		6,000
Year to 31 December 1999 profit		9,000

The terminal loss for s388 purposes is:

	£	£
6 months to 30 September 2002 (year of cessation)		(8,000)
Add: overlap relief		(5,000)
6 months to 31 March 2002		
– balance of loss of final period	(4,000)	
– *Less*: profit (3/12 × £8,000)	2,000	(2,000)
		(15,000)

The terminal loss can be set against profits from the trade in any of the years (and in this order) 2002/03, 2001/02, 2000/01 and 1999/00. The loss could be offset as follows:

2001/02	8,000
2000/01	6,000
1999/2000 (balance)	1,000

The balance of the loss for the year to 30 September 2002 (£2,000) can be claimed under s380 ICTA 1998, if the trader has other income or gains chargeable to tax in 2002/03 or 2001/02. If there is sufficient other income another option would be to claim the whole of the loss of £17,000 (including overlap relief) under s380. The loss cannot be claimed more than once.

6.3.3   Transfer of business to company

There is a limited carry forward of trading losses where a business is incorporated, whether previously carried on as a sole trader or in partnership. A loss carried forward under s386 ICTA 1988 can be set against income derived from the company, whether by way of dividends or otherwise (which would include employment income). The following requirements must be met:

(a)   The consideration for the transfer for the business must be solely or mainly the allotment of shares. Creating a director's loan account for a large part of the consideration could, therefore, result in a loss of this relief entirely.

(b)   The individual must beneficially own the shares throughout the year of assessment (or from the date of transfer to the following 5 April in the first year) and the company must also carry on the same business throughout that year as well.

> **Tax tip**
>
> Given a choice between remuneration and dividends, the loss of repayable tax credits will usually mean that remuneration is a more effective way of using a loss carried forward under s386 ICTA 1988.

6.4   Foreign trades

Where a trade is carried on wholly abroad, such that any profits are assessable under Schedule D Case V, s391 ICTA 1988 provides a restricted relief for any losses. Broadly, the various loss relieving provisions apply in the same way as a trade or profession taxable under Schedule D Case I or II. A restriction is contained in s391(2), providing that relief can only be given against foreign pensions or chargeable overseas earnings under s23 Income Tax (Earnings and Pensions) Act 2003. This effectively limits the income available to what might be called overseas earned income, excluding, therefore, other employment income and investment income.

7 Schedule D Case VI and anti-avoidance

7.1 Schedule D Case VI

7.1.1 Charging provisions

There are two broad types of amount that are chargeable to tax under Schedule D Case VI.

(a) Income falling within s18 ICTA 1988, which charges tax 'in respect of any annual profits or gains not falling under any other Case of Schedule D and not charged by virtue of Schedule A or by virtue of ITEPA 2003 as employment income, pension income or social security income'.

(b) Various specific statutory provisions which treat Case VI as a dumping ground where a charge to tax is required but the amount does not fall naturally under any of the other charging provisions. This applies in particular to tax charged by various anti-avoidance provisions. The structure of income tax requires any taxable amounts to fall under one of the schedules (or case) to be part of total income. Case VI is also used to recover any excess reliefs, such as the double taxation relief adjustment under s804(5B) ICTA 1988, and taxes particular receipts such as the enterprise allowance under s127 ICTA 1988.

This chapter deals with income falling under (a) above, gains in connection with land that could be assessed under s776 ICTA 1988 being an example of a specific statutory provision in (b), together with a brief mention of other anti-avoidance provisions.

7.1.2 Principles determining whether a Case VI charge arises

On the face of it, the charging provision in s18 ICTA 1988 is very wide. It has, though, been limited in certain ways by decisions of the courts. These determine that:

(a) Any sum must be payable by virtue of some legal right such as a contract or quasi-contractual right enforceable by a court. A mere gift cannot be assessed under Case VI (although it has been held that tips can be assessed as earnings in relation to employments and gifts in connection with a trade, etc., may be assessable under Schedule D Case I or II). Authority for this is *Bloom* v *Kinder* (1958) 38 TC 77. In the later case of *Dickenson* v *Abel* (1968) 45 TC 353, the only question at issue was whether or not a secret profit of £10,000 paid to an individual for his assistance in recommending the offer made by a purchaser of land was under an enforceable contract.

(b) The sum must have the quality of income, albeit a casual profit which will not recur. In *Leeming* v *Jones* (1930) 15 TC 333 the Commissioners had held that the purchase and resale of Malaysian rubber estates was not assessable under Case I. The Revenue then mounted an argument for assessment under Case VI. This was rejected. The following extract from the judgment of Lawrence LJ in the Court of Appeal was approved generally.

> 'In the case of an isolated transaction of purchase and resale of property there is really no middle course open. It is either an adventure in the nature of trade, or else it is simply a case of sale and resale of property.'

Nowadays, such a gain could be subject to capital gains tax or possibly under Case VI by virtue of s776 ICTA 1988.

(c) If a sum falls within Case VI, it is taxable in the year the amount is actually received (see *Grey* v *Tiley* (1932) 16 TC 414 where commission was paid over two years).

Decisions of the courts include the following instances where an assessment was made under Schedule D Case VI.

Sums received from authorship

In *Hobbs* v *Hussey* (1942) 24 TC 153, the taxpayer sold the serial rights in his life story to *The People* for £1,500, after his retirement as a solicitor's clerk. This was held to be assessable, being more in the nature of the performance of services. Similarly, the taxpayer also failed in *Housden* v *Marshall* (1958) 38 TC 233 and *Alloway* v *Phillips* [1980] STC 490, in which the wife of one of the Great Train Robbers sold her story to a national newspaper.

However, in other cases the courts have held that a lump sum was not taxable, being a capital receipt. In *Trustees of Earl Haig* v *CIR* (1939) 22 TC 725, consent was given to a biographer to use the late Earl Haig's diaries, in consideration for one-half of the profits, receiving advance royalties which proved to be the only sums received. This was regarded as a partial realisation of a property right, reversing the decision of the Special Commissioners. There was a similar finding in *Beare* v *Carter* (1940) 23 TC 353.

One-off services

The courts have held the following to be taxable under Case VI:

- guaranteeing a company's overdraft for 2½ per cent of amount guaranteed (*Ryall* v *Hoare* (1923) 8 TC 521);

- insurance agency commission (*Hugh* v *Rogers* (1958) 38 TC 270);

- underwriting commission (*Lyons* v *Cowcher* (1926) 10 TC 438); and

- arranging a meeting between owner and a client, following a social occasion. The taxpayer was paid part of the net profits, and assisted in the negotiations. The Court of Appeal found an enforceable contract for services (*Brocklesby* v *Merricks* (1934) 18 TC 576).

The Revenue view on the taxation of commission, cash backs and discounts is given in SP 4/97 with further comment in *Tax Bulletin* February 1998. Sums received by an ordinary retail customer in relation to the purchase of goods or services does not give rise to a taxable receipt but commission for introducing others, where under an enforceable contract, is assessable.

The Revenue failed in the following cases:

- *Bradbury* v *Arnold* (1957) 37 TC 665, where a third party paid a theatrical producer for introducing him and providing the opportunity of a share in the profits from producing ice shows. The sum was held to be more in the nature of a capital receipt; and

- *Scott* v *Ricketts* (1967) 44 TC 303, where again the sum received was held to be a way of realisation of an asset, being a sum paid to the taxpayer to surrender any rights he might have from negotiations with the other party to develop a site.

7.2 Section 776 ICTA 1988

7.2.1 Overview

This provision came into being in 1969 to counter complex avoidance schemes, illustrated by *Ransom* v *Higgs* [1974] STC 539, which reached the House of Lords. There is a preamble in s776(1) to the effect that this section is enacted to prevent the avoidance of tax by a person concerned with land or the development of land, although the courts have determined that a tax avoidance motive as such is not required for the section to bite. If there is avoidance when judged objectively, albeit unwittingly, there can be a charge. This was a particularly fearful provision when income tax rates were significantly higher than capital gains tax but became less onerous when the rates of tax merged in 1988. However, the introduction of taper relief in 1998, and in particular the beneficial effect of business taper relief where an asset has been held for just two years, has again potentially widened the gap between the two taxes.

7.2.2 Broad circumstances in which the section can apply

The section is very widely drafted and in principle applies to any gain of a capital nature obtained from the disposal of land wherever any of the following circumstances apply:

- land, or any property deriving its value from land, is acquired with the sole or main object of realising a gain from disposing of the land;

- land is held as trading stock; and

- land is developed with the sole or main object of realising a gain from disposing of the land when developed.

Given the anti-avoidance nature of the provision, it is stated that the provision can apply not only to capital gains on the disposal of the land by the person acquiring, holding or developing the land, but also any connected person or where there are arrangements or schemes whereby a gain is realised by any indirect method or, when it is a series of transactions, by any person who is a party to, or concerned in, the arrangement or scheme. Other parts of s776 and s777 supplement the basic provisions to make them as wide as possible, and in particular so that they take account of any method, however indirect, by which any property or right is transferred or transmitted, or the value of any property or right is enhanced or diminished.

The particular complexities are seen as necessary to protect the Revenue in the case of diversion schemes. The Revenue give an example in the *Inspector's Manual* at paragraph 4736 of a purchase of land for eventual resale being diverted through a non-UK resident company based in a tax haven. The Revenue could not in practice assess the non-UK resident company although there might be an argument that s739 ICTA 1988 applies, but only if a trading profit as such arises to the offshore company. The Revenue could invoke s776 to tax the UK resident as a person who has given an opportunity of realising the gain to the offshore company, applying s776(8) ICTA 1988.

The section applies to all persons whether UK resident or not, if the land is in the UK. In the case of non-residents, s777(9) empowers the Revenue to direct that income tax should be withheld at the basic rate although in practice completion could well have taken place before the Revenue are aware of the transaction.

7.2.3   Instances where the section could apply

The reference to the section applying where land is acquired with the sole or main object of realising a gain or developing land with that object, suggests that the transaction could fall within Schedule D Case I as a trading transaction, albeit of a one-off nature. As can be seen in Chapter 2, the matter is very much one for the Commissioners hearing the evidence and some of the decisions will appear difficult to reconcile. As also mentioned, given that this is a question of fact, the Commissioners must either make an error of law or produce a result that is perverse on the evidence for their decision to be reversed on appeal.

However, if the Revenue are unsuccessful in their arguments for a Schedule D Case I assessment, they cannot simply raise a s776 Schedule D Case VI charge as an alternative. The *Inspector's Manual* at paragraph 4723 makes it quite clear that the section is not an alternative to Case I in simple transactions of purchase of land by UK residents and resale to unconnected UK persons. This applies whether or not there have been works on the land prior to sale. In these simple cases there has been no avoidance of Schedule D Case I tax because if it did not amount to trading, there can be no avoidance. This could be seen as a generous interpretation given that a lesser amount of income tax would be payable if the transaction is not within Case I and so in that sense there has been avoidance. The interpretation is, though, in line with the history of the section and the complex provisions to catch indirect methods of realising a gain.

Similarly, the reference to the section applying to land where held as trading stock seems odd at first sight given that if land is held in that capacity, it will always give rise to a Schedule D Case I charge. This again can be reconciled by the overall thrust of the provisions which can catch transactions affecting the value of land, such as shares in companies. In the case of a disposal of shares in a company holding land as trading stock, any gain arising to the holder of shares is not assessable under s776 where the land is disposed of by the company in the normal course of its trade and so as to procure that all opportunity of profit in respect of the land arises to that company.

In practice, apart from complex avoidance transactions, the section is most likely to bite where an owner sells land but participates in the development profit. This aspect is dealt with in more detail in the next section.

7.2.4   Development participation arrangements

The *Inspector's Manual* refers to these arrangements in the somewhat inelegant phrase, "slice of the action" schemes. This falls naturally within the third type of transaction mentioned in s776(2), where land is developed with the sole or main object of realising a gain from disposing of the land when developed. Almost certainly, a landowner wishing to maximise the value of his land would not see this as tax avoidance but a simple commercial transaction, particularly so if the land in question has been held for many years. The Revenue acknowledge that the basic sale of the land cannot be subject to income tax but simply seek to tax the extra profit under Case VI. Practically speaking, the avoidance nowadays arises largely because of taper relief for capital gains tax purposes, given that the top rate applying of 40% applies irrespective of whether or not there is a capital gain or income tax profit (although clearly the use of capital losses and the annual exemption are also factors).

The circumstances are best illustrated by way of an example (see example **7.1** opposite). The Revenue's view is supported by the decision in *Page v Lowther* [1983] STC 799. The predecessor section at the time was headed, 'Artificial transactions in land'. Moreover, the fact that there was no intention to avoid tax on the part of the landowner was of no avail. There had been a long lease of land granted to a developer and under the contract part of the amount was received on the grant of sub-leases for a capital sum to the eventual purchasers was paid by the developer to the landowner. The Revenue assessed this successfully under Case VI, their view being that in this situation the landowner is effectively receiving a share of the proceeds of something that is a trading activity and which apart from s776 would be of a capital

Example 7.1

Mr and Mrs Farmer bought the freehold of 400 acres in 1970, which they have farmed commercially throughout. In 2001 they entered into an agreement with developers in relation to 20 acres of land on the basis that they would receive a fixed amount of £400,000 per acre of developable land if planning consent is granted for a minimum of 80 houses and that in addition they will receive 10 per cent of the sale value of each house. Planning consent is granted in August 2003 at which point the land is conveyed to the developers, Mr and Mrs Farmer receiving their fixed sum of £8 million. Subsequently, they receive £500,000 in 2004/5 and £1,000,000 in 2005/06 being a 10 per cent share of the sale proceeds. Assume that at the date when planning consent is granted, the land with that consent is worth £600,000 per acre.

Given the use of the land and the period of ownership, Mr and Mrs Farmer are clearly entitled to full business asset taper relief, so that with the 40 per cent top rate their effective rate is now 10 per cent. However, the Revenue are likely to take a different view in relation to the contingent sums receivable on development as falling with s776.

The Revenue will accept that the gain up to the point before the intention to develop the land was formed is subject to capital gains tax only and which would include the whole of the fixed payment of £400,000 per acre, even though at that time the land did not have planning consent and so would not have been worth that amount. The reason for this is that that sum is not conditional upon development and would be payable irrespective of the amount received on the sale of the houses.

The additional sums of £500,000 in 2004/05 and £1,000,000 in 2005/06 will, though, be subject to income tax under Schedule D Case VI, the basis of assessment being when the sums are received (applying *Yuill v Wilson* [1980] STC 460).

Had they simply agreed to sell the land according to its market value of £600,000 per acre when planning consent was granted (or in practice a percentage to allow some profit to the developer in incurring the cost of obtaining planning consent), the gain would be subject to capital gains tax only. This would, though, be quite a different commercial arrangement. There is a danger in some instances that the additional profit from the 'slice of the action' is more than countered by the additional tax payable, especially when, in principle, the land can benefit from business asset taper relief for capital gains tax purposes.

nature. Again, there is avoidance albeit that, on a subjective basis, the landowner was not aware of this.

However, there are clearly limits to s776. It will not apply in the common situation where a landowner, who has owned land for many years, grants an option to a developer to acquire the land once planning consent is obtained and where the proceeds are dependent upon the value of the land with planning consent. The gain in this situation arises solely from the sale of the bare land and not from its development. The developer will retain the entire profits from the development, taking all the risks and in particular the ability to sell the completed units and receive the price of each unit.

7.2.5 Other points

Section 776 cannot apply to a gain accruing to an individual which would have been exempt from capital gains tax under the private residence provisions but for s224(3) TCGA 1992, which disapplies the exemption where the acquisition of a dwelling house was made wholly or partly for the purpose of realising a gain from its disposal.

There is clearance procedure generally, given by s776(11) but it is, as usual in such circumstances, important that there has been full and accurate disclosure of all material facts and other matters which could have a bearing on the matter. Unusually, though, the application is made to an inspector of taxes rather than the Board. The inspector has 30 days to notify the applicant whether or not he is satisfied that the gain is or is not chargeable to tax under s776. In practice this clearance procedure is rarely used although if a transaction will only take place on the basis that s776 is not applicable, clearance would be particularly relevant.

7.3 Other anti-avoidance provisions

There are also other anti-avoidance provisions that could apply in the context of trades, professions or vocations. In very broad terms these are:

(a) Transactions or arrangements effected to exploit the earning capacity of an individual pursuing any profession or vocation. If one of the main objects of the transactions is the avoidance of income tax and the individual receives a capital amount, that amount can be treated as income chargeable under Schedule D Case VI. Generally, see ss775 and 777 ICTA 1988.

(b) Sale of land and lease back where the rent payable under the lease exceeds a commercial rent. Any deductions for tax purposes cannot exceed the commercial rent (s779 ICTA 1988).

(c) The assignment or surrender of a lease to a landlord for a capital sum in conjunction with the grant or assignment to the lessee of another lease of the same property for a term not exceeding 15 years. Section 780 ICTA 1988 can treat part of the capital sum as a trading receipt or taxed under Schedule D Case VI in other cases. The amount so taxable varies on a straight line basis according to the length of the new lease, the shorter the term the greater the amount taxed as income.

(d) The conversion of capital into deductible income payments in connection with the leasing of any asset, which in particular could include plant or machinery. Section 781 ICTA 1988 taxes the person receiving the capital sum under Schedule D Case VI. The sale and lease back of assets is covered by s782 ICTA 1988 rather than s781, to disallow the excess of the actual hiring payment over the commercial rent.

(e) Schemes designed to create deductible interest payments when in reality there is no economic cost to the payer. The wording of s787 ICTA 1988 is wide but the Revenue have indicated that they would not normally apply this to commercial transactions even where borrowings have been organised in a tax effective manner, provided there is true interest payable.

8 Income from property

8.1 Scope of charge and general principles

8.1.1 Income within Schedule A

A distinction must be drawn between land in the UK and overseas property. Section 15 ICTA 1988 is the main charging provision for Schedule A, which deals with land in the United Kingdom. Income from overseas property is charged under Schedule D Case V. Section 65A ICTA 1988 has the broad effect of applying the basic Schedule A rules to overseas property income.

Under para 1(2) of s15 the exploitation of land in the UK is to be treated as a business and para 1(3) provides that:

> 'All businesses and transactions carried on or entered into by a particular person or partnership, so far as they are businesses or transactions the profits of which are chargeable to tax under this Schedule, are treated for the purposes of this Schedule as, or as entered into in the course of carrying on, a single business.'

This means that the receipts and expenses derived from all UK properties held by an individual are aggregated to produce for each year a profit or loss from that deemed business. A similar principle applies to overseas properties. Two separate property accounts should be prepared as UK and overseas property lettings are treated as separate businesses (s64A(5) ICTA 1988).

The following comments apply to all property income except where otherwise indicated in **8.8** in relation to overseas properties.

For a further discussion on Schedule A matters see Tax Digest 149 *Income from Property*.

8.1.2 Property income subject to tax

The starting point is para 1(1) of s15(1) ICTA 1988 which provides, for Schedule A purposes, that:

'Tax is charged under this Schedule on the annual profits arising from a business carried on for the exploitation, as a source of rents or other receipts, of any estate, interest or rights in or over land in the United Kingdom.'

Rents or other receipts include amounts derived from licences to occupy or otherwise use land or exercise any other right over land.

Without clarification, the basic charging provision could extend to activities beyond mere land ownership. It is specifically provided, therefore, that the following are not within Schedule A:

- profits arising from the occupation of land (commercial woodlands are exempt from tax);
- profits charged under Schedule D Case I from farming and market gardening;
- similarly, profits from mines quarries and other concerns specified in s55 ICTA 1988; and
- rent chargeable under Schedule D by virtue of ss119 and 120 ICTA 1988 (re mines, quarries, etc.).

Schedule A also includes furnished lettings and it is expressly stated that any sum payable for the use of furniture is treated in the same way as rent, together with associated expenditure.

A well-cited aphorism is that income tax is a tax on income. Thus, in principle capital receipts are not within the charge to tax. A statutory exception to this is the treatment of premiums, etc., which to some extent are brought within the charge. Premiums are dealt with later in 8.7. A case on the distinction between capital and income is *McClure* v *Petre* [1988] STC 749. Captain Petre received £76,125 under agreements with motorway contractors for allowing them to enter his land and deposit sub-soil. The contractors agreed to lay drains and restore the land. It was held that these receipts were capital, as on the facts the land was ruined for agricultural use and planning permission for development would not be granted. The capital value of the land had been reduced in return for a one-off payment.

That case can be distinguished from the earlier case of *Lowe* v *J W Ashmore* (1970) 46 TC 597 where it was held that receipts from the selling off of turf were income. There was nothing to suggest that the turf removed could not be regrown, so there was the possibility of recurrence.

8.1.3 Basis period

The basis period is the same as the tax year of assessment. For example, the tax year 2003/04 is based on the profits of the property business for the year to 5 April 2004. There is no objection to a taxpayer preparing accounts for a different year, but the results must then be apportioned to arrive at the profits for a year to 5 April. In practice, there seems little merit in choosing an accounting date other than 5 April unless there are compelling non-tax reasons.

The exception to this is where the property income is part of a trading partnership. That situation is dealt with in Chapter **9** on partnerships.

8.2 Computational aspects

8.2.1 Basic rule

Section 21A(1) ICTA 1988 provides that the profits of the Schedule A business are computed in the same way as a trade under Schedule D Case I. The accruals basis of accounting applies together with other sound principles of commercial accounting practice. Chapter **4** dealing with the computation of profits for trading purposes is, therefore, relevant to property income. Section 21A(2) spells this out in more detail, specifying the enactments which are relevant as a consequence of this general provision.

In IR 150 paragraph 90, the Revenue state that they will accept accounts prepared on a cash basis where the gross receipts of the rental business do not exceed £15,000. That basis must be used consistently and produce an overall reasonable result, not differing substantially from the strict earnings basis.

Certain consequences of this general rule are worthy of specific comment.

For a discussion of deductible expenditure see Tax Digest 172 *Maximising Tax Allowances on Property Expenditure*.

8.2.2 Rental income

Rents under a lease or tenancy are the most likely form of receipt in a property business. Commonly, rent is paid in advance but sometimes it is paid in arrears. Account must be taken of that. For example, a quarter's rent due on 25 March 2003 in advance should be carried forward for inclusion in the accounts of the year to 5 April 2004, apart from the 11 days up to 5 April 2003.

It may not be possible to determine precisely the rent accrued for a year because of rent review negotiations. Rent reviews are normally backdated to the date of the review, so consideration must be given to bringing in the amount estimated to be due from that date to the following 5 April.

Where a property is bought or sold it is usual to make an apportionment of the rent in advance or in arrears between the vendor and purchaser. This is usually dealt with in the completion statement. Section 40 ICTA 1988 sets out how such apportioned amounts (including apportioned expenses) should be treated. Any amount apportioned to or from a person should be brought into the letting business accounts as a payment or receipt, as the case may be, at the date to which the apportionment is made.

Example 8.1

V sells a commercial property to P for completion on 31 March 2004, having received a quarter's rent of £5,000 in advance on 25 March 2004.

Six days of this can be retained by V (i.e., £330) and the balance is accounted for by V to P (i.e., £4,670). The effect of s40(4A) ICTA 1988 is that P brings in the full amount of £4,670 into his letting account for the year to 5 April 2004, even though in fact most of this relates to a period after 5 April 2004.

Correspondingly, V will bring into his accounts for the same year the net amount of £330.

8.2.3 Improvements, alterations and repairs

Following normal Schedule D Case I principles, capital expenditure is not deductible (unless eligible under the capital allowances system). Thus, alterations and improvements to the property are not deductible as such, but repairs and maintenance expenditure is fully allowable. This is dealt with in more detail in Chapter 4 dealing with trades, as the same principles apply.

One exception that did exist to the trading principles was that for Schedule A purposes, concession ESC B4 allowed a deduction for notional repairs where obviated by improvements, etc. This concession was withdrawn with effect from 6 April 2001. In *Tax Bulletin* of June 2002 the Revenue give their views on when work on property amounts to a repair. In particular they will accept that the replacement of a part of the entirety by the nearest modern equivalent is allowable, such as the replacement of single glazed windows by double-glazed equivalents.

If a property is also occupied by the taxpayer as well as being let in part, Revenue practice, as set out in paragraph 254 of IR 150, is to review exceptionally heavy expenses to ensure that there is a proper attribution to produce a fair result when taken in the round. An example would be rewiring, where the property has been let for only part of the period. This practice works both ways so that a higher attribution may be appropriate where a property was wholly let for most of the period and owner-occupied in part for a relatively short period.

8.2.4 Interest paid

The treatment of interest paid is far more favourable than existed before 1995. Provided interest is incurred wholly and exclusively for the purposes of the letting business, it is deductible as an expense. Bank overdraft interest can also be allowed together with normal bank charges. The accruals basis applies so that interest charged in arrears and bridging 5 April should be apportioned, even though paid in the subsequent year.

The borrowing requirement giving rise to the interest must be related to the properties in some way, whether to purchase a property, improve it or to meet running costs. The mere fact of charging a loan against a property as security does not satisfy the deductibility requirements. It is the use to which the loan has been put so that if, for example, an individual borrowed £50,000 secured on a property to buy a racehorse, the interest on that loan would not be deductible.

Interest paid to a non-resident bank, for example, can also be deducted. The more restrictive provisions of s82 ICTA 1988 are specifically excepted from applying to letting businesses. There may, nevertheless, be a requirement to deduct income tax at source in making payment to a non-resident under s349(2) ICTA 1988, subject to the provisions of a relevant tax treaty.

Incidental costs in obtaining loan finance wholly and exclusively for a property let on a commercial basis are deductible.

8.2.5 Legal and professional costs

The same principles apply as for a trade. In the context of a letting business, the fees in relation to the following matters would be deductible (see IR 150 paragraphs 213 to 221).

- insurance valuations;
- negotiation of rent reviews;
- evicting a tenant in order to relet the property;
- accountancy fees in preparing the letting business accounts;
- the first letting or subletting of a property for one year or less; and
- renewing a lease for less than 50 years (excluding a proportion relating to the payment of any premium), provided the new lease is broadly similar in terms to the previous one.

Expenses relating to the following are not deductible:

- purchasing or selling a property;
- architect's and surveyor's fees, etc., in improving a property;
- the first letting or sub-letting of a property for more than one year; and
- planning applications (unless for example to carry out repairs where listed building consent is required).

8.2.6 Premiums

If a tenant who has paid a premium taxable on his landlord under Schedule A in turn sublets the property, a deduction can be made for the part taxable on the landlord in accordance with s37 ICTA 1988. This should not be confused with the payment made on the assignment of a lease from a previous tenant, even if it is described as a premium.

In the case of reverse premiums, Schedule 6 para 2(3) FA 1999 treats amounts received after 8 March 1999 as a revenue receipt derived from land (unless taxable under Schedule D Case I or II).

8.2.7 Void periods and uncommercial lettings

A property may be unoccupied for a variety of reasons, such as inability to let the property or owing to alteration works. There may not be any rental income but the revenue expenses relating to the property are still deductible, as part of the overall expenditure of the letting business.

If a property is let uncommercially, such as to a relative, some restriction may be required. The Inland Revenue cannot require a notional market rent to be included in the accounts but if the expenditure exceeds the letting income they may argue that the excess is not incurred wholly and exclusively for the purposes of the business. An adjustment may be required for this, therefore, but not so as to create a surplus on that letting. However, if an expense is incurred partly, at least, for personal as well as business reasons, it may be non-deductible under the wholly and exclusively rule.

8.2.8 Capital allowances

As usual, depreciation is not an allowable expense. In principle, capital allowances can be claimed. In the case of a factory, industrial buildings allowances may be in point and for other expenditure plant and machinery allowances may be available. For example, a landlord may have office equipment, such as a computer, which he uses or machinery for maintenance. Allowances will be available in the same way as a trade, applying a 5 April basis period.

In the case of residential lettings, though, there is a specific statutory prohibition against a claim for capital allowances where the plant or machinery is for use in a dwelling house (s35 CAA 2001). Instead, by concession the Revenue allow a wear and tear deduction equal to 10 per cent of the rents (ESC B47). For this purpose, expenses normally borne by a tenant such as council tax and water rates, are netted off. An exception to the general bar on capital allowances is qualifying furnished holiday lettings, dealt with separately below. Alternatively, the renewals basis could be used, but without any deduction for the initial expenditure. The wear and tear allowance is the usual method in practice. Whichever method is adopted, it should be applied consistently to all furnished properties rented out. If a house is not let with sufficient furniture to justify the wear and tear allowance, the renewals basis is the only effective method of obtaining relief for the replacement of items that are included in the letting. The renewals allowance also applies to the renewing of plant and machinery normally included as part of a dwelling, whether furnished or unfurnished, such as central heating systems.

Example 8.2

X owns a residential house let furnished for £1,000 per calendar month and a factory at £20,000 p.a. plus VAT. There is a review on the factory effective from 6 October 2003, increasing the rent to £27,000 p.a. plus VAT. Surveyor's fees for negotiating the rent are £1,175 (incl. VAT). Other expenses paid in the year are £750 for decorating the house, paid in May 2003 for work completed in the previous March, and a new fridge/freezer £200. X also paid water rates of £300 for the year to 31 March 2004, and house contents insurance of £600.

X borrowed £80,000 to purchase the factory which cost £150,000 plus VAT to build in 1995. Interest at a variable rate to 30 June 2003 was 7% and 6% from that date. X elected to waive exemption for VAT purposes.

His Schedule A accounts for the year to 5 April 2004 are:

		£
Rent – house 12 months at £1,000		12,000
Rent – factory six months at £20,000 p.a. and six months at £27,000 p.a.		23,500
		35,500
Less: Expenses		
Water rates	300	
Rent review fees (excl. VAT)	1,000	
Insurance	600	
Interest payable (£80,000 at 7% for three months and 6% for nine months)	5,000	
Accountancy fees (say)	500	
Wear and tear of house (10% × (£12,000–£300)),	1,170	
Capital allowance on factory (4% × £150,000)	6,000	(14,570)
Net surplus – assessable under Schedule A		20,930

Notes

1 VAT on factory rents is payable to Customs & Excise, and input tax recovered. The figures are, therefore, included net of VAT.

2 The redecoration of the house relates to the previous year and would have been deductible then.

3 The new fridge/freezer is a replacement and is covered by the wear and tear allowance.

8.2.9 Relief for conversion of parts of business premises into flats

Schedule 19 FA 2001 added a new Part 4A to the Capital Allowances Act 2001, to create a new relief for capital allowances purposes where certain types of building are converted or renovated so as to create a qualifying flat for residential purposes. There are, however, many detailed rules that must be met. The following is a very broad summary and attention must be paid to those rules in the legislation in a given case. The following references are to Part 4A CAA 2001.

Relief is only available in respect of expenditure incurred on or after the day on which FA 2001 was passed (11 May 2001). The person incurring the qualifying expenditure is entitled to an initial allowance of up to 100 per cent under s393H. The allowance is given in the year of assessment in which the expenditure is incurred but will be withdrawn if, in the event, the flat does not prove to be a qualifying flat. Where the whole initial allowance is not claimed, a writing-down allowance is available for later periods under ss393J to K, at the rate of 25 per cent of the expenditure (or until the allowance has been given in full). A balancing event can give rise to a charge or allowance under ss393M to P but only if that event occurs within seven years of the time when the flat was first suitable for letting as a dwelling. Balancing events include the sale of the relevant interest in the flat; death of the person incurring the expenditure; demolition of the flat; and the flat ceasing to be a qualifying flat. The value to be brought into account depends upon the nature of the balancing event as set out in s393O. The allowances and charges are deductible or taxed as the case may be in determining the results of the individual's Schedule A business. The purchaser of a flat that qualified for this relief cannot make a claim for allowances.

It is clearly important to be able to determine the expenditure that can qualify for these allowances. In essence, 'qualifying expenditure', requires the following:

- capital expenditure on the conversion of part of a qualifying building or qualifying flat;

- alternatively, the renovation of an existing flat in a qualifying building where that flat will become a qualifying flat;

- in either case, the part of the building or flat mentioned above must have been unused (or used only for storage) throughout the period of one year ending with the date on which the works begin;

- the flat must be self-contained and divided horizontally from another part of the building;

- the building in which the flat is contained must have at least most of its ground floor authorised for business use and be not more than four storeys above the ground floor. Those storeys should, when the building was constructed, have been intended for use primarily as one or more dwellings;

- the building must have been constructed before 1 January 1980, although an extension after that date and before 1 January 2001 will not disqualify it;

- the flat must be suitable for letting as a dwelling and for the purpose of short-term lettings (not more than five years) with its own access. It must not have more than four rooms (ignoring kitchen, bathroom, and most hallways, etc.);

- the flat must not be a high value flat or a part of a scheme involving the creating of such flats. Section 393E defines the meaning of high value flats, which depends upon the number of rooms and whether the flat is in Greater London or elsewhere – broadly, a flat whose notional rents exceeds £480 per week in London and £300 per week elsewhere cannot qualify, with lower rents applying for smaller flats;

- the flat must not be let to a person connected to the individual who incurred the expenditure.

It may be asked why this relief is given as a capital allowance rather than as a simple deduction in arriving at Schedule A business results. However, one particular advantage of this system is that under s41 TCGA 1992 the expenditure qualifying for capital allowances can also be deducted in arriving at a chargeable gain (although there is a restriction if a loss arises for capital gains tax purposes). Moreover, capital allowances can be included in a loss claim against other income (see **8.5** below).

8.3 The nature of the letting business including jointly owned property

8.3.1 Identifying the letting business

A letting business would ordinarily commence at the earliest on the first occasion when an individual completes on the purchase of a property for the purposes of letting. If the property is vacant, it is arguable that the business does not commence until the first letting. This is largely academic, because any pre-commencement expenditure should be allowable when the business commences, on the same lines as pre-trading expenditure. The point is likely to be more relevant where the property is a qualifying furnished holiday letting if there is a potential claim for a loss in the initial period.

That letting business continues for as long as an individual has a property either let or available for letting. The cessation of a rental business is more problematical. In practice this is likely to be of particular relevance if there is a loss brought forward. If the letting business ceases, those losses will disappear. Even if the same individual acquires a property for letting at a later date that will be treated as a new, and separate, letting business.

This is a question of fact and clearly it is in the interests of a taxpayer to argue that the same business continues where he has losses not otherwise relievable. The practice of the Revenue is to treat the business as having ceased if there is an interval of more than three years, unless there is convincing evidence to the contrary. If the gap is less than three years then, as a rule, they will regard the business as continuing but there should, nevertheless, be evidence of attempts to acquire other properties. Generally, see IR 150 paragraphs 313 to 321.

If the letting business has ceased the normal rules for post-cessation receipts and expenditure apply, as for a trade.

8.3.2   Identifying the person(s) carrying on the business

All properties forming part of a person's letting activities are treated as a single business. Hence, there is a pooling of all receipts and expenditure in the same way as if they were a single trade. If an individual is also involved as a partner in letting activities then the activities of that partnership are treated as a single business, quite distinct from any letting activities carried on by that individual in his sole capacity. Whether or not there is a partnership in the strict sense of the word, and how joint ownership is dealt with, is considered in the next section.

Another situation that might arise in practice is that of an individual letting properties and also being entitled to property income as the life tenant of a trust. In that situation the letting activities of the trust are normally assessed on the trustees in that capacity, which would be a separate letting business. The main implication for this is again that a loss on one business could not be set against a profit on the other. The analysis might be different if the trustees have delegated their powers of leasing and management to the life tenant under their statutory powers, which is less likely in most instances in practice.

The consequence is the same even where the rents are deemed to be those of the settlor having an interest in the settlement and, therefore, within the settlement provisions of s660C ICTA 1988. The rental income is charged on the settlor under Schedule D Case VI. If the settlor is also the life tenant and actually carries on the trustees' Schedule A business, by virtue of delegation to him, he may be able to merge the two together.

8.3.3   Jointly owned property

Is joint ownership of property a partnership? If it is, that is a separate letting activity.

The definition of partnership is considered in more detail in Chapter **9**. In the majority of cases the simple joint ownership of property does not constitute a partnership. There must be a high level of activity. For example, two individuals might join together to establish a programme of purchasing properties for letting on an extensive scale, probably borrowing considerable sums. They might also have offices from which they conduct the letting activity. In that situation, a partnership could well exist, but that is likely to be the exception.

Otherwise, where property is simply jointly owned, each individual should take into his own letting business his share of the rents and expenses of the jointly owned property. A separate partnership return is not required.

If a trading partnership also has letting income, that letting income is ordinarily treated as part of a separate Schedule A business. That letting business is distinct from the letting activities of individual partners. As explained in Chapter **9**, the computation of the income can be quite different as well, involving different basis periods together with overlap relief.

8.4 Property letting as a trade

8.4.1 General

Generally speaking, letting of property would not amount to a trade except in the case of furnished holiday lettings in the UK, where there is a statutory exception, explained below. Running a guest house or providing bed and breakfast can amount to a trade, where the services offered are beyond those of a normal landlord. An individual may be carrying on a separate trade of providing services in its own right distinct from the letting activities, but only where the services are well beyond those normally provided by a landlord.

In practice, a caravan site proprietor can treat income from letting caravans as trading receipts where the operational activities amount to trading (ESC B29).

8.4.2 Letting of surplus property by a trader

By concession, rent from accommodation which is temporarily surplus to current business requirements can be treated as part of the Schedule D Case I or Case II activities, as appropriate. The circumstances are restricted as set out in IR 150 paragraph 502, as follows:

- the premises must be partly used for the business and so a separate property which is wholly surplus must be dealt with under Schedule A;

- the rental income must be comparatively small; and

- the rent must be from surplus business accommodation only and not land.

In the case of a property developer, he may let, on a temporary basis, a property he has constructed owing to depressed market conditions. The letting income is nevertheless assessed under Schedule A. If the expenses exceed the rental income, the loss can be deducted as part of his Schedule D Case I activities.

A similar position arises where a trader takes on a lease as part of his trade but the property becomes surplus. The rent he pays remains deductible as a Schedule D Case 1 expense, but any rents received will be assessed under Schedule A (net of expenses). If a loss arises he may deduct that loss in arriving at his trading profits (IR 150 paragraph 506).

3 Furnished holiday lettings in the UK

A Schedule A business may include the commercial letting of furnished holiday accommodation in the UK. In that case, s503(1) ICTA 1988 treats the profit from that letting as if it were a trade chargeable under Schedule D Case I.

The main advantage of this treatment is that a loss arising can be set against other income and not restricted to rental profits. Any profits made are also eligible for making personal pension contributions. There are also considerable capital gains tax advantages, as explained in the *Capital Gains Tax* volume at **18.3**.

The basic conditions which must be met for this treatment are as follows:

(a) The letting must be on a commercial basis with a view to the realisation of profits. Funding of a property in such a way that the interest cost is always likely to produce a loss probably means that the letting does not qualify. This was the conclusion of the Special Commissioners in rejecting the taxpayer's claim in *Brown v Richardson* [1997] STC (SCD) 233.

(b) The accommodation must be available for commercial letting to the public generally as holiday accommodation for at least 140 days in the year of assessment.

(c) The period of actual letting in that year must be at least 70 days.

(d) In any period of at least seven months, the property should not normally be in the same occupation for a continuous period exceeding 31 days.

(e) A claim can be made to average holiday accommodation properties for the purposes of meeting the 70 day actual letting test.

(f) Overseas properties do not qualify for this treatment.

Where a property is acquired during a year, the above tests are applied to the period of 12 months from the date the property is first let. If a property ceases to be let as furnished accommodation then the test is applied to the 12-month period to the date it ceased to be let.

> **Tax tip**
>
> It is important that a furnished holiday letting is on a commercial basis. Projections should be prepared to establish, if need be at a later date, that the letting is commercial and can make a profit. In particular, borrow at such a level which can be justified commercially.
>
> The Revenue would normally expect there to be a reasonable and realistic expectation of profit within five years from the date of commencement. The Revenue approach is set out in *Tax Bulletin* of October 1997.

8.5 Losses

A Schedule A or Schedule D Case V letting business adopts trading principles to determine the business results. Nevertheless, the profit or loss arising is not from a trade, remaining within Schedule A or Schedule D Case V as appropriate.

This is particularly relevant where a loss arises. It follows that such a loss cannot be deducted against other income of the taxpayer. There are exceptions as set out below. Otherwise, a Schedule A loss can only be carried forward against future profits from the same letting business (s379A(1) ICTA 1988). A Schedule D Case V loss can only be set against profits from the same Schedule D Case V letting business. Property letting losses cannot be carried back.

Exceptions are the following cases:

(a) A loss arising from a furnished holiday accommodation letting treated as if it were a trade under s503(1) ICTA 1988 can be dealt with in the same way as any other trading loss. Thus, it can be set against other income for the same tax year or the preceding tax year. Relief can also be given under s381 ICTA 1988 against other income in the three preceding years, subject to meeting the commerciality test in s381(4). However, no relief is given under s381 if any of the accommodation in respect of the deemed trade was first let by the same individual as furnished accommodation (whether qualifying under s503 or not) more than three years before the beginning of the year of assessment in which the potential s381 loss arises. In principle, terminal loss relief is also available for a loss in the final year.

(b) Capital allowances (net of balancing charges) can be claimed against other income for the tax year of loss or the following year under s379A(3) ICTA 1988. Such a loss cannot exceed the loss in the Schedule A business. Capital allowances on plant and machinery must also rise in connection with a letting to a person whose use is for trading purposes.

(c) Section 379A(3) also applies to 'allowable agricultural expenses' in relation to agricultural land in the UK. The definition of 'allowable agricultural expenses' includes maintenance, repairs, insurance or management of the agricultural estate, but does not include interest payable.

Tax tip

A taxpayer incurs a Schedule A business loss in the year to 5 April 2004 of £12,000. Capital allowances included in that loss amount to £7,000.

By making a claim, £7,000 of that loss can be set against other income under s379A(3) ICTA 1988. The remainder of the loss will be carried forward against future profits from the letting business.

If his letting business also included agricultural land and the allowable agricultural expenses amounted to £6,000, the maximum loss against other income would be the actual Schedule A loss of £12,000.

8.6   Rent-a-room

To encourage the letting of part of an individual's home, s59 and Sch 10 Finance (No.2) Act 1992 provide an exemption in prescribed circumstances for rental income derived from such lettings. The provisions only apply to the letting of an individual's only or main residence for the time being. Thus, if the individual has moved out and is letting the entire property the exemption will not apply. Although not explicit in the legislation, the letting should be for residential purposes and not, for example, used as office accommodation. The Revenue have made this clear in *Tax Bulletin* of August 1994, to counteract recommendations from some advisers to take advantage of rent-a-room where an individual's company uses part of his house for office purposes. The manner in which relief is given depends upon whether or not the 'basic amount' for the year of assessment is exceeded. The current 'basic amount' is £4,250. Thus:

(a) If the total amount in the year from the letting, including not only rental income but also charges for meals, cleaning, laundry and goods and services of a similar nature, does not exceed £4,250, the receivables and expenditure in relation to the letting are ignored for Schedule A purposes. Thus, any profit is not taxable but neither is any loss allowable.

It may not suit an individual to apply these provisions, such as where a loss arises on the letting. Schedule 10 para 10 permits the individual to elect not to apply rent-a-room for a particular year of assessment. The election must be made within 12 months from 31 January next following the end of the year of assessment. A fresh election must be made for later years, if appropriate.

(b) If the total sum of gross receipts and meals, etc., exceeds £4,250, the individual may elect to be taxed as if the profit from the letting were equal to the difference between the total sums receivable and £4,250. This election must also be made within 12 months from 31 January next following the end of the year and will continue to have effect until withdrawn. Such notice is deemed to have been withdrawn if, in a later year, the total sums receivable do not exceed the basic amount for the year.

If a property is jointly owned the 'basic amount' of, currently, £4,250 is reduced to one half, i.e., £2,125. If three individuals own a house in which they all live it would seem that each of them has a limit of £2,125.

If the period of letting is less than 12 months, the current basic amount of £4,250 is also reduced to £2,125 if some other person lets accommodation in the same residence in any period of 12 months and which includes the individual's period of letting. If an individual moves in a tax year and both houses qualify for relief, the 'basic amount' applies to the total rents from both properties.

8.7 Premiums

A landlord may ask for a capital sum in return for granting a lease, usually in addition to rent. If the lease does not exceed 50 years then part of that premium is treated for tax purposes as if it were rent. That part is then brought into the letting business accounts on the date the lease is granted. If the premium is paid by instalments, the landlord can elect to pay the tax on the premium by such instalments as the Revenue agree (s34(8) ICTA 1988).

In the straightforward case of a premium, the Schedule A part is calculated by deducting from the premium the fraction represented by the number of complete years in the duration of the lease (less one year) divided by 50. Thus, if a premium of £20,000 is charged for a lease of 10½ years, the Schedule A (rent) element is £16,400

$$\left(\text{i.e., £20,000 less}\left(\frac{10-1}{50}\right)\right).$$

The legislation also deems other transactions to involve the payment of a premium. These prevent avoidance of tax. Briefly, the circumstances covered are as follows:

(a) Where the landlord imposes an obligation on the tenant to carry out improvement work on the premises (not being repairs which would otherwise be deductible if the landlord incurred them), the landlord is deemed to have received a premium equal to the increase in the value of his reversionary interest arising because of the tenant's obligations.

Example 8.3

L grants a lease of office premises for 25 years from 6 October 2003 at an initial annual rent of £30,000 p.a. The lessee is required to carry out various improvements to the premises which cost £25,000, but only increase L's freehold reversion value by £20,000.

L is deemed to receive a premium of £20,000, being the increase in value of his reversionary interest. A fraction of this, being $\dfrac{25-1}{50}$ (48%), is not treated as rent.

Thus, for the year 5 April 2004 L's letting business would include rent of £15,000 and taxable premium £10,400, i.e., £25,400

The non-Schedule A part of the premium will be brought into account for capital gains tax purposes.

(b) Where, under the terms subject to which a lease is granted, the tenant pays a sum in lieu of rent for any period or as consideration for the surrender of the lease, a premium is deemed to have been received by the landlord equal to the sum paid. When the sum is paid in lieu of rent, the duration of the lease is deemed to include only the period for which the sum is payable.

(c) A sum payable by the tenant (otherwise than by way of rent) as consideration for the variation or waiver of any of the terms of the lease is treated as a premium received when the relevant contract is entered into. In applying the formula to compute the Schedule A element, the duration of the lease is treated as the period for which the variation or waiver has effect.

(d) If the landlord could have obtained an additional premium based on values prevailing for the time the lease was granted, 'the amount foregone' can be treated as if it were a premium on a subsequent assignment of the lease. The income element of the premium is treated as income of the assignor. This deeming can apply to successive assignments, to the extent of the total 'amount foregone'. The deemed premium is brought into account when the sum payable on the assignment becomes payable (s35 ICTA 1988).

(e) If the freeholder of land simply sold his interest for, say, £200,000, he could build in a provision to have the property bought back for, say, £160,000 at a future date. This type of transaction is seen as equivalent to a premium, and s36 ICTA 1988 would deem that difference in price of £40,000 to be a premium. It is reduced by 2 per cent for each complete year (other than the first) in the period between the sale and the future date of re-purchase. This provision also covers the situation where the right to purchase back is granted to a person connected with the vendor.

As mentioned, a premium can only be treated as rent if the duration of the lease does not exceed 50 years. It would in some cases be relatively easy to draft a lease which, nominally at least, exceeds 50 years but which in reality is for a much shorter period. Hence, s38 ICTA 1988 sets out detailed rules for determining the duration of a lease for these purposes. In particular, if the terms of the lease or any other circumstances render it unlikely that the lease will continue beyond a date falling before the expiry of the term of the lease, the lease is treated as having been granted to the date the lease is likely to end in practice. However, if the premium truly reflects the grant for the full term, no adjustment is required.

Section 38 also applies in the opposite way to treat a lease as having been granted for a longer period, if the lease includes provision for the extension of the lease at the election of the tenant.

These rules for the duration of the lease are applied based on facts known or assertainable at the grant of the lease, or at the date of the contract for a variation or waiver where s34(5) ICTA 1988 applies.

8 Overseas properties

Schedule D Case V charges tax in respect of income arising from possessions out of the United Kingdom. Property overseas is a possession and is therefore chargeable under that case. Schedule A, as has been mentioned above, is confined to United Kingdom property. Section 65 ICTA 1988 provides that the relevant income is to be computed on the full amount of the income arising in the year of assessment, whether brought to the UK or not.

Section 65A ICTA 1988 enacts further provisions specifically in relation to land outside the UK where the income:

> '. . . arises from a business carried on for the exploitation, as a source of rents or other receipts of any estate, interest or rights in or over land outside the United Kingdom.'

The remainder of s65A provides for the Schedule A rules to be adopted in computing the income for the purposes of Schedule D Case V. Thus, the overseas activities are treated as one single business, but that business is distinct from the actual Schedule A business. Hence, there can be no offset of losses on an overseas property against profits on a UK property (and vice versa).

Section 65A(6) prevents the application of ss80 and 81 ICTA 1988 in computing the profits of an overseas property business. This exclusion could effectively deny certain costs of travel from the UK to the overseas property, unless the wholly and exclusively test is met applying normal principles. Travelling between properties overseas should, though, be allowable applying normal trading principles.

The general law of property overseas is likely to be quite different to that in the UK. Section 65A(8) recognises this to ensure that the treatment of receipts in connection with overseas properties are dealt with in the way which most closely corresponds with the result that would be produced for Schedule A purposes in the UK. In particular, a premium or its overseas equivalent would be brought into account by applying the premium rules in ss34 to 38 ICTA 1988.

Finally, in principle overseas property income can only be assessed on a UK-resident individual. That individual may be domiciled outside the UK in which case the remittance basis of taxation will be relevant, in the same way as any other foreign income. This is dealt with in Chapter **10**.

> **Example 8.4**
>
> Z owns a villa in Spain which, owing to poor local market conditions, is only let for two months in the year 2003/04. As a result she incurred a net loss of £1,500. She also owns a UK flat that is let. The net profit on that flat for 2003/04 is £3,500.
>
> Her Schedule A profit is £3,500, which is fully taxable. The £1,500 loss arises on an overseas property and must be kept separate. It can only be carried forward against a future letting profit from overseas properties.

8.9 Non-resident landlords

8.9.1 Basic principle

The source of Schedule A income is clearly in the UK and hence the Inland Revenue have a claim to tax on that income. This is irrespective of the country of residence of that individual. Moreover, tax treaties between the UK and other countries grant primary taxing rights to the country in which the property is located (usually referred to as immovable property).

The potential difficulty of the Inland Revenue is one of collection. If the individual is not in the UK, enforcement may become a practical impossibility. The Revenue must, therefore, have provisions to ensure the collection of tax.

Section 42A ICTA 1988 provides the Inland Revenue with the authority to make regulations to assist in the collection and assessment of tax in these circumstances. The detailed regulations are contained in the Taxation of Income from Land (Non-residents) Regulations 1995 SI 1995/2902.

From 1 April 2001, the Revenue have been administering this scheme (as well as other aspects of non-residence) through a new centre for non-residents.

8.9.2 Persons liable to account for tax

The Revenue may require an agent or tenant to deduct tax and pay it over in accordance with the regulations, in which case they must do this or risk the consequences. Even without such a notice, there is an automatic requirement to account where:

(a) The agent is in the UK and has power to receive income in respect of the UK property, or has control over the direction of that income. Thus, he does not need to actually receive the income to be made liable but simply have some power over it. An agent whose activities are confined to legal advice or services cannot be made liable, but, by implication, any professional person acting beyond those activities could become liable. Any involvement of such a professional in relation to an overseas property could place them at risk, unless care is taken.

(b) If there is no such agent, a UK-based tenant is liable, but only if the sums he pays to the non-resident exceed in total £5,200 p.a. (apportioned where less than one year). This is a relatively low sum nowadays and it should be noted that relevant sums must be aggregated, which would include not only rents but also premiums.

8.9.3 Deducting income tax and accounting for it

An agent should, within 30 days of first becoming an agent in relation to an overseas property owned by a non-resident, register with the Revenue. He must then make a tax calculation for each calendar quarter (i.e., 31 March, 30 June, etc.).

For each such quarter the agent accounts for income tax at the basic rate on the excess of the rents and other Schedule A amounts he receives for the property over the expenses paid by him or by another at his direction. He must be reasonably satisfied that the expenses are deductible. Expenses paid by the landlord, such as loan interest, cannot be dealt with in this way. The landlord must submit a return and claim repayment of overpaid income tax.

The return must be submitted within 30 days after the end of the quarter and an annual return not later than 5 July after the year end (31 March). A certificate must be provided to the non-resident landlord, to ensure the proper credit for tax deducted. In the case of a tenant making payment to a non-resident, he simply deducts income tax at the basic rate from the rents, applying the same quarterly and annual rules as for an agent.

Proper records must be kept by relevant agents and tenants and these can be inspected by the Revenue.

8.9.4 Payment of rent without deduction of income tax

To avoid the deduction of tax and the practical implications of this, there are provisions whereby payments can be made gross to a non-resident without deducting income tax. In that case, the non-resident makes a self-assessment return in the same way as any other individual, accounting for tax on the usual dates and in accordance with the usual provisions.

The Revenue must consent to gross payment. This is dealt with by completing form NRLI, which contains details regarding the non-resident. This includes a statement that:

- the individual has complied with all UK tax obligations imposed on him prior to the date of the application; or

- he has not had any such obligations imposed on him; or

- he does not expect to be liable to pay UK income tax for the year in which the application is made.

He must also give undertakings that he will:

- notify the Revenue if he does become liable to pay tax;

- comply with all UK tax obligations imposed on him;

- inform the Revenue if his usual place of abode ceases to be outside the UK;

The Revenue can refuse an application, subsequently ask for further information or withdraw approval that has been given.

9 Partnerships

9.1 Meaning of partnership

9.1.1 Partnership Act 1890

Section 1 Partnership Act 1890 defines partnership as:

> '. . . the relation which subsists between persons carrying on business in common with a view of profit.'

Section 2 then expands upon this definition, setting out certain rules to which regard must be had, as follows:

(a) Simply owning property jointly does not itself create a partnership.

(b) Neither does the sharing of gross returns create a partnership, whether or not the property from which those returns are derived is held jointly.

(c) On the other hand, the receipt by a person of a share of the profits of a business is prima facie evidence that he is a partner, although this is not conclusive. In particular, it is specified that an employee or agent receiving a share of the profits under his contract is not by virtue thereof a partner.

(d) The receipt by way of annuity of a portion of the business profits by a dependant of any deceased person does not create a partnership. Neither does lending money where the rate of interest varies with the profits, nor the receipt of an annuity or a portion of the profits in consideration of the sale of goodwill.

As can be seen, simply owning property jointly does not create a partnership. This is why in the majority of cases there is not a separate Schedule A business merely because property is jointly owned.

Whether or not there is a partnership is a question of fact based on the application of these basic legal principles. The existence of a partnership is often questioned where between related parties, especially husband and wife.

9.1.2 Identifying a partnership

There are potentially two questions. Does a partnership exist and if so from what date?

When minor children are involved, the Revenue would need some convincing that they are truly partners. In *Alexander Bulloch and Co v CIR* [1976] STC 514, the partners purported to bring into partnership their two daughters aged 14 and 15. An agreement had been made in January 1974 and the year in dispute was 1972/73. The Court upheld the Special Commissioners' view that, for the particular year in question, there was no concluded agreement for the daughters to become partners. There was no evidence of acceptance of responsibility as partners. Clearly, the younger the individual the greater the evidential burden, as there is some point where there is little likelihood of understanding the nature and responsibilities of being a partner.

The Revenue can also question whether or not there is truly a partnership between spouses. Simply preparing accounts and tax returns as if partners is not sufficient. A partnership agreement is helpful evidence but not conclusive. There ought to be some external evidence such as notifying creditors, bankers and ensuring that all contracts are entered into by the partners. It does not matter that one spouse does not have the same technical skills as the other, as one can provide valuable management and administrative services, leaving the other to deal with the operational side. The importance of evidence is shown by *Saywell* v *Pope* [1979] STC 824. Two partners introduced their wives into partnership and agreed that they had become partners in April 1973. However, creditors were not informed and there were no drawing facilities on the bank account. Neither was there any evidence that the wives did anything in their capacity as partners. The agreement itself was not actually signed until June 1975. The General Commissioners' finding that there was no partnership in April 1973 was supportable on the evidence.

An earlier case on this topic is *Dickenson* v *Gross* (1927) 11 TC 614. A farmer entered into a deed of partnership with his three sons, on the basis of an equal division of profits. The farmer purported to let two farms to the partnership at a rent but in fact nothing was paid. No accounts were prepared and cheques were signed solely by the farmer. No distributions of profit were ever made. Again, it was held that no partnership existed on the facts. Although a partnership deed had been prepared it was simply set on one side and disregarded.

The sons could have enforced their rights under the deed but they did not do so.

Even if a partnership does, in fact, exist does it matter that one spouse receives a greater share of profits than the level of activity might justify between parties at arm's length? There is an argument that the 'settlement' provisions of Part XV ICTA 1988 could apply. This is on the basis that the introduction of the partner, or the terms, are not commercial. Thus, there is a possibility that a larger part of the profits of the partnership can be deemed to be those of the main partner, as settlor, as he has retained an interest. To avoid this type of argument, it should be ensured that the spouse in question is involved in the partnership and that the share can be justified. Assuming unlimited liability as a partner is itself a factor. The Revenue in *Tax Bulletin* of April 2003 have stated clearly that they do regard the 'settlement' provisions as being in point where wives are brought into partnership. They give the example of two husbands in partnership as second-hand car dealers who then introduce their respective wives as partners, the wives doing no work for the partnership, which has no employees. The Revenue would regard this as having the element of bounty required to treat the husbands as taxable on the profits as previously. However, the Revenue view is being contested strongly by many in the profession.

For a discussion of capital gains tax matters relating to tax partnerships see the *Capital Gains Tax 2002/2003*.

9.1.3 Joint ventures

Merely labelling a relationship as a partnership is not conclusive. A declaration in a contract that the parties are not entering into a partnership may be helpful in a marginal case. If the facts clearly point the other way then in law a partnership could exist. A joint venture, where there is no continuing business as such, can amount to a partnership. Two cases illustrate this.

In *John Gardner and Bowring, Hardy & Co Limited* v *CIR* (1930) 15 TC 602, London and Glasgow coal merchants entered into an agreement, during a coal strike, whereby the London firm bought cargo from overseas and the Glasgow dealers carried out the marketing. The London merchants discharged the cargoes to the venture at cost and expenses of purchase and marketing were deducted in arriving at the profit. Neither party was bound to purchase any particular coal. It was held that a partnership existed in relation to the venture, rejecting arguments that this was merely a normal purchase arrangement.

In *Fenstone* v *Johnstone* (1940) 23 TC 29, the taxpayer wished to buy and develop land, with the financial aid of another, who received 50 per cent of the profits. That other party also assisted in the development and sale of the land. It was also held here that a partnership existed in relation to the one venture.

Example 9.1

A builder who ordinarily carries out contracting work has the opportunity of buying a piece of land on which to build houses. He does not have the finance and arranges that an acquaintance will supply the money to purchase and develop the land. The builder provides all the materials and labour. They agree to share profits made on the sale of the houses equally, but after allowing agreed figures for interest on the funds supplied by the financier and management of the site by the builder.

On these facts, there could well be a partnership. If the financier had simply lent money at an interest rate, perhaps geared to profitability, this might not constitute him a partner. If his return is dependant upon a profit, this is more consistent with a partnership. In the words of s1 Partnership Act 1890, they are carrying on business in common with a view of profit.

In addition to income tax aspects, they will also need to consider VAT. They are likely to require a separate registration for the purposes of that tax.

9.1.4 Types of partners

In the normal case, all partners are general partners in that they share profits and losses according to their agreement. They are often referred to as equity partners, to distinguish them from salaried partners in other cases.

The expression 'salaried partner' is in some ways an unfortunate one, as the exact meaning in a given case cannot be gleaned from the description itself. If all this means is that a partner's share of profit is fixed but he is actively involved in the partnership itself, attending partners' meetings and voting, then he could well be a partner in the strict sense of the word. This is particularly so if, on the facts, he would not be entitled to any profit if the partnership broke even or made a loss. If, on the other hand, the salaried partner is entitled to his salary, come what may, that salary may properly be assessable as employment income (with PAYE etc.). In that situation, the other partners should execute a deed of indemnity, as that partner could nevertheless be liable to the outside world for any debts, as he is held out to be a partner.

A less common arrangement is that of a limited partnership. Ordinarily, any partner has unlimited liability for the debts of a partnership. If one or more partners cannot meet their share, the remaining partners are liable. However, under the Limited Partnerships Act 1907 it is possible to create a limited partnership. Provided there is a least one general partner, having unlimited liability, the other partners can limit their liability to the amount they agree to contribute as capital. Such a partnership must be registered under the Act and a limited partner does not have any right to take part in the management of the business. If the requirements of the Act are breached, then every limited partner is liable in the same way as a general partner. This type of arrangement became popular as part of arrangements to exploit capital allowances. Legislation has now been introduced to restrict certain reliefs (see **9.6** and see **9.7** below for the treatment of LLP's)

9.1.5 The partnership agreement

It is up to the partners to agree between them how the partnership is to be administered, profits and losses shared how they deal with outgoing partners. Indeed, there are usually many other matters that need to be agreed and are usually dealt with in comprehensive agreements. Such an agreement will always prevail provided it is not a sham and is lawful. An agreement can be oral or implied by the conduct of the partners.

If there is no written or oral agreement, or if the agreement is not sufficiently comprehensive, the provisions of the Partnership Act 1890 will come into play. In particular, this provides for a dissolution of the partnership rather than an orderly procedure when a partner wishes to leave. Profits and losses are divided equally in the absence of agreement to the contrary. A partner is not entitled to interest on capital but is entitled to interest on a loan to the partnership. The partners can always vary the arrangement from time to time as they agree. It is clearly better for this to be in writing to avoid argument at a later date.

Given that the income tax provisions follow the partnership division of profit, it is essential to know how profits and losses are divided.

9.1.6   Other matters

The fact of a partnership has many consequences. Being a partner means that an individual is potentially liable for all the debts of the partnership, if the others cannot pay. This is particularly relevant where husband and wife become partners. There may well be tax savings in doing this, by making use of one spouse's personal allowances and basic rate band (albeit with an increased National Insurance cost). There can also be an advantage in pension provision if the earnings cap is otherwise exceeded. However, these advantages are acquired at a price. If the business in question contains risks, and particularly those which cannot be insured, then if everything goes wrong the combined assets of husband and wife are jeopardised. If only one of the parties to the marriage is in business, at least the other spouse's share of the assets is protected. In certain professions, it is not possible for one spouse to be a partner, because they lack the appropriate qualifications. Moreover, if the Revenue invoke the 'settlement' provisions mentioned in **9.1.2** above, there will be no tax saving but the commercial risks will still be there. See also **9.2.5** below.

9.2   Determining the partnership taxable profits and losses

9.2.1   Partnership accounts and tax returns

Until 1997/98, an assessment for income tax was made on the partnership as such. It made every partner potentially liable for the tax debts of all the other partners if they could not pay. That is no longer the case.

However, the partnership accounts, and partnership tax return based thereon, is a starting point for taxing the partners. Given that they share the profits or losses there has to be a mechanism for determining the results which are to be divided. Thus, a separate partnership tax return is issued, which divides the profits and losses between the partners. Each individual includes his share on his own tax return and computes his tax liability accordingly. The partnership return does not itself compute any liability to tax. Indeed, it would not be possible to do so. The administrative aspects of this are dealt with in Chapter 12 on returns and records.

9.2.2 Particular matters in computing the partnership profits, etc.

The results of the partnership are computed in the same way as a sole trader, applying the principles set out in the chapters dealing with computation of trades and professions, including capital allowances.

Interest on capital and partners' salaries are merely factors taken into account in the allocation of profits. They cannot be deducted in arriving at the Schedule D Case I or II profits. However, a partner may lend monies to the partnership quite distinct from his capital. He may also act as landlord in letting the partnership have the use of premises. In these cases, the interest and rent paid would ordinarily be treated as a deductible expense in the same way as if paid to a third party. The receiving partner will simply bring in that share as untaxed interest and the rental income into his property business.

In some instances, notably the medical profession, partners have made separate claims for personal expenses. This is effectively part of the way in which they distribute the profits, requiring certain expenses to be incurred by those partners rather than borne by the partners in their overall profit sharing ratios. Such expenses must be included in the partnership return in the same way as any other expense, otherwise there is no means of obtaining tax relief. One consequence of this is that all partners become involved in claiming those expenses, the details of which may not be known to them. In practice, therefore, care should be taken in agreeing the expenses that an individual partner can claim.

A similar principle applies to capital allowances on machinery or plant, which is not partnership property as such. Section 264 CAA 2001 provides for the same allowances and charges to be made for the purposes of the trade as if it had been partnership property (unless let to the partnership). There is no disposal on a sale or gift between partners of such machinery or plant, provided it continues to be used for the partnership trade.

In practice there are certain types of expenses which can present problems. One example is private motoring and another is wife's wages. Strictly, each partner should maintain a record of his business mileage and the exact proportion claimed, including capital allowances. In practice this may be more difficult, particularly in larger partnerships. There must, though, be some arrangement to ensure that the deduction made for motor expenses is reasonable. This should be kept under review. Otherwise, an inspector of taxes could dispute the amount claimed and then challenge earlier years. In the case of wife's wages, these must be justified and not simply be allocated in profit sharing ratios. This might be an appropriate method in some cases, but it is important that for each spouse the amount paid is supported by reference to the actual duties.

By concession, incidental directors' fees dealt with as part of the partnership profits can be included in the Schedule D Case I/II results rather than as employment income. The Revenue should be asked to agree this treatment (ESC A37).

For a discussion of accounting policies to be adopted by partnerships see Tax Digest 183 *The New Rules for Taxing Professionals.*

9.2.3 Allocation of profits or losses

As mentioned above, there is no partnership assessment as such from 1997/98 onwards. The treatment of partnerships is dealt with in s111 ICTA 1988. The first three subsections are important:

'(1) Where a trade or profession is carried on by persons in partnership the partnership shall not, unless the contrary intention appears, be treated for the purposes of the Tax Acts as an entity which is separate and distinct from those persons.

(2) So long as a trade or profession is carried on by persons in partnership, and any of those persons is chargeable to income tax, the profits or losses arising from the trade or profession ("the actual trade or profession") shall be computed for the purposes of income tax in like manner as if –
   (a) the partnership were an individual; and
   (b) that individual were an individual resident in the United Kingdom.

(3) A person's share in the profits or losses arising from the actual trade or profession which for any period are computed in accordance with subsection (2) above shall be determined according to the interest of the partners during that period.'

This effectively means that having established a partner's share of the profit for a given year, he is then taxed as if that profit were from a sole trade. This has the consequence of applying the commencement and cessation rules. Once an incoming partner is beyond the special rules in the opening years, his basis period for assessment will be the same as the continuing partners. A partner also has his own overlap relief, so that under the actual year basis he will pay tax on the actual profit (as adjusted for tax purposes) he has earned as a partner. Unlike the old preceding year basis, he cannot effectively be taxed on profits for a year in which he is not a partner.

Example 9.2

The AB partnership has been in business for many years drawing up its accounts to 30 September each year. M joined the partnership on 1 July 2002. The tax adjusted profits for the year to 30 September 2002 are £150,000. Prior charges on profits are as follows:

	Interest on capital £	Salary £
A	5,000	21,000
B	4,000	17,000
M (from 1 July 2002)	1,000	2,000

The balance of the profit is allocated equally between A and B until 30 June 2002 and from that date as 35% each to A and B and 30% to M.

The tax adjusted profits of £150,000 are allocated as follows:

	Total £	A £	B £	M £
Interest on capital	10,000	5,000	4,000	1,000
Partners' salaries	40,000	21,000	17,000	2,000
Balance to 30 June 2002	75,000	37,500	37,500	–
3 months to 30 September 2002	25,000	8,750	8,750	7,500
	150,000	72,250	67,250	10,500

In the above example, A and B will be assessed on profits of £72,250 and £67,250 respectively for the year 2002/03, on the actual year basis. M's position is more complicated because he became a partner in that year, which is dealt with in **9.2.4**.

9.2.4 Changes in partners

Previously, the introduction or leaving of a partner involved an automatic cessation of the partnership business, with adjustments to cessation and opening years, unless a continuation election was signed by all the relevant individuals. Section 113(2) ICTA 1988 now provides that if there is a change in the persons carrying on a trade then subsection (1) of that section is not to treat it as having been discontinued, and a new one as set up and commenced, if

> '... a person engaged in carrying on the trade, profession or vocation immediately before the change continues to be engaged immediately after it.'

Similarly, s263 CAA 2001 provides continuity for capital allowance purposes where there is such a change in partners.

Thus, if the partnership business continues as a question of fact there is no cessation or commencement, provided at least one partner continues. This is also the case if a sole trader brings into partnership another individual. If the two are then carrying on the business there is no cessation. The sole trader would effectively be taxed as if nothing had changed, apart from allocating part of the profit to the incoming partner. The incoming partner will be dealt with by applying the commencement rules. The following is an example of an individual joining a partnership.

Example 9.3

The profits of the AB partnership are as stated above for the year to 30 September 2002 and are £210,000 for the year to 30 September 2003 of which M's share is £60,000.

M is taxed as if his share were from a separate sole trade which he commenced on 1 July 2002. He is taxed as follows:

	£	£
2002/03 (1 July 2002 to 5 April 2003)		
Part of year to 30 September 2002	10,500	
6/12 × £60,000 (year to 30 September 2003)	30,000	40,500
2003/04 – year to 30 September 2003		60,000
His overlap relief is 6/12 × £60,000 (i.e.,		30,000
1 October 2002 to 5 April 2003)		

If a partner leaves the partnership and other partners continue the same trade, etc., the position is effectively reversed. Throughout he is taxed as if he were a sole trader. The cessation rules apply to affect the year of leaving, bringing in any overlap relief. For partners in the year 1996/97, the transitional year to the actual year basis, a partner's overlap relief is his share of the tax adjusted profits (before capital allowances) from the end of the basis year ending in 1996/97 to the following 5 April. For example, for a partnership with an accounting year to 30 June, a partner's overlap relief is based on his share of the profits from 1 July 1996 to 5 April 1997. This means that, as with all individuals, he is only assessed on the profits he earns from 6 April 1997 to the date of cessation.

Example 9.4

Assume that M, referred to in the previous two examples, leaves the AB partnership on 30 September 2007. His share of the tax adjusted profits for the year to 30 September 2007 is £80,000.

The only tax year affected by his cessation is the year 2007/08 and he will be assessed on:

	£
Year to 30 September 2007	80,000
Less: overlap relief (as above)	(30,000)
Net assessable Schedule D Case I profit	50,000

9.2.5 Bringing a spouse into partnership

The risk of a Revenue attack under the 'settlement' provisions on the introduction of a spouse into partnership has already been mentioned. Assuming this is not an issue on the particular facts, any resulting tax saving may not be obvious. Indeed, depending upon the accounting year there could be an immediate cashflow disadvantage because of the opening year provisions that will apply to the tax year in which the spouse becomes a partner, especially when National Insurance contributions are also taken into account. Even in an ongoing year, the overall saving is often seen by clients as less than they thought, particularly when the total assets of the marriage are put at risk. The other spouse's personal allowance can be used by paying a salary of that amount, if justifiable, which will also give an entitlement to the basic and second state pensions.

Example 9.5

H brings W into partnership as an equal equity partner on 1 October 2003, drawing up accounts to 30 September in each year. Results as adjusted for tax purposes for the relevant years are:

Year to	£
30 September 2003	120,000
30 September 2004	150,000

Had no change been made, H would be assessable as follows:

2003/04	120,000
2004/05	150,000

By bringing W into partnership the assessable profits become:

2003/04	H – year to 30 September 2003	120,000
	W – period to 5 April 2004 6/12 × 150,000 × 1/2	37,500
		157,500

2004/05	H – year to 30 September 2004 1/2 × 150,000	75,000
	W – ,, ,, ,, ,, 1/2 × 150,000	75,000
		150,000

New overlap relief is created for W of £37,500 but the immediate effect is an additional income tax (and Class 4 National Insurance) charge for 2003/04.

9.2.6 Some partners having profits and others having losses

It is perhaps possible, depending upon the provisions of a partnership agreement, for there to be an overall profit in the partnership but one partner actually bears a loss. This could arise if there are prior charges on profit which exceed the profit. It is suggested that in most agreements this should not happen, the prior charges being abated so as not to create a loss.

However, if under the partnership agreement a loss does arise, the partner incurring that loss cannot obtain tax relief. Otherwise, the other partners would have profits greater than the actual profits of the partnership. Section 111 ICTA 1988 only provides for the allocation of a person's share in the profits or losses arising from the actual trade. If there is no loss as such, then there is nothing that can be allocated to him. His only course of action in practice would be to ask for an equitable adjustment between the partners, so he receives the tax benefit of the loss. If this were not done, the partners having the profit would effectively receive part tax free.

Conversely, if a partnership has a loss, it is not possible to allocate that loss in such a way, for tax purposes, so that one partner is taxed on a profit when the overall result is a loss.

9.2.7 Non-trading income

The above sets out the position for dealing with trading or professional profits under Schedule D Case I or II. A partnership's income could also include other sources, which are taxed under different provisions. In that case, s111(7) and (8) provide that a person's share in any untaxed income from one or more sources (or losses for that matter) are to be computed for each individual partner as if they derived from a sole trade or profession that commenced when he became a partner. This does not turn such sources of income into trading profits, this rule applying only to compute the assessable amount. The practical advantage is that the normal partnership accounting year applies as the basis period for computing the untaxed income. The cessation and commencement rules, including overlap relief, also apply in the same way as a trade, etc. If overlap relief on ceasing to be a partner gives rise to an excess, that excess can be deducted against the individual's income for that year (s111(9)).

Example 9.6

In the year to 30 June 2003 a partnership has the following profits:

	£
Schedule D Case I	150,000
Schedule A from letting surplus properties	20,000
Taxed interest on bank deposit	8,000 (gross)

In the year to 5 April 2004 the gross bank deposit interest is £11,000.

Assuming that there are no new partners or retiring partners, the share of profit for each partner for the year 2003/04 will be based on the following:

	£
Schedule D Case I – year to 30 June 2003	150,000
Schedule A – year to 30 June 2003	20,000
Taxed interest – year to 5 April 2004	11,000

Where taxed income is received, such as interest, it is allocated between the partners on the tax year basis and not according to the accounting year.

9.3 Financing the partnership

9.3.1 Borrowing by partnership or by individuals

Clearly, there are commercial considerations which are likely to override tax aspects. If a partnership borrows then all the partners are jointly and severally liable, whereas if an individual borrows and introduces the sum as capital, he alone is responsible. Individual borrowing is off balance sheet, which can make a partnership appear sounder financially than it perhaps really is. If partners have substantial personal borrowings, they will need to receive a certain level of profits simply to service those loans. Thus, partners' interest on capital may in practice be no more than interest payable to third parties by another name.

If a partnership borrows and the interest is incurred wholly and exclusively for the purposes of the trade, interest is deductible on an accruals basis, in the same way as any other expense. If the overall capital and current accounts for the partners are overdrawn, the Revenue may seek a disallowance to reflect the net overdrawn amount. This is no different from a sole trader with an overdrawn capital account.

If, instead, an individual partner borrows and pays the sum into the partnership as capital, there is no relief under Schedule D Case I or II. He must make a personal claim under s362 ICTA 1988. That section gives relief for a loan to an individual that is used to defray money applied in purchasing a share of a partnership; contributing money to the partnership whether by way of capital or loan; or paying off another loan eligible for such relief. If capital is returned the loan is deemed to be repaid to that extent under s303 ICTA 1988. The important point for this purpose is that the relief under s362 is given according to the interest paid in the actual year to 5 April, whereas partnership interest will be given according to the partnership year. Another difference is that relief under s362 is given for amounts paid, and not amounts accrued. There could be a timing advantage, especially if a partnership year is early in the tax year, such as 30 April.

> **Tax tip**
>
> Additional monies are required for partnership purposes in April 2003, the partnership having an accounting year to 30 April. If the partnership borrows there will be no or minimal interest relief in the tax year 2003/04 as this is based on the year to 30 April 2003. If the individual partners borrow and increase their capital in the partnership, they can claim interest paid in the year to 5 April 2004. Moreover, their Schedule D Case I/II profits are not affected for pension contribution purposes.

Partners may have substantial capital accounts in the partnership, but large borrowings outside for an unallowable purpose (such as their private house). They could consider refinancing the partnership by reducing capital accounts, allowing the individual partners to repay their unallowable borrowings. The partnership could subsequently borrow for business purposes that arise later, the interest being deductible. Some care needs to be taken as there ought to be some commercial purpose, without money simply going around in a circle. There is a risk the Revenue could seek to apply s787 ICTA 1988, an anti-avoidance provision. The Revenue successfully argued this point before the Special Commissioners in *Lancaster* v *IRC* [2000] STC (SCD) 138, involving an inter-spouse loan.

9.3.2 Tax reserves

Up to and including 1996/97, the partnership income tax liability was, for Schedule D Case I and II purposes, a partnership liability. It was essential, therefore, for tax to be withheld in the partnership and appropriate provisions made. Given that there is no longer a partnership liability, but merely an individual one, there is a case for making no provision whatsoever in the accounts of the partnership. In that situation, tax would simply be dealt with as part of partners' drawings.

There are, though, dangers with this approach. If partners are allowed to draw all or the majority of their profits, there is a risk that some partners might not put tax monies aside. In an extreme case, the Inland Revenue could bankrupt them, with practical consequences to the partnership. A professional person may automatically be excluded from membership of his professional body and bankruptcy will treat his interest in the business an asset to be realised by a trustee in bankruptcy. Alternatively, the continuing partners would have to club together to bail out the insolvent partner. In practice, it is suggested that it is prudent to continue as if nothing has really changed. Monies for tax could be retained in a partnership bank account and only released as and when tax liabilities are due. This is made relatively simple because there are two payment dates in the year as a rule, being 31 January and 31 July. The partnership agreement should be amended to reflect this, or at least a minute of a partners' meeting made.

There is also a potential cessation liability, even though over the life of a partner's interest in the partnership he will pay tax on no more than he has earned. This arises because of the interaction of overlap relief with the cessation year. If profits are much higher in the year of cessation than they were in the year of commencement, there could be a relatively substantial amount taxed in that year of cessation. For example, in his first year in practice to 30 April 2001 a partner's share of profit might be, say, £20,000. With improvements in his share and inflation, when he retires 20 years later on 30 April 2021 his profit for that final year might be £200,000. He will be taxed on the whole of that year's profit less his overlap relief, leaving nearly £182,000 assessable. If tax had been retained on a payment basis, insufficient sums may be available to meet this final liability. Retention in the partnership accounts could, therefore, be extended to deal with this, which has the effect of a partner bearing tax for each accounting year on the profits he has actually earned rather than the actual taxable amounts. If the year-end is 31 March, this problem does not arise. On the other hand, if profits are rising there is an overall cash flow disadvantage to the partnership.

Some would argue that this is an over-paternalistic approach. Provided partners are reminded of this potential liability no particular problems should arise. Moreover, if a partner has substantial capital in the firm, net of borrowings, then he should have sufficient cash resources to meet his tax liability. There are no hard and fast rules, provided the matter is properly considered by partners. Surprises should be avoided. The sudden death of a partner could itself cause problems if he has not properly provided for his family. There is a possibility that his final tax liability will exceed his capital account in the firm, to be financed somehow out of his estate. His dependants may be unaware that he had effectively been using tax reserve money for living expenditure.

9.3.3   Retirement provision

Strictly, it is up to each partner to make his own pension arrangements for retirement. It is relatively rare these days for the partnership itself to make retirement provision, such as by way of annuities. Many old agreements provide for annuities, but these are gradually being watered down as the years go on. Section 628 ICTA 1988 contains specific provision for retirement annuities paid under a partnership agreement (or acquisition of partnership business). Given that the main effect of this to treat the annuities as earned income, this is largely academic nowadays as there is no longer an investment income surcharge.

A partnership agreement could make it mandatory for a partner to make a given level of contribution to a personal pension scheme, by withholding sums otherwise available for drawings. Some partners will resent this approach, believing that retirement provision is a matter for them personally, and that there are many other ways of achieving the same end result. However, the last thing a continuing body of partners would wish is an impecunious partner, as they may feel a moral responsibility to do something or succumb to the pleas of dependants. The problem is largely avoided by ensuring that at least a minimum amount is set aside each year. Another advantage is that pension benefits can be taken from age 50, which might fit neatly with a proposal for early retirement, or a reduced level of income.

If a partnership should find itself in financial difficulties, and partners are aged 50, there is always the option of taking the maximum 25 per cent lump sum, at least in part, if other funds are not available. This is a last resort as clearly the funds are likely to perform better if allowed to grow until the intended date for retirement. With the possibility of pension draw down, this could become an attractive option if necessary.

9.4   Mergers and demergers of partnerships

9.4.1   Mergers

For commercial reasons, two partnerships may decide to merge and continue as a single operation. They are likely to be in the same line of business, but not necessarily so. Advantages may come from the combination of different skills or rationalisation of branches, for example.

On the other hand, the merger may be such that a brand new business has been created, the old businesses falling by the wayside. The Revenue view is set out in SP 9/86.

Where, on the facts, the result of the merger is a new business, different in nature from either of the previous businesses, there will be a cessation of the old businesses and a commencement of the new one. This may not have quite the dire consequences under the pre-actual year basis of assessment, but nevertheless different tax liabilities could arise. The cessation of the old businesses triggers overlap relief. New overlap relief would then be created applying the commencement rules under s61 ICTA 1988. There are also implications for capital allowances, possibly triggering balancing adjustments.

In practice, it is perhaps more likely that the new partnership succeeds to the businesses of the old partnerships, where similar in nature. This would be so if two firms of solicitors or accountants merged. In that case, the choice is either to apply the cessation rules to both businesses and the commencement provisions to the combined operation, or treat both businesses as continuing throughout. If the second option is chosen, there is likely to be a change of accounting date for at least one of the old businesses. The change of accounting date rules in s62 ICTA 1988 should be applied first, adopting the new partnership year end.

The above provisions apply equally where businesses previously carried on by sole traders are merged and subsequently carried on in partnership.

9.4.2 Demergers

The business of a partnership may be divided up, with one or more partners going one way with part of the business and the others going the other way. In this situation, there is likely to be a cessation of the partnership business with two (or more) commencements. This would also apply if there are only two partners and they become sole traders as a result of the demerger. A case demonstrating this is *Connelly & Co* v *Wilbey* [1992] STC 783.

However, on the facts it is possible that there is a recognisable business which in fact continues. In that case, there would be no change to the basis of assessment, except that the results of that business will inevitably exclude the part hived off to an outgoing partner(s). The part hived off is a separate business to which the commencement rules apply.

The Revenue do not accept that a business can simply be divided on a demerger and treated as if they had always been two or more separate businesses.

9.5 Overseas aspects

9.5.1 Partners ceasing to be resident for UK tax purposes

Under s112(1B) ICTA 1988, there is a deemed cessation and commencement on an individual partner becoming or ceasing to be resident in the UK. This only applies where the trade or profession is carried on wholly or partly outside the UK, and only affects the partner in question.

A loss arising before the change of residence can be carried forward under s385 ICTA 1988 and set against future profits from that trade. The main impact of this rule, therefore, is to apply the cessation rules on the date of change of residence, with overlap relief, and then apply the commencement rules, with the special basis for the first two years of assessment.

9.5.2 Other consequences of trade, etc., carried on wholly or partly outside the UK

Section 112(1) has the effect of treating a partner who is not resident in the UK as liable to income tax only on the profits arising from that part of the trade actually carried on in the UK. The overall results of the partnership have to be divided between those from trading in the UK and those from trading outside it. A non-resident partner is taxable on his share of UK source profits.

Where the control and management of the trade, etc., is situated outside the UK and any of the partners is an individual resident, but not domiciled, in the UK, the profits arising outside the UK are treated as if they were from a foreign possession, taxable under Schedule D Case V. The consequence of this is that the remittance basis of this assessment can apply to the extent of the profits from that part of the trade, etc.

9.6 Special situations

Persons other than individuals can be in partnership. For example, individuals could be in partnership with a company. Sections 114 to 116 ICTA 1988 contain special rules for this, which, following the move to self-assessment, apply principally for the purposes of computing the company's share in the profits. A company is liable to corporation tax and the individual partners to income tax on their share of the profit as computed applying the basic rule in s111 ICTA 1988.

Section 117 ICTA 1988 restricts the loss relief available to a limited partner. The broad effect of this is to restrict interest payments or losses against profits other than those arising from the trade, to the amount of the limited partner's capital contribution to the partnership at the end of the year of assessment in which the interest is paid or the loss arises.

Finally, it is possible for trustees in that capacity to be partners with others. This is comparatively rare but not unknown, particularly in farming.

9.7 Limited liability partnerships

It is now possible to create a limited liability partnership (LLP) under the Limited Liability Partnerships Act 2000, which came into force on 6 April 2001. Many of the rules, particularly those of a detailed nature, are contained in the Limited Liability Partnerships Regulations 2001. An LLP, in terms of structure, has more similarities with a limited liability company, especially given that an LLP has a separate corporate existence under the Act. In practice, it is likely that only the larger partnerships will consider incorporation as an LLP.

For tax purposes, though, an LLP is, in very broad terms, treated in the same way as a partnership. The Act has added ss118ZA, ZB, ZC and ZD to ICTA 1988. In particular, the new s118ZA provides that a trade, profession or business carried on by an LLP with a view to profit shall be treated as carried on in partnership by its members and not by the LLP as such.

A distinction is drawn for certain purposes between an LLP which carries on a trade and one carrying on any other activity, such as a profession. The broad effect of s118ZC is that, in the case of the trade, a trading loss can only be set against other income to the extent of the greater of the amount subscribed by that member and the amount of his liability on a winding up.

10 International aspects

10.1 Relevance of residence for tax purposes

In principle, individuals who are resident in the UK are subject to tax here on their worldwide income, whether brought to the UK or not. The only exception to this is the case of non-domiciled individuals in relation to foreign source income, who are only taxed to the extent of the income brought to the UK. In the case of individuals not resident in the UK, they are only liable to UK income tax on UK source income and even in that instance, the provisions of a relevant tax treaty with the UK must be considered.

This inherent territorial limitation can been seen from the various charging provisions and in particular s18 (1) ICTA 1988 regarding Schedule D;

> 'Tax under this Schedule shall be charged in respect of –
> (a) the annual profits or gains arising or accruing –
>   (i)   to any person residing in the United Kingdom from any kind of property whatever whether situated in the United Kingdom or elsewhere and
>   (ii) to any person residing in the United Kingdom from any trade, profession or vocation, whether carried on in the United Kingdom or elsewhere and
>   (iii) to any person, whether a Commonwealth citizen or not, although not resident in the United Kingdom from any property whatever in the United Kingdom or from any trade, profession or vocation exercised within the United Kingdom'

Reference has been made elsewhere in this book in relation to international aspects and in particular the following:

1. The limitations imposed by the decisions of the courts where there is trading outside the UK (see **2.1.4**).

2. The implications for non-resident individuals who are trading in the UK (**2.4.6**).

3. Non-resident partners where a trade is carried on wholly or partly outside the UK, where a partner is non resident or non domiciled (**9.5**).

4. Income from letting of property and other receipts where either the individual is not resident in the UK (**8.9**) or the property is overseas in the case of a UK resident individual.

It is clear, therefore, that determining an individual's residence status is key to establishing the basis of taxation, particularly where there is income arising outside the UK. Domicile becomes relevant also for non-UK source income but only once it has been established that the individual is UK resident.

10.2 Residence and domicile

10.2.1 Residence

This is a general term and there is no special definition for individuals who have trading or property income although the extent of their activities in the UK could itself be a factor in determining residence. There is no statutory definition of residence but the following statutory provisions must be considered in determining an individual's residence status:

- Section 334 ICTA 1988 determines that every Commonwealth or Republic of Ireland Citizen is to be taxed as a UK resident if he has left the UK for the purpose only of occasional residence abroad.

- Section 335 ICTA 1988 allows residence to be determined without reference to a place of abode maintained in the UK if the individual works full-time outside the UK (apart from incidental duties) in a trade, profession, vocation, office or employment.

- Under s336 ICTA 1988 a person in the UK for some temporary purpose and not with a view to establishing his residence is not treated as resident in the UK unless here for six months in any tax year (and again ignoring a place of abode in the UK).

An individual's residence status is determined for each tax year. In a case involving a popular musician, *Reed v Clark [1985] STC23*, the High Court held that the individual was not resident in the UK for a particular tax year when he did not set foot in the UK at any time in that year. The Special Commissioners had decided that he was not resident and the judge decided that that was the only true and reasonable conclusion on the facts. Thus, there could be no charge tax under Schedule D on his income as a variety entertainer. In particular, the judge held that it could not be said that he had left the UK for the purpose only of occasional residence abroad. There had been a distinct break in the pattern of his life, not having visited the UK at all in the tax year. Difficult questions can, though, arise on particular facts to determine an individual's residence status, as this is largely a question of fact. The Revenue have, though, given some guidance in their booklet IR20. In the early editions of IR20 the Revenue gave particular guidance on employees going abroad to work full-time under a contract of employment. They have now extended that practice if an individual leaves the UK to work full-time in a trade, profession or vocation and similar conditions are met to employees who leave the UK. Those conditions, rewritten to be consistent with a trading individual, are:

- absence from the UK and the period of full-time working abroad both last for at least a whole tax year; and

- during the absence any visits made to the UK
  - total less than 183 days in any tax year, and
  - average less than 91 days of tax year. The average is taken over a period of absence up to a maximum of four years and in practice the Revenue do not normally count days spent in the UK because of exceptional circumstances beyond the taxpayers control, such as illness of a taxpayer or a member of his immediate family.

If these conditions are met the individual is regarded as neither resident nor ordinarily resident in the UK from the day after the day of departure to the day before returning to the UK at the end of the period spent on business abroad. The Revenue practice in arriving at the number of days spent outside the UK is to ignore days of arrival in and departure from the UK, except in applying the concessionary split year treatment. Strictly, based on a decision of the courts, the calculation should include part days in the UK.

As indicated, for income tax purposes the Revenue by concession will split a tax year between a resident and non resident period, although strictly residence must be considered for an entire tax year. Full details are given in IR20 so that no liability to UK income tax will arise from the time the individual leaves the UK for full-time work abroad, a trade, profession or vocation up to the date of return.

In practice, though, it may be difficult to fall within the similar practice for employments in IR20, which is more likely to be relevant where an individual is performing personal services and so can quite easily be based abroad without having a permanent establishment in the UK. For example, even though an individual can satisfy the Revenue that he has ceased to be UK resident applying normal principles but has a trading establishment in the UK, the Inland Revenue will still seek income tax on the profits derived from that establishment. Where resident in a country with a tax treaty with the UK the essential question is whether that trading establishment amounts to a permanent establishment in treaty terms. The profits derived elsewhere in the world would not, though, be subject to UK income tax for a non-resident. If the individual's main source of income from the trade is derived in the UK still, and there are regular visits made to the UK, it may be more difficult to establish non-residence. However, even in that situation, a double tax treaty with a tie-breaker provision, where the individual could be regarded as resident under the domestic laws of both countries, would determine in which of those countries the individual is resident in applying the treaty.

10.2.2   Non-resident entertainers and sportsmen

Payments made to non-resident entertainers and athletes in relation to activities performed in the UK in that capacity can be subject to a withholding tax of 22 per cent. Payments in respect of the proceeds and the sale of records deriving from a sound recording are paid gross. It is up to the person making the payment to deduct income tax and submit the appropriate returns to the Inland Revenue. The deduction of tax is subject in turn to any relevant provision to the contrary in a double taxation agreement. The rules are contained in ss555 to 558 ICTA 1988 and the regulations in Income Tax (Entertainers and Sportsmen) Regulations 1987 SI 1987/530, to which reference should be made for the detailed rules.

It should be borne in mind in particular that a payment to a person controlled by the entertainer such as a company in which that individual holds the shares, is deemed to have been made to the entertainer himself. This prevents the possibility of simple avoidance by the interposition of an intermediary. The relevant activities are deemed to be performed in the course of a trade, profession or vocation exercised in the UK and to be a separate source of profits assessable under Schedule D Case I or II. This gets over any argument that the source of the income from the activities is where the individual is based abroad. Most treaties in fact allow the country in which the activities are actually performed to tax that income. Even though deduction at source is only at the basic rate, the individual could be liable to higher rates as the limitation on liability does not apply to trading type income.

10.2.3   Domicile

Domicile is relevant in instances where an individual, even though resident and/or ordinarily resident in the UK has an overseas source of income. If such an individual is not domiciled in the UK, then on making a claim no liability to UK income tax arises in respect of foreign source income unless and to the extent that the income is remitted to the UK.

In the context of trading or property income, this could be relevant where, for example, an individual has a let property that is situated outside the UK. However, if that property is in the Republic of Ireland, the remittance basis is not available. Section 68 ICTA 1988 provides that, in the case of property situated and profits arising in the Republic, the income charge under Schedule D Case V is to be computed on the full amount of the income arising in the year of assessment. In the case of trading income arising in the Republic, this is also on the arising basis but could be on the full amount arising or on an average of such a period as the case may require and as may be directed by the inspector. In practice, that ought to be on the same basis as a trade carried on in the UK assessed under Schedule D Case I or II. Section 65 (3) ICTA 1988 provides that income charged under Schedule D Case V on income which is immediately derived by a person from the carrying on by him of any trade, profession or vocation either solely or in partnership should be computed by applying the rules applicable to Schedule D Cases I and II.

Where the remittance basis is relevant, the very wide definition in s65 ICTA 1988 must be borne in mind. In particular, s65 (5) requires tax to be computed for Schedule D Case V purposes:

> 'On the full amount of the actual sums received in the United Kingdom in the year of assessment from remittances payable in the United Kingdom, or from property imported or from money or value arising from property not imported, or from money or value so received on credit or on account in respect of any such remittances property, money or value brought or to be brought into the United Kingdom, without any deduction of or abatement other than is allowed under the provisions of the Income Tax Acts in respect of profits charged under Case I of Schedule D.'

Subsections (6) to (9) extend the meaning of remittances to cases involving the lending of money, where the individual is ordinarily resident in the UK. For example, if an individual borrows in the UK and repays the debt outside the UK he is treated as having remitted the sum applied outside the UK. This also applies to money lent outside the UK which is brought here to the extent that income arising from securities or possessions outside the UK is applied in reducing that debt. Section 65 (7) also catches money brought to the UK from loan monies whether that loan is cleared in whole or in part before the monies are brought here.

Whether or not income has been remitted, whether directly or indirectly, is a question of fact. The onus is on the taxpayer to prove that what has been remitted is from a non taxable source (*Scottish Provident Institution v Allan* (1903) 4TC 591). In consequence, it is usual for a non-domiciled individual to open separate banks accounts to clearly distinguish sums derived from sources that could potentially be subject to UK income tax if remitted here.

It is clear that great care must be taken on detailed matters. For example, in *Timpson's Executors v Yerbury* (1936) 20 TC155, a UK resident individual assessable on the remittance basis directed US trustees to pay quarterly sums to her children out of her income entitlements. This was carried out by bills of exchange drawn on a London bank payable to the order of the children's UK bankers, the taxpayer's accounts with the trustees being debited in dollars when each bill of exchange was drawn. The Court of Appeal held that the taxpayer had remitted sums to the UK because they remained her income to the date of encashment of the bills being exchanged. She was, therefore, entitled to the income when it reached the UK and until encashment could have directed the income elsewhere. Thus, it is vital for gifts to UK individuals to be made wholly outside the UK so it is clear the remittances by these individuals are from their own funds and not from a UK resident's funds. The taxpayer achieved this in *Carter v Sharon* (1936) 20 TC229, because under Californian law a banker's draft became the taxpayer's daughter's irrevocable property at the latest when it was posted in California. The relevant provisions were also considered by the Court of Appeal in *Grimm v Newman* [2002] STC 1388. The Revenue were not a party to this case but in essence it was held that a gift outside of the UK by a non-domiciled individual which was then used by the recipient to acquire an interest for her in a house in the UK along with the taxpayer did not constitute a remittance. It is a basic principle of UK tax law that income tax can only be charged in the year of assessment if the source exists at some time in the year. This does not apply to employment income nowadays but could be relevant to trading or property income, although in practice it is far easier to apply this principle to deposit accounts.

This still leaves the question as to whether or not an individual is domiciled in the UK. This is a concept of general law especially on the application of international law principles and must be distinguished from residence, which is more of a temporary status compared to the enduring nature of domicile. In essence, individuals are domiciled in the country where they have a permanent home, intending to remain there indefinitely. Unlike residence, an individual can only have one domicile at any one time. At birth an individual acquires a domicile of origin, which would normally follow that of their father, and so the place of birth is irrelevant. Thus, a child born in the UK to a father who is currently in a trading operation in the UK, but who was domiciled in Spain will also have a Spanish domicile. This domicile of origin will continue as a domicile of dependency and will follow that of the person on whom they are legally dependent. As a matter of law an individual must follow this dependency rule until attaining 16 years of age. On attaining 16 years of age, an individual can then acquire a new domicile of choice although there is perhaps a presumption of continuing a domicile of origin or dependency until there is definite evidence to the contrary. This would involve leaving the current country of domicile and settling in another country on a permanent or indefinite basis.

10.2.4 The future

Along with the Budget speech in April 2003, the Revenue issued a discussion paper inviting consultation on the definition of residence and domicile. There has been concern regarding the difficulties of defining those terms in practice as well as the perceived overall fairness in terms of tax liabilities where that can be a determining factor. Two individuals can be dealt with quite differently even though in substance their circumstances are virtually the same. There is every possibility, therefore, that the present basis will change.

10.3 Other matters affecting individuals

10.3.1 Personal allowances available to non-residents

Section 278 (1) ICTA 1988 states that no personal and other allowances under Chapter 1 Part VII ICTA 1988 shall be given to any individual not resident in the United Kingdom. However, subsection (2) provides the following exceptions where the individuals are:

- Commonwealth citizens;

- nationals of the European Economic Area;

- persons who are or have been employed in the service of the Crown, any missionary society or a territory under Her Majesty's protection;

- residents of the Isle of Man or Channel Islands;

- individuals who have previously been resident in the UK and are resident abroad for the sake of their health or the health of a resident family member; and

- a widow or widower whose late spouse was in the service of the Crown.

A double tax treaty may also give allowances to a resident of a country, even if not falling within the above categories.

10.3.2   Limit on individual's income tax

The move to self assessment brought with it a significant change in the income tax chargeable on individuals not resident in the UK. These rules are also in turn subject to the provisions of a relevant double tax treaty. In principle, s128 FA 1995 provides that the maximum UK income tax chargeable on a non residence shall not exceed the aggregate of the following:

(a) tax chargeable on total income after deducting 'excluded income' and disregarding personal allowances; and

(b) the tax deducted at source from 'excluded income' including tax credits. Excluded income is defined by s128 (2) ICTA 1988 as income chargeable under:
    - Schedule D Case III
    - Schedule F
    - Schedule D Case VI by virtue of s56 ICTA 1988 (transactions and deposits)
    - Certain pension income chargeable under the Income Tax (Earnings and Pensions Act) 2003 where either a UK social security pension or under a retirement annuity contract and other pensions described as other employment related annuities in ss609 to 661 of that Act.
    - Various social security benefits otherwise taxable as set out in

s660 of the Income Tax (Earnings and Pensions) Act 2003 other than taxable income support or jobseeker's allowance.

- Other income falling within s127(2) and (3) ICTA 1988 where carried out through a broker or investment manager (other than as a Lloyd's Underwriter).

Thus, it can be seen that neither trading income assessable under Schedule D Case I or II nor property income assessed under Schedule A can be excluded income and so is fully taxable on a non-resident individual, which could, therefore, be taxed at up to 40 per cent where relevant. It is necessary, therefore, to carry out two calculations because all s128 does is impose a maximum. Bringing all income into charge, even though excluded income, could in some cases produce a lower liability because of the benefit of personal allowances.

10.4 Double taxation relief

10.4.1 General principles

A UK resident individual is subject to income tax on worldwide income with the exception, as mentioned above, of non-domiciled individuals to the extent that they can claim the remittance basis. Income arising abroad could have suffered foreign tax either by deduction at source or by direct assessment. To avoid double taxation the UK has entered into treaties with many countries of the world. A treaty may provide that certain types of income are not subject to tax in the country of source, in particular interest income which may exempt or taxed at a reduced rate. As a general rule, though, profits on trades carried on through a permanent establishment in the country are subject to tax there as well as income from land situated in that country. As has been explained elsewhere in this book, there is no substitute for reading the actual treaty between the UK and the country in which the source arises.

If there is no treaty or the treaty does cover the particular income, unilateral relief can be claimed under s790 ICTA 1988. This provides credit for tax paid under the law of a foreign country where computed by reference to income arising there. Credit relief is usually preferable but on occasion, such as where losses arise, it may be better to treat foreign tax as an expense under s811 ICTA 1988.

10.4.2   Restrictions on relief

First, under s794 ICTA 1988 the individual must be UK resident except in the case of Isle of Man or Channel Islands tax when the individual can be resident either in the UK or in any of those territories.

Secondly, s796 ICTA 1988 limits the credit to the UK income tax on that income. The broad effect of this section is to compute the UK income tax as if the income were the top slice of an individual's total income. Where there is credit from more than one source, the calculation is applied successively to each source but ignoring amounts already applied under this provision (otherwise excess relief could be given if the effect of income falling into the basic rate band is not taken into account). Deductions from total income can be applied in the most effective manner. Pensions contributions deductible by virtue only of the inclusion of foreign source profits or net relevant earnings are treated as reducing those profits in computing UK tax for offsetting of foreign tax.

Example 10.1

A sole trader commences on 1 January 2003 and in the year to 31 December 2003 has profits of £30,000 on which foreign tax of £4,000 is paid. This will be assessed as follows with the appropriate tax credit:

	Assessable Profit £	Foreign Tax £
2002/03 3 months to 5 April 2003	7,500	1,000
2003/04 first 12 months	30,000	4,000

Assume that the trade continues until cessation on 31 December 2009, the profit for the final year being £40,000 on which foreign tax of £7,000 is paid. The profit assessable in 2009/10 will be as follows:

	£
Profit for the year to 31 December 2009	40,000
Less Overlap Relief	(7,500)
Net Profit Assessable	32,500

The foreign tax of £7,000 is reduced by the additional £1,000 allowed on commencement, producing a net credit of £6,000. Had there been no foreign tax paid in the final period, the tax payable would have been assessed under Schedule D Case VI to produce tax chargeable of £1,000 (s804 (5) B)(a) and (b) ICTA 1988).

10.4.3 Overlap profits

If trading activities are carried on outside the UK there are special rules to give credit for overlap profits (ie where the same profit is taxed in part in two successive years of assessment as on a commencement of trade). This could also apply to non-trading income of partnerships. Under s804 ICTA 1988 credit for overseas tax on an overlap profit is allowed for both years. However, there are provisions to ensure that overall no more relief is claimed for overseas tax than is actually borne. The provisions involved and the broad effect is best illustrated by an example.

11 Pension contributions

11.1 Overview

The area of pensions in general is a complex one, mainly because of the different types of schemes available. This chapter is concerned only with the taxation aspects of pension contributions, although it will touch briefly upon other areas by way of background. Not only are there specific taxation rules for pension contributions, but the schemes themselves have tax advantages, if they are of an approved nature. The income and gains of an approved scheme are not normally subject to taxation, except that from 2 July 1997 schemes have no longer been able to reclaim tax credits on UK dividends. They can also be liable to tax on profits if found to be trading. The Savings, Pensions, Share Scheme Section of the Inland Revenue oversees pension schemes. Significant changes to pensions legislation are expected following the publication of a green paper in December 2002. A further announcement has indicated that the changes will not take effect until 6 April 2005.

It is very important in practice to identify the type of scheme to which an individual is contributing. An individual employer could make contributions either in his capacity as an employer or for his own benefit. If there is a scheme for employees, the contributions could be either under a retirement benefits scheme operated by the employer or to an employee's personal pension (whether under a group personal pension or individual scheme). The only sure way to determine the nature of any payments to a pension scheme or life insurance company is to read the relevant documentation. If that is not clear, it may be necessary to contact the financial adviser involved in setting up the scheme.

A self-employed individual, whether a sole trader or in a partnership, can provide for his own retirement by making payments to a personal pension scheme or possibly a retirement annuity scheme. If the first time an individual makes a contribution for his own benefit is after 30 June 1988 this would have to be into a personal pension arrangement, as new retirement annuity schemes cannot be established after that date. However, existing retirement annuity arrangements can continue and the differences are mentioned below.

The method of giving tax relief varies according to the type of scheme. An employer obtains relief for contributions benefiting his employees as a deduction in arriving at Schedule D Case I/II profits, in the same way as any other expense except that the accruals basis does not apply. This also includes personal pension contributions to employee schemes. However, in no circumstances can a pension payment for the benefit of the employer be treated as a trading expense. To be eligible for income tax relief the rules mentioned later in this chapter for personal pension or retirement annuity contributions must be met.

11.2 Personal pensions

11.2.1 General

Personal pensions schemes first became available from 1 July 1988. Until then, retirement annuity contracts could be made which are described in **11.3** below. Personal pension schemes are appropriate in particular for self-employed individuals.

The personal pension rules were changed considerably with effect from 6 April 2001, to coincide with the introduction of what are called 'stakeholder pensions'. However, for tax purposes a 'stakeholder pension' is simply a type of personal pension. The Government is keen to encourage individuals to make provision for their retirement and particularly in the case of lower paid individuals. The new 'stakeholder pension' is designed to encourage this by imposing various regulatory requirements, especially in relation to the charges made by life insurance companies.

The changes made to the rules with effect from 6 April 2001 by Schedule 13 FA 2000 are so significant that to rely on past knowledge can be dangerous. A new approach to the whole subject is required, to take account of the following principal changes:

- there is far more flexibility in making contributions, particularly given that contributions can in some cases be based on net relevant earnings for earlier years;

- for contributions up to £3,600 per annum gross, there is no requirement for any relevant earnings;

- the carry forward of unused relief for six years has been abolished;

- the carry back of contributions has been restricted; and

- the self-employed deduct income tax at the basic rate in paying contributions.

11.2.2 Main features

In general terms, there are two areas which are relevant to personal pension schemes. The first is in deciding the maximum contributions that can be paid (and on which income tax relief is available). The other issue is to determine how the fund that has been accumulated can be used for the benefit of the individual. Unlike retirement benefit schemes, there is no limit on the total benefit that can be drawn under a personal pension policy. The limits are instead based on the level of contributions, dealt with in more detail in **11.2.3** below. In practice, the pension benefits are determined by the size of the fund built up by the contributions and the investment growth thereon.

The following is a summary of the main features of personal pension schemes:

- the contributions grow in a fund that is generally free of taxation, albeit that tax credits on dividends can no longer be reclaimed;

- the benefits can be taken at any age from 50 to 75 (possibly earlier than 50 if ill-health intervenes or the individual is in a special occupation);

- up to 25 per cent of the value of the fund can be taken as a tax-free lump sum;

- the remainder is then used to purchase an annuity from a life company, although by taking what is called income drawdown it is possible to defer the purchase of the annuity until 75 years of age. Drawdown allows an individual access to the fund and in particular the lump sum, although a pension within defined parameters must also be paid from the fund. If the individual dies before buying the annuity, the value of the remaining fund is returned subject to income tax at 35 per cent under s649B ICTA 1988. Schedule 13 FA 2000 made drawdown more flexible;

- whether or not a spouse's pension is bought is up to the individual and is not compulsory. There is no requirement to build in escalation of pensions in payment;

- life assurance can be written under the personal premium rules. For contracts made after 5 April 2001, the limit is 10 per cent of the aggregate contributions made in that year. For contracts made before 6 April 2001, the limit is 5 per cent of an individual's net relevant earnings for the year (s640(3) ICTA 1988 as amended);

- if contributions exceed the maximum allowable for tax relief purposes, the excess must be refunded under s638(3) ICTA 1988; and

- all contributions paid by individuals to their own scheme are paid after deduction of income tax at the basic rate. Until 6 April 2001, deduction at source was only relevant to employees.

11.2.3   Income tax relief

Until 6 April 2001, contributions were limited by two factors, being the net relevant earnings of the individual for the year of assessment in question and the percentage limit applied to that individual based on age. Although net relevant earnings and age remain relevant, it is now possible to make contributions based on net relevant earnings for an earlier year. The definition of net relevant earnings is set out in **11.2.4** below and the remainder of this part sets out the rules for determining eligibility to make contributions and the maximum contributions payable for any year of assessment.

Eligibility to make contributions

An individual can make contributions at any time during a year of assessment if:

- he has actual net relevant earnings for the year; or

- for some part of the year he is not in pensionable employment to which s645 ICTA 1988 applies and the residence requirement is met.

The residence requirement is met if the individual is in any of the following categories:

- at some time in the relevant year resident and ordinarily resident in the United Kingdom;

- at some time during the five preceding years of assessment resident and ordinarily resident in the United Kingdom and had that status when the personal pension arrangements in question were made; and

- at some time in the year the individual performs Crown employment duties, or a spouse of such an individual.

Maximum contributions for a year

Any individual not in pensionable employment for the whole of a year (subject to the concurrent membership exception) can pay £3,600 gross per annum into a personal pension scheme irrespective of the actual net relevant earnings for the year. Indeed, a person without any occupation can pay up to that amount, including minors.

An individual can pay a sum greater than £3,600 per annum, depending upon actual or deemed net relevant earnings for the year and the percentage limit based on age. The minimum percentage limit is 17½ per cent, with higher percentages as follows for those aged 36 or over at the start of the year of assessment:

Age on 6th April of tax year	%
36–45	20
46–50	25
51–55	30
56–60	35
61 and above	40

An explanation of actual and deemed net relevant earnings, with examples, is given in **11.2.4**.

Method of giving income tax relief

Previously, contributions to personal pension schemes were deducted from net relevant earnings. Given the greater flexibility in making contributions, particularly where there are no relevant earnings at all, this method of giving relief had to change. Income tax relief is now given as follows:

- Basic rate income tax relief is given from 2001/02 onwards by deduction at source and failure to deduct at source will mean the loss of basic rate relief. Currently, this gives relief at 22 per cent and is available whether or not the individual is a taxpayer. This now applies to everyone, including the self-employed.

- Higher rate income tax relief is given by increasing the basic rate limit band for the year.

To be eligible for basic rate relief, the requirements of the Personal Pension Schemes (Relief at Source) Regulations 1988 SI 1988/1013, as amended by SI 2000/2315, must be met. Application forms of pension providers are designed with a view to meeting those requirements.

Example 11.1

Assume that for the year of assessment 2003/04 a self-employed individual decides to make gross personal pension contributions of £5,000, being his maximum limit. In making payment to the pension provider, he deducts basic rate of 22%, so that he actually pays £3,900. Higher rate relief on £5,000 is given by increasing the basic rate limit from £30,500 to £35,500.

A practical issue is the need for the taxpayer to provide 'requisite evidence' if contributions exceed £3,600 gross per annum. This includes evidence of earnings such as a self-assessment return, or accounts for a specified s646B ICTA 1988 basis year (see below). A self-employed taxpayer could have difficulty in supplying such information for a current year if he wishes to base contributions on the earnings of that year. That would be appropriate if there were no relevant earnings previously that could be a 'basis year' or if earnings are expected to increase for that current year. To pay the maximum contributions may require using the carry back provisions mentioned in **11.2.5**.

11.2.4   Net relevant earnings

As indicated, contributions in excess of £3,600 gross per annum can be based on actual or deemed net relevant earnings. It remains necessary to compute the actual net relevant earnings for a given year, although the actual net relevant earnings for an earlier year can be used as the basis for contributions in later years.

Meaning of net relevant earnings

It is first necessary to determine whether or not an individual has relevant earnings for a year, which are defined by s644 ICTA 1988 to include:

- general earnings, which include benefits in kind;

- income from property which is attached to or forms part of the emoluments of an office or employment;

- income chargeable under Schedule D and immediately derived by the individual from the carrying on or exercise by him of his trade, profession or vocation;

- inventor's income from patent rights treated as earned income under s529 ICTA 1988; and

- profits from the commercial letting of furnished holiday accommodation in the UK (s503(2)(b) ICTA 1988).

The following are not treated as relevant earnings:

- anything chargeable under ITEPA 2003 arising from the acquisition or disposal of shares;

- amounts taxable under s403 ITEPA 2003 (termination, etc., payments);

- earnings from an investment company that the individual (or with connected persons) controls;

- earnings arising to an individual where at any time in the previous 10 years he has been a 20 per cent shareholder and director ('controlling director') and received benefits under a retirement benefits scheme by virtue of past service with the company. For more details see s644(6A) to (6F) ICTA 1988; and

- earnings from pensionable employment, falling with s645 ICTA 1988, unless the benefits are restricted to death in service benefits, such as a lump sum on death or surviving spouse's pension.

Section 646 ICTA 1988 then determines the meaning of 'net relevant earnings', which put simply are the relevant earnings after deducting the following:

- amounts not deductible for Schedule D Case I purposes because they fall within s74(m), (p) or (q) ICTA 1988;

- deductible expenses of employees; and

- trading losses from activities which would constitute relevant earnings if a profit were made. If a trading loss is set against income other than relevant earnings and contributions are made in that year, the loss so deducted is set off against net relevant earnings in later years, applying s646(5) ICTA 1988.

In any case, the net relevant earnings cannot exceed the earnings cap under s640A ICTA 1988, which for the year 2003/04 is £99,000. This earnings ceiling applies to the total net relevant earnings in a year from all activities added together. There is no reason why an individual cannot both be in pensionable employment and pay personable pension contributions based on self-employed earnings.

185

Deemed relevant earnings

This is one of the most important features introduced by FA 2000. In broad effect, it replaces the old six year carry forward of unused relief, with what could be seen as surprising ramifications.

Section 646B ICTA 1988 has been added and provides that, by meeting certain administrative type requirements, it is to be presumed that the net relevant earnings for a basis year are also the net relevant earnings for each of the succeeding five years of assessment. To do this, the individual must provide the 'requisite evidence' to the scheme administrator of the actual net relevant earnings for the basis year. A basis year can be superseded by providing the requisite evidence for a later year, which in turn becomes the new basis year for the succeeding five years of assessment, and so on.

Example 11.2

X, born 10 March 1951, decided to reduce his level of activity as a solicitor in practice. As a result, his net relevant earnings for 2003/04 are £50,000. For earlier years those earnings were:

	£
2002/03	90,000
2001/02	85,000
2000/01	112,000
1999/00	87,000
1998/99	62,000

He could provide evidence to the pension provider of his earnings for 2000/01, which would then become his 'basis year'. He could, therefore, pay personal pension contributions as if his actual earnings for 2003/04 were £112,000, although the earnings cap would apply to deem those earnings to be £99,000. His age on 6 April 2003 was 52 and so his relevant percentage is 30%.

His maximum personal pension contribution for 2003/04 is:

30% × £99,000 = £29,700

He could also base his contributions for 2004/05 and 2005/06 on earnings of £112,000, subject to the earnings cap for those years.

For 2006/07 and 2007/8 he could provide requisite evidence of his earnings for 2002/03 of £90,000. This example ignores the changes that could arise from the implementation of the December 2002 green paper.

The percentage that is based on age for the year of assessment will then be applied to the net relevant earnings for the year, including those presumed under s646B ICTA 1988. This provision is particularly relevant where an individual's profits reduce or fluctuate. It is quite possible, therefore, for an individual to pay higher level contributions without any actual net relevant earnings for a year. As explained above, tax relief is given by deduction at source for the basic rate and by extending the basic rate limit band to give higher rate relief. An individual with substantial dividends could, therefore, obtain income tax relief at 44.5 per cent.

Cessation of actual relevant earnings

Section 646D ICTA 1988 can extend the period for basing contributions on deemed net relevant earnings for a further five years. It will usually apply where an individual ceases the source giving rise to the relevant earnings. Strictly, it applies where there is a year of assessment for which there are no actual relevant earnings, including loss making years, and which preceded a year in which there were such earnings. This is called the break year. Then for the next five years, contributions can be based on the actual net relevant earnings for any of the six years of assessment preceding that first year in which there are no actual net relevant earnings. There is the same requirement as in s646B to provide the requisite evidence of net relevant earnings. Generally, s646D can only apply where the break year is 2001/01 or later.

In effect, this means that one high year of actual net relevant earnings could form the basis of contributions not only for that year but for the succeeding five years under s646B and for five years thereafter under s646D, where there has been a cessation of relevant earnings. However, the rules can work in an arbitrary manner because the five year post cessation period would be broken if the individual has any actual relevant earnings in a year of assessment, which could include small amounts from casual employment, as an example. It would also be broken if the individual is in pensionable employment to which s645 ICTA 1988 applies throughout a year of assessment.

In practice, these changes are likely to benefit the better-off individual, because of the need to have sufficient resources to pay the maximum contribution available. Moreover, pension contributions are particularly beneficial to an individual who is a higher rate taxpayer and especially so if the resulting taxable pension (after taking the maximum tax-free lump sum) will be subject to tax at the basic rate only.

> **Tax tip**
>
> A practical problem in making use of the presumption of higher net relevant earnings is that the individual may not have the funds available to meet the maximum contributions.
>
> An individual could consider taking the benefits from other personal pension policies and use the tax-free lump sum (and pension) to pay contributions. Advice must be taken on this especially on the policy terms such as charges, but otherwise this could be of advantage to a higher rate taxpayer.

At one time the Revenue took the view that where an earlier year is chosen as the basis year, the net relevant earnings are capped by the ceiling for that basis year and not the year for which payments are made. The Revenue changed their view and accept that the relevant cap is that for the year for which payments are made.

11.2.5 Carry back and carry forward

For contributions made up to 5 April 2001, s641 ICTA 1988 provided considerable flexibility in carrying back a contribution so as to treat it for all purposes as if paid in the previous year (or in some cases the year before that).

No election under s641 is possible for contributions paid after 5 April 2001. Instead s641A ICTA 1988 gives a more limited facility. That section provides that a contribution paid by 31 January at the latest in any year may be carried back and treated as if paid in the preceding year of assessment. However, the election, which is irrevocable, must be made at or before the time when the contribution is paid. Form PP43 should be completed and supplied to the pension provider with the contribution payment.

The carry forward of unused relief for six years has been abolished for the year 2001/02 and subsequent years.

11.2.6 Other points

(a) In most cases, contributions are paid to a life company to invest in their pooled funds, although the contributor does have the choice as to the type of fund. However, for the more sophisticated individual a self-invested personal pension plan (SIPP) may be attractive, as it gives greater choice as to the areas in which funds are invested. For example, this could include the purchase of a freehold property which is leased at a full commercial rent to the trader by the product provider operating the SIPP. Residential property is not permitted nor loans to the member, partnership or connected company.

(b) An individual does not have to take the benefit of all his personal pension policies at the same time. This is known as phased retirement, which is not too dissimilar from the income drawdown arrangements mentioned above. This could allow an individual to partially retire or defer converting all his available funds into an annuity, particularly if it is believed that annuity rates might improve in later years, or if there is concern about the life expectancy of a spouse.

(c) There are concessional rules for doctors and dentists, assessed under Schedule D Case II, but who also pay compulsory contributions to the NHS scheme on their NHS earnings. This allows them to pay premiums either on the excess over the equivalent NHS earnings (being the pension contributions to the NHS × 100/6) or by disregarding tax relief on the NHS contributions and claim up to the maximum allowed under the personal pension and retirement annuity rules.

11.3   Retirement annuity contracts

11.3.1   Essential features

As mentioned above, these arrangements ceased to be available from 1 July 1988, except that contributions to existing contracts can continue. Moreover, in many cases it is also possible to pay a single premium or vary the contributions without affecting the status. The legislation is contained in ss618 to 626 ICTA 1988. These arrangements are not affected by the changes to personal pension schemes from 6 April 2001. In particular, it will still be possible to carry forward unused relief for six years.

Retirement annuity contracts are the forerunner to personal pension schemes and apply to the same type of individuals, including the self-employed. The main differences compared to a personal pension scheme are as follows:

- the age range at which benefits can be taken is normally 60 to 75 years of age;

- the maximum lump sum is three times the pension payable on an annual basis in arrears after taking the lump sum;

- a retirement annuity fund can be transferred to a personal pension scheme but not the other way about;

- there is no income drawdown facility, but this can be achieved indirectly by transferring to a personal pension scheme;

- there is no earnings cap;

- the definition of relevant earnings and net relevant earnings is slightly more beneficial, but mainly for the benefit of employees;

- if contributions are overpaid (i.e., exceed the maximum of net relevant earnings) the excess cannot be returned to the contributor;

- all contributions are paid gross;

- tax relief is given by setting contributions against actual net relevant earnings for the appropriate year of assessment;

- tax deductible contributions must be based on actual net relevant earnings for the year. There is no provision to base contributions on earnings of an earlier year; and

- the percentage maximum based on net relevant earnings according to age is as set out below.

Age on 6th April of tax year	%
51 to 55	20
56 to 60	22½
61 and above	27½

The rules for carry back and carry forward of contributions remain as previously and are not affected by the changes to the personal pension scheme rules.

Section 619(4) ICTA 1988 provides that contributions paid under a retirement annuity contract in one tax year can be carried back and treated as if paid in the earlier year. Thus, there is no requirement as for personal pensions to make the payment by 31 January following. Moreover, if there are no net relevant earnings in the immediately preceding year of assessment, the carry back could be to the year before that. The election to carry back must be made before 31 January after the year of assessment in which the contributions were actually paid.

Where an individual has not paid the maximum contributions under retirement annuity contracts for earlier years, s625 ICTA 1988 allows the carry forward of unused relief for six years, on a first-in first-out basis. However, to make use of this carry forward of relief, the individual must make the maximum contribution in the year for which relief is to be given, before he applies the amounts unused for earlier years. The interaction with personal pension contributions must be taken into account as explained below.

It is possible for the tax-free lump sum under retirement annuity contracts to be up to one-third or so of the value of the fund. However, the recent decreases in annuity rates have meant that the lump sum is often less than 25 per cent (the standard maximum for personal pension schemes) and so for many individuals there is little to choose between the two. Indeed, in taking benefits it might be better to transfer first to a personal pension scheme, even with the same life company. All factors must be considered, though, before making a transfer; additional charges could arise or guarantees lost, as examples. The other reason for continuing contributions to retirement annuity contracts is that the earnings cap does not apply. For very high earners, higher contributions can be paid to retirement annuity contracts than to personal pension schemes. For individuals whose earnings do not reach the earnings cap, higher contributions can be paid under personal pensions at age 36 and above. Personal pensions have the added advantage from 2001/02 of basing contributions on net relevant earnings of an earlier year.

11.3.2 Payments to both personal pensions and retirement annuity contracts

Many individuals still contribute to retirement annuity arrangements, having been in existence for many years, and top up through personal pensions. There are some complex transitional provisions applying in this situation, set out in s655 ICTA 1988. These provisions are not easy to decipher but the main aim is to ensure that an individual cannot make maximum payments under both types of arrangement. Briefly, they work in the following way:

(a) The maximum that can be relieved under personal pensions is reduced by retirement annuity payments made in the same year (or deemed to have been made by virtue of a carry back election).

(b) Unused retirement annuity relief carried forward is reduced by payments made into personal pension schemes. It was held by the

Special Commissioners in *Brock* v *O'Connor* [1997] STC (SCD) 157 that if personal pension payments exceed the maximum retirement annuity relief in a given year, that excess is to be treated as also utilising unused retirement annuity relief from earlier years.

An individual with very high earnings in some years and who also makes payments under both retirement annuity and personal pension contract can, with appropriate use of carry back claims, increase his maximum overall contribution limit.

Tax tip

Assume that in 2002/03 an individual's assessable trading profits were £60,000. He is aged 40 and pays regular premiums of £2,000 under retirement annuity contracts and £3,000 to personal pension schemes. For the year 2003/04, taxable profits are £200,000.

On the Revenue's interpretation, paying personal pension contributions automatically brings in the earnings cap, not only for personal pension payments but also, by a sidewind, payments under a retirement annuity contract. This view is debatable, in the author's view, but is clearly that of the Revenue. However, if the personal pension payment of £3,000 in the year to 5 April 2004 is paid by 31 January 2004 it could be carried back to 2002/03. The earnings cap for 2003/04 cannot apply to that year because there are no personal pension payments as a result of the election.

This means that the individual could pay a total of £35,000 under retirement annuity contracts for 2003/04 (£200,000 × 17 1/2%), of which £2,000 is a regular contribution. Had he not done this, his maximum overall contribution for that year would have been £19,800 (£99,000 × 20%). He will be restricted, though, to the life company(ies) with which he has retirement annuity arrangements, which is a factor to be taken into account.

---

12 Returns and records

12.1 General

This chapter and the next are concerned with the administration of the tax system in so far as relevant to income tax.

The taxes management system was once relatively relaxed compared to the present day. The rules are now far more rigid and particularly so following the introduction of self-assessment. Income tax rates are much lower than they were 25 years ago but on the other hand greater efforts are made to collect taxes, imposing penalties and interest for failure to comply. Interest has become automatic and so too are certain penalties.

The authority of the Inland Revenue is derived from s1 TMA 1970, which provides that income tax, as well as corporation tax and capital gains tax, is under the care and management of the Commissioners of Inland Revenue. The Revenue must administer the system according to the law but they do have a wide discretion. As part of this discretion, they can relax the strict application of the law when it is clearly unsuitable. These relaxations are generally included in extra-statutory concessions. It is not unknown, though, for the Revenue to take a concessionary view in particular cases, not strictly within a published concession, to avoid an unjust or wholly impractical consequence.

An example of a concession on the administration of the tax system is ESC A19. The Revenue may agree not to collect tax that is due where they fail to make proper and timely use of information supplied by a taxpayer. As a rule, this concession will only be applied if the taxpayer could reasonably have believed that their tax affairs were in order and the arrears are notified more than 12 months after the end of the tax year in which the Revenue received the information.

12.2 Tax returns

12.2.1 Personal return

Section 8 TMA 1970 is the Revenue's authority to require a person to 'make and deliver' a tax return. That return:

- must contain such information as may reasonably be required in pursuance of the notice; and

- may also require the submission with the return of such accounts, statements and documents, relating to information contained in the return, as may reasonably be so required.

The tax return under self-assessment is in standard format but the core return does not contain all the appropriate pages for various types of income. It is up to the taxpayer to request the appropriate pages and complete them. Examples are trades, etc., and income from property.

In the ordinary course, the tax return must be submitted by 31 January following the end of the relevant year of assessment. Thus, the return for the year to 5 April 2003 must be submitted by31 January 2004. However, if a notice requiring completion of a return is not given until after 31 October following the end of the tax year, the filing date is three months after the day on which the notice is given. Thus, the taxpayer will always have at least just under three months to complete a return from the time it is received.

In addition to declaring details of income, s9 TMA 1970 now requires that every return under s8 TMA 1970 must include self-assessment. This means that the return must state the tax payable, including not only income tax but also capital gains tax and Class 4 National Insurance contributions. However, provided the tax return is submitted to the Revenue by 30 September following the end of the year at the latest, there is no obligation to go the next stage of actually computing the tax liability. The Revenue then undertake this process. Neither is there such an obligation if the return is made within two months of issue, where the notice is given after 31 July.

The tax return should be signed in person by the individual. In practice, the Revenue accept the signature of an attorney of the taxpayer in cases of physical or mental incapacity.

12.2.2 Partnership returns

Although there is no longer a partnership assessment as such, it is essential for there to be a mechanism for the profits of a partnership to be reported centrally. There is also a corresponding obligation on each individual partner to include his share of profits in his own tax return submitted under s8 TMA 1970.

The obligation to complete a partnership return is in s12AA TMA 1970. That section applies where a trade, profession or business is carried on by two or more persons in partnership. A notice to complete a return can be given to any partner, to include:

- such information as may reasonably be required in pursuance of the notice; and

- such accounts and statements as may reasonably be so required.

In practice, the notice will be given to the partner nominated to receive it or his successor nominated by a majority of the partners.

The time limit is also 31 January as a rule, or three months later if the notice to complete the return is given after 31 October. However, if a partnership includes one or more companies, the return cannot be required before 12 months after the accounting period.

The return must include details of each person who has been a partner for the whole or part of the period and s12AB(1) TMA 1970 specifies particular details which should be included with the return such as the amount of income, etc., from each source, income tax deducted or tax credits and charges on income of the partnership.

12.2.3   Electronic lodgement of tax returns

Section 115A and Schedule 3A TMA 1970 make provision for the electronic filing of tax returns. The Revenue must approve submission in this way and a signed hard copy must be retained. It should be possible to file electronically the basic tax return and any attachments. Supporting documents may be sent in hard copy form and in practice, provided this is within one month of the electronic submission of the return, are regarded as accompanying the return for s29 TMA 1970 disclosure purposes. The Revenue practice on electronic lodgement is dealt with in detail in SP 1/97. Section 132 FA 1999 contains provisions to facilitate electronic communications generally and s139 and Schedule 8 FA 2000 enable incentives to be provided.

12.2.4   Incomplete returns and provisional figures

A return does not meet the filing obligations if it is incomplete, including failure to sign the return or if pages are missing. The Revenue might immediately identify missing pages if a tick has been made to the effect that such pages should be attached. In *Tax Bulletin* of

October 1998 the Revenue indicate when they will give some degree of forbearance to taxpayers. If a return is submitted in good time, obvious matters might be spotted on a cursory review. The taxpayer could then still meet the deadline. Difficulty arises where returns are submitted near the deadline of 31 January and sent back for resubmission. For 2000/01 returns, provided a return met the 31 January 2002 deadline, the taxpayer was given 14 days in which to resubmit it. If that deadline was met, the original time limit was deemed to have been complied with. The Revenue stress that any such oversight must be genuine and not simply to buy further time.

A return is also strictly incomplete if it includes provisional figures. If such figures are included simply for the convenience of the taxpayer, the Revenue will regard the return as incomplete. However, in genuine cases, where taxpayers have done all they reasonably could to obtain the final figures, the Revenue will accept estimates. Once the actual figures are established, these must be notified. One particular area where provisional figures may be necessary is where an accounting date ends close to the deadline (such as within three months) or even bridges that submission deadline, such as for new partners (in that the accounting date is not chosen by them but by the partnership generally). The fact of provisional figures should be declared in the additional information box of the tax return together with a date by which the final figures will be provided. Failure to adjust a provisional figure in good time could prompt an enquiry.

12.2.5 Obligations if the Revenue do not issue a tax return

The Revenue do not send out tax returns to every taxpayer. There are many instances where to do so would serve no purpose, such as repayment cases. It should be noted that there is a separate claim form for repayment of tax, which does not of itself create any obligation. It is up to the taxpayer to claim a repayment. However, if such a taxpayer has been sent a normal tax return, which requires completion, it cannot be ignored. If nothing else, submission will establish that the Revenue cannot impose a fixed £100 penalty for tardiness.

It is quite possible, though, that an individual not normally within the charge to tax by assessment becomes liable, such as on the commencement of trading. There are also requirements to pay Class 2 National Insurance contributions and perhaps register for Value Added Tax purposes, which are likely to predate the income tax deadline.

A person cannot escape taxation by keeping quiet. Section 7 TMA 1970 imposes an obligation to notify the Revenue of chargeability to tax in situations where a return has not been issued. Notice of chargeability must be given by 5 October following the end of the relevant year of assessment. All that happens then is that the Revenue will issue a return for completion, which will have to be submitted by 31 January or three months after the date of issue if later.

If a liability to tax does arise, and notification by 5 October has not been given, the taxpayer becomes liable to a tax-geared penalty not exceeding the tax outstanding and not paid on or before 31 January following the end of the year. In practice, the Revenue are not likely to charge 100 per cent penalty or even get near it, other than in exceptional circumstances. Nevertheless, failure to notify the Revenue by 5 October runs the risk of a penalty, as well as interest in the normal course for late payment. All is not lost, though, if notification is not made in time but payment can be made by 31 January.

Tax tip

An individual has not been sent a return for the year 2003/04. He had been an employee for many years until commencing a trade on 1 June 2003, which is profitable, he fails to notify the Revenue by 5 October 2004 but his accountant realises this in early January 2005.

Both interest and the tax-geared penalty can be avoided by making a payment on account to the Revenue by 31 January 2005. If there is any uncertainty as to the exact figure, it will be better to overpay rather than underpay. Failure to give notice by 5 October 2004 means that any tax outstanding after 31 January 2005 is at risk for the tax-geared penalty, whatever the good intentions of the taxpayer.

12.2.6   Revenue power to determine tax

If a return has not been submitted by the filing date, s28C TMA 1970 gives the Revenue the power to make what is effectively an estimated self-assessment. This must be made to the best of an inspector's information and belief, but once made is treated for all purposes as an open self-assessment. Tax must be paid accordingly, until superseded by the actual self-assessment. No determination or superseding self-assessment can be made more than five years after the filing date or, in the case of self-assessment, more than 12 months after the date of determination.

12.2.7 Penalties for late submission

Under s93 TMA 1970 the basic penalty for failing to meet the filing deadline (usually 31 January following the end of the year) is £100 for personal or trust returns. A further £100 penalty can be imposed if the return has not been submitted within six months. For longer delays of in excess of one year from the filing date, a tax-geared penalty not exceeding the tax owed can be imposed.

In any event, a penalty cannot exceed the tax which is actually owed at the filing date in the case of the fixed £100 penalties. This means that if a taxpayer cannot for some reason quite meet the deadline he could pay the tax he believes is owed and if that clears the liability in full, no penalty can be imposed (s93(7) TMA 1970).

In extreme cases, the Revenue have power to apply to the General or Special Commissioners, who can impose a further penalty of up to £60 per day, under s93(3) TMA 1970. As soon as the outstanding return has been submitted, no penalty can be imposed under these particular rules for past failures.

In the case of partnership returns, s93A TMA 1970 also provides for a £100 fixed penalty. However, each partner is liable for this and there is no provision which can reduce the penalty to a lower figure depending upon the tax owed. This is for the simple reason that the partnership return does not of itself compute a tax liability, as that is the responsibility of each individual partner. If individual returns are also late, the combined penalty could be up to £200 per partner.

There is limited scope to appeal to the Commissioners against a penalty imposed under s93 or s93A TMA 1970. The Commissioners cannot reduce the penalty to a lower figure but simply set the penalty determination aside if they believe that the taxpayer had a reasonable excuse. In practice, the Revenue would first consider the matter, to see if the excuse is reasonable within their guidelines. In their booklet SA/BK6, the Revenue indicate that the following could amount to a reasonable excuse:

- tax return not received;
- serious illness;
- loss of tax records through fire, etc;
- death of the taxpayer or of a close relative; and
- misleading advice from the Revenue.

On the other hand, the Revenue would not accept as reasonable claims of pressure of work, failure of a practitioner to do the work or lack of understanding. However, the Revenue's view of what is reasonable would not necessarily be upheld by the Commissioners. Whether or not the amount at risk is worth the expense of disputing a penalty is another matter. However, the expense may be worthwhile in the case of large partnerships, given the penalty that can be imposed on each partner.

On reasonable excuse generally, this continues until the excuse ceases. At that time, the failure should be remedied without unreasonable delay (s118(2) TMA 1970).

In practice, the Revenue have to date slightly relaxed the strict filing date, which is usually 31 January following the end of the tax year. Their practice for 1999/00 returns is set out in *Tax Bulletin* of April 2000, following in particular the Special Commissioners' decision in *Steeden* v *Carver* [1999] STC (SCD) 283. In that case, the taxpayer's return for 1996/97 was handed in to the tax office in mid-morning of 2 February. The taxpayer and her agents had relied upon Revenue advice that they would accept the return as delivered in time if placed in their letter box before the post was opened on that day. The Special Commissioner held that there was a reasonable excuse throughout the period of default. The Revenue indicated that 2000/01 tax returns received on Friday 1 February 2002 would not give rise to a penalty.

12.2.8 Other tax returns

Various other provisions of the Taxes Acts can require the submission of returns for particular purposes. Many of these are required under the PAYE regulations.

Sections 13 to 19 TMA 1970 give the Revenue the power to require information under the following broad headings:

- persons receiving taxable income belonging to others (such as trustees mandating income directly to a life tenant) – s13;

- return of lodgers and inmates – s14;

- return of employee's emoluments – s15;

- payments made by a person carrying on a business for services rendered, etc. – s16;

- agency workers under Income Tax (Earnings and Pensions) Act 2003;

- interest paid by banks – s17;

- interest paid by other persons gross – s18;

- other payments including from public funds – s18A; and

- information for Schedule A purposes (such as to tenants regarding the terms under which they occupy land) – s19.

In addition to these, there are many other provisions under which documents or information must be provided to the Revenue. Non-compliance runs the risk of a penalty. Section 98 TMA 1970 is headed 'Special Returns, etc.' although many of the requirements are common place. Section 98 draws a distinction between situations where the Revenue must give notice to a person to produce documents or information, as listed in Table 1 of that section. In other instances, the requirement exists without the need for a formal notice, as set out in Table 2. For example, s660F ICTA 1988, listed in Table 1, provides that an officer of the Board may give a notice to any party who is a 'settlor' to provide such particulars as the officer thinks necessary for purposes of the 'settlement' provisions. A taxpayer need do nothing until he receives such a notice. On the other hand, any matter within Table 2 must be met without waiting for the Revenue to ask for the information and failure to comply could lead to a penalty.

The maximum penalty for failing to comply with a notice in Table 1 or supply information as required by any of the statutory provisions in Table 2 is £300, under s98(1)(i) TMA 1970. The effect of s100(2) TMA 1970 is that the Revenue must commence proceedings before the General or Special Commissioners for this penalty and the Commissioners can set the penalty at the appropriate level up to the maximum. If failure continues after the imposition of the initial penalty, an officer of the Board can, under s100(1) TMA 1970, make a determination imposing a penalty of up to £60 for each day on which the failure continues after the day on which the initial penalty was imposed. There is a right of appeal to the Commissioners against such a determination under s100B TMA 1970, who can reduce or increase the amount determined by the officer.

Where under the statutory provision the penalty is required to be of a particular amount the Commissioners' jurisdiction is limited. If the penalty is correctly imposed they cannot use their discretion to reduce it to a lower figure. For example, late PAYE returns will incur a fixed penalty under s98A TMA 1970, according to the number of employees.

Penalties carry interest under s103A TMA 1970. Generally, the Revenue have the discretion to mitigate any penalty, under s102 TMA 1970.

12.3   Record keeping

Self-assessment also introduced, for the first time, a statutory requirement to keep and maintain records for the purposes of tax returns. The detailed provisions are contained in s12B TMA 1970. The basic requirement is that any person who may be required to submit a return whether a personal, trustee or partnership return, must:

* keep all such records as may be requisite for the purpose of enabling him to make and deliver a correct and complete return for the relevant period; and

* preserve those records for the required period of time.

Thus, there is a dual obligation, first, to create the records and, having created them, retain them. If the person was carrying on a trade, profession or business, whether alone or in partnership, the records must be preserved for nearly five years ten months from the end of the year of assessment. A person who lets property is treated as carrying on a

---

Example 12.1

A sole trader draws up accounts to 30 April in each year. In relation to the tax year 2003/04 he must, therefore, maintain and preserve the following:

his business records for the year to 30 April 2003, which means that in reality records will be retained for part of nearly seven years; and

details of other income for the year to 5 April 2004.

These records must be maintained until 31 January 2010.

However, if enquiries are made into the return and for some reason the enquiries are not completed by 31 January 2010, the records must be preserved until the Revenue's enquiries are treated as completed (s12B(1)(b) TMA 1970).

trade for this purpose under s12B(6) TMA 1970, and must preserve all records for the longer period. It is not only the records applicable to the business which must be retained for nearly six years but records relating to other parts of the return, such as dividend counterfoils. For other taxpayers, the retention period is 12 months from 31 January next following the end of the year of assessment.

It is unlikely, therefore, that records need to be maintained for longer than a period of nearly six years. However, when a taxpayer is investigated and fraud or neglect alleged, there is often benefit in having retained papers for a longer period. This is more of a practical matter as there is no obligation to retain them, unless in the middle of an enquiry. Indeed, the most likely situation where an enquiry will be in progress when the normal time limit expires will be non-business taxpayers. Another situation is where s12B(2A) TMA 1970 applies. This states that if a notice to complete a return is issued after the normal date for preservation, any records held at the date of the notice must be retained until the time when an inspector is no longer able to make enquiries into the return.

Revenue guidance on record keeping can be obtained from SA/BK3 (for self-employed) and SA/BK4 (a general guide). These explain the records the Revenue expect taxpayers to maintain. Section 12B(3) TMA 1970 states in general terms the business records that must be kept and preserved to include:

- records of all amounts received and expended in the course of the trade, etc;
- the matters in respect of which the receipts and expenditure take place;
- where goods are involved, records of sales or purchases of goods made in the course of the trade; and
- all supporting documents (invoices, etc.).

Section 12B(4) permits copies to be retained rather than originals. The Revenue accept that microfilm or optical imaging systems serve this purpose. However, there are a few instances where originals must be maintained as set out in s12B(4A) TMA 1970:

- dividend counterfoils;
- tax deduction certificates;

- sub-contractors' certificates of tax deduction; and

- evidence of foreign tax paid.

Full details can be obtained from the Revenue booklets referred to above. If in doubt, do not destroy. Many business taxpayers are involved in VAT, which has created the need to maintain a proper accounting system. However, if an accounting system is not adequate there will be a breach of the basic requirement to maintain appropriate records.

Failure to maintain or preserve records as required can render the taxpayer liable to a penalty of up to £3,000. The Revenue will take a reasonable view and look at each case. They state in the booklets that the full penalty will be charged in only the most serious cases, such as where records have been deliberately destroyed to obstruct an enquiry. The Revenue cannot impose a penalty for failure to maintain the original records where required by s12B(4A) TMA 1970 if other documentary evidence can be furnished.

12.4 Claims

Many provisions of the Taxes Acts require a claim to be made within the time limit specified in the particular provision. For example, loss relief claims against other income under s380 ICTA 1988 must be made by 31 January next following the end of the year of assessment. If a specific provision does not prescribe a particular period, the general rule under s43(1) TMA 1970 is that the claim must be made not more than five years after 31 January next following the year of assessment. Thus, a claim for 2003/04 with no specific time limit must be made by 31 January 2010.

Most claims should be made with the return or an amendment to a return if in time. If not, Schedule 1A TMA 1970 specifies the various procedural matters which must be met. These include the following:

- the Revenue may determine the form in which a claim should be made;

- if the claim is for repayment of tax the claimant must have documentary proof that the tax has been paid;

- the claim must include a declaration to the effect that all the particulars given in the form are correctly stated to the best of the information and belief of the claimant;

- the Revenue may also require that the claim includes the delivery of such accounts, statements and documents which are reasonably required; and

- generally, records must be maintained for the purpose of enabling a correct and complete claim to be made and also preserved for the relevant period.

There are provisions to enable the Revenue to amend a claim within nine months of its making for any obvious errors or mistakes and the taxpayer may amend the claim within 12 months. The Revenue also have powers to enquire into claims under para 5 Schedule 1B and under para 6 they can also call for documents. Having given notice to enquire into a claim or amendment, the officer of the Board will in due course issue a closure notice under Sch 1A para 7 TMA 1970 (as amended by FA 2001). This will either accept the amendment or amend or disallow the claim. The taxpayer has, as usual, a right of appeal.

If the Revenue make an assessment under s29 TMA 1970 other than for the purpose of making good a loss of tax owing to the fraudulent or negligent conduct of the taxpayer (or his agent) then under s43A TMA 1970 an extension is given to the normal time limits for making a claim. An example would be a discovery made by an inspector where the basis on which the taxpayer has prepared his assessment was tenable. In these cases the time limit is extended to one year from the end of the tax year in which the assessment is made. However, this extension does not apply where the effect would be to alter the tax liability of another person without their consent (s43B TMA 1970). Section 43A is extended by FA 2003 to include late claims where a return is amended.

12.5 Error or mistake claims

Section 33 TMA 1970 provides relief to a taxpayer who alleges that an assessment (including a self-assessment) was excessive by reason of some error or mistake in a return. The claim must be made not later than five years after 31 January next following the relevant year of assessment. Relief is not automatic as the Revenue are required to look into the matter and make such repayment as is reasonable and just. No relief can be given if the liability was based on the practice generally prevailing at the time or if the error or mistake is made in a claim included in the return. In *Wall v IRC* [2002] STC (SCD) 22, the Special Commissioner decided that an error or mistake claim can be made notwithstanding an agreement with the Revenue preceding a self-assessment amendment.

Under s33(3) TMA 1970 the Revenue must have regard to the relevant circumstances and are allowed to take into account tax years other that those to which the claim relates.

A corresponding claim can be made under s33A TMA 1970 where a person alleges that the tax charged in their self-assessment was excessive by reason of some error or mistake in a partnership statement. A claim must be made by the representative partner not later than five years after the filing date, asking for relief. This provision and also s33 only apply to errors in a return. In the case of claims s42(9) TMA 1970 permits a supplementary claim within the time allowed for the original claim, where the taxpayer subsequently discovers an error or mistake.

There have been further developments in the law of restitution as applied in taxation law. Another judgment of Park J, in *Deutsche Morgan Grenfell Group Plc* v *IRC* [2003] STC 1017, sets out that in his view there is no reason why the recent extension by the House of Lords to recognise a claim in restitution to recover money paid under a mistake of law should not extend to money paid to the Revenue. If this decision is not reversed on appeal, it could cut across the various time limits imposed by the Taxes Acts, where a mistake of law can be demonstrated, and in particular in the area of error or mistake claims where a tax return was prepared on the basis of the prevailing practice that is subsequently proved to be wrong in law.

12.6   Appeals to Commissioners

Most appeals against assessments, amendments, penalties and the like are initially made to the General Commissioners. However, an appeal against a decision of the Board must be made to the Special Commissioners in certain circumstances specified by statute, such as s705 ICTA 1988 in relation to transactions in securities. Section 46B TMA 1970 also specifies particular questions that are within the jurisdiction of the Special Commissioners, including matters in relation to the 'settlement' provisions, administration of estates and s740 ICTA 1988 on transfer of assets abroad. Section 46C TMA 1970 also confers jurisdiction on the Special Commissioners regarding certain claims included in the returns, particularly double taxation relief.

The Special Commissioners determine these particular issues because of their technical and specialised nature. The General Commissioners are comprised of non-experts, serving voluntarily on a part-time basis, without any requirement for any particular knowledge. The Special Commissioners on the other hand are remunerated and are appointed on account of their legal knowledge and experience (including barristers who have practised in tax).

Even though an appeal is within the competence of the General Commissioners, it is possible for the taxpayer to exercise his right to elect under s46(1) TMA 1970 for the appeal to be heard by the Special Commissioners instead. However, under s31 TMA 1970 the General Commissioners can review the election to ensure that the taxpayer is not simply playing for time. On the other hand, if the case is regarded as of sufficient complexity or likely to be lengthy, the General Commissioners can transfer the proceedings to the Special Commissioners, with their agreement. Procedural matters are now set down in statutory instruments, being the Special Commissioners (Jurisdiction and Procedure) Regulations 1994 SI 1994/1811 and the General Commissioners (Jurisdiction and Procedure) Regulations 1994 SI 1994/1812. The rules are very detailed and should be studied by a practitioner intending to argue a case before the Commissioners. All hearings of the General Commissioners are in private. Hearings before Special Commissioners are in public unless an application is made for a private hearing. Decisions of the Special Commissioners can now be published, although in the case of a private hearing the name of the taxpayer will not be disclosed.

Both the Special and General Commissioners have power, in regulation 10 of their respective regulations, to direct that particulars or books, accounts or other documents should be provided within the time specified in the notice. Penalties can be imposed for failure to comply.

13 Payment, interest and surcharge

13.1 Payments under self-assessment

13.1.1 Payment on account

Section 59A TMA 1970 provides that payments on account of income tax for a year of assessment are to be made on 31 January in the year and 31 July immediately after the end of the year, if the following requirements are met:

- the person was assessed to income tax under s9 TMA 1970 for the previous year;

- the total tax assessed exceeded the income tax deducted at source (including tax credits and PAYE deductions);

- the difference between those two amounts (being the actual income tax payable to the Revenue under self-assessment) was at least £500; and

- that tax payable was also at least equal to 20 per cent of the person's total income tax liability.

The last two points are set out in the Income Tax (Payments on Account) Regulations 1996 SI 1996/1654. If, following the above tests, income tax was payable, which exceeded the two limits, then 50 per cent is due on 31 January in the year and the other 50 per cent on 31 July following the year end. If there was no income tax liability in the previous year, or below the £500 and 20 per cent limits, no payments on account are required. Although not strictly relevant to this volume, payments on account are not required for capital gains tax.

A taxpayer may have an exceptional year, which he knows will not be repeated, or for some other reason he expects his income tax liability for the following year to be less than the previous year. In that situation he can, at any time up to 31 January following the year of assessment, make a claim to either eliminate or reduce his payments on account. Section 59A(3) or (4) TMA 1970 also require the claim to state the grounds for believing an adjustment is required. The Revenue must accept this claim, provided the grounds are acceptable

---

Example 13.1

In 2002/03 a sole trader's self-assessment return is based on the following:

	£	£
Total income tax liability for the year		25,000
Less: tax deducted at source from interest received		(2,000)
Net tax due		23,000

Applying s59A TMA 1970, payments on account for 2003/04 are payable as follows:

31 January 2004	11,500
31 July 2004	11,500

---

on their face, and each of the two payments on account is adjusted by one half of the overall reduction claimed. However, care must be taken in making such a claim because if an incorrect statement is made fraudulently or negligently, then under s59A(6) TMA 1970 the tax-payer is liable to a penalty on the difference between the tax paid by him and the amount he would have paid had the statement been correct. Evidence should be kept of the basis on which the reduction claim has been made, such as management accounts. The financing costs of carelessness could be very substantial, as interest will also be payable on the tax reduction in addition to any penalty. Given that the Revenue pay supplement on excessive payments on account it is safer to pay slightly more, as falling short incurs a liability to interest at a much higher rate.

Specific provision is also made in circumstances where the s9 TMA 1970 assessment is made late or the Revenue assess under s29 TMA 1970, to ensure that payments on account for the following year are made on the same basis as self-assessments made in time (s59A(4A) and (4B) TMA 1970).

13.1.2 Balancing payment

The self-assessment return is normally required by 31 January follow-ing the end of the year of assessment. That is also the date on which a balancing payment of income tax (and full payment of capital gains tax) is due. The final liability for the year is the tax liability less payments on account. If payments on account and tax deducted exceed the liability, the balance is repayable (excluding of course tax credits on dividends). Strictly, the Revenue have until 31 January to repay, although they will make repayments earlier in practice if the return is submitted in good time. However, if a return is enquired into by the Revenue, no repayment need be made until the enquiries are treated as completed (although provisional repayments can be made in the interim at the discretion of the Revenue).

Tax owed to the Revenue is not payable on 31 January in the following circumstances:

- If notice of chargeability under s7 TMA 1970 is given by 5 October and the notice to complete the return under s8 or s8A TMA 1970 is not given until after 31 October. In that case the tax is payable (or repayable) at the end of three months from the date the notice to complete the return is given (s59B(3) TMA 1970).

- In the case of an amendment to a person's self-assessment, the tax payable (or repayable) by virtue of the amendment is due 30 days from the day on which the notice is given, if later than the normal due date.

- If the Revenue assess, the tax is payable 30 days after the date of the assessment (s59B(6) TMA 1970).

13.1.3 Discovery assessments and amendments to self-assessment returns

Where an appeal is made against a discovery assessment under s29 TMA 1970, application can also be made under s55 TMA 1970 to postpone all or part of the tax charged by that assessment, where there are grounds for believing that the assessment is excessive. Otherwise, the tax charged by the assessment is payable irrespective of the appeal. A postponement application can be agreed with the inspector but otherwise it will be determined by the Commissioners. The application to postpone should be made within 30 days after the date of issue of the assessment and at any time thereafter if there is a change in the circumstances of the case.

There are new rules to determine when tax is payable after an amendment or correction to a self-assessment contained in Schedule 3ZA TMA 1970, which was inserted by FA 2001. The basic rule is that any tax payable (or repayable) as a result of the amendment or correction is payable 30 days after the day on which the notice or correction is given where later than the normal due date under self-assessment. This rule applies whether the amendment is made by the taxpayer, the Revenue on a closure notice or under s9C TMA 1970 (jeopardy assessment). Section 55 TMA 1970 also applies to amendments made by the Revenue, allowing the tax to be postponed in the same way as a discovery assessment.

It is important not to confuse the date when the Revenue can actually collect tax and the date from which the interest runs as explained in the next section.

13.2 Interest and surcharges on unpaid tax

13.2.1 Interest

Interest is charged automatically from the due date tax is payable to the date it is paid. The due dates are determined as follows, under s86 TMA 1970:

- payments on account on 31 January or 31 July, as adjusted by claims to reduce such payments, as to 50 per cent each instalment;

- the balancing payment is due on the later of 31 January after the end of the tax year and the date by which the return is due if the Revenue do not issue the return until after 31 October, under s59B(3) TMA 1970; and

- by concession, where an individual dies before a payment is due, interest is calculated by reference to the date of probate or letters of administration (ESC A17).

There are provisions to ensure that a double charge to interest cannot arise where a claim has been made to reduce payments on account. As mentioned above, interest runs on any reduction from the payment on account date and so s86(4) to (6) TMA 1970 provide that interest on any balancing payment is to be calculated as if the unreduced payments on accounts had been made on the due dates. If tax is discharged, interest under s86 is recalculated as if the tax had not been charged in the first place (s91 TMA 1970).

It should be noted that the date from which interest runs is not necessarily the same as the day on which tax is payable. Interest will always run from the dates determined under the above rules even where tax is not collectable until 30 days have expired from the making of an amendment or an assessment by the Revenue.

The calculation of the appropriate interest rate is dealt with by the Taxes (Interest Rate) Regulations 1989 SI 1989/1297. Broadly, this is the average of the base lending rates of the main clearing banks, rounded to the nearest whole number, plus 2.5 per cent. For example, if the average base lending rate is 5.75 per cent, the interest chargeable on unpaid tax becomes 8.5 per cent. Under s90 TMA 1970 this interest is not deductible for any tax purpose and so becomes a high rate of interest compared to deductible borrowings. On the other hand, an individual paying credit card rates of interest would find the Revenue's rate cheaper, except that the Revenue does not regard itself as a bank!

Section 88 TMA 1970 has been repealed, not only for tax under self-assessment but also for earlier years where the assessment is made after 5 April 1998. Section 86(2)(b) TMA 1970 also applies to earlier years, with the consequence that the due date for interest purposes is 31 January following the year of assessment. Most assessments for earlier years will be made by the Revenue on account of fraud or neglect but this provision also applies to late assessments raised where the taxpayer is not culpable. Thus, an assessment made for 1995/96 on 31 March 2002 carries interest from 31 January 1997.

These provisions are also applied to late payment of capital gains tax (see the *Capital Gains Tax* volume paragraph **21.3**).

13.2.2 Surcharge

As a further incentive to make payments of tax within a reasonable time, s59C TMA 1970 allows the Revenue to impose a surcharge of 5 per cent of any tax unpaid 28 days after the due and payable date. Any tax which remains unpaid after six months from the due and payable date is subject to a further surcharge of 5 per cent of the tax then outstanding. In the typical case, this means that tax paid on 1 March or 1 August will attract a surcharge. However, the surcharge provisions only apply to balancing payments under s59B TMA 1970 or income tax not postponed under s55 TMA 1970 (such as where the Revenue assess). No surcharges are levied on late payments on account. The Revenue must formally impose a surcharge, against which a taxpayer can appeal. Apart from simply confirming the surcharge, the only action the Commissioners can take is to set aside the charge, provided they believe that the taxpayer had a reasonable excuse for non-payment. The inability to pay tax is not a reasonable excuse, under s59C(10) TMA 1970. Interest is payable on a surcharge from 30 days after the date of imposition. An appeal must be made within 30 days of imposition. A surcharge is not imposed if the tax outstanding is subject to a tax geared penalty, such as under s95 TMA 1970 (s59C(4) TMA 1970).

13.3 Interest on repayments of tax

The right to interest on tax repayments (known as repayment supplements) for individuals and trustees is set out in s824 ICTA 1988. The right to a supplement is also extended to the repayment of surcharges under s59C TMA 1970 and penalties. Supplement is not due on tax paid voluntarily.

It is important to determine the date from which the right to interest runs. Section 824(3) to (4A) ICTA 1988 sets this out as follows:

- if the repayment is of income tax paid on account under s59A TMA 1970 or the repayment of income tax (other than tax deducted at source) the date is that of actual payment;

- for tax deducted at source, 31 January after the year of assessment; and

- for penalties or surcharges, the actual date of payment.

A person could have made various payments during the course of a year, including payments on account, balancing payments and income tax suffered at source. A repayment is deemed to have been made in the following order:

- first, the balancing payment made under s59B TMA 1970 (usually therefore on 31 January following);

- secondly, equally between the two payments on account made under s59A TMA 1970; and

- thirdly, as the repayment of income tax deducted at source.

For repayments made after 11 May 2001, FA 2001 amends s824 to allow a right to a repayment supplement following a claim affecting an earlier year in connection with the carry back of losses, farmers' averaging or creative artists' averaging. This only applies where a repayment is made after 31 January following the later year in relation to the claim. Repayment supplement will then be calculated from that date of 31 January following to the date of repayment.

The rate of interest on tax repaid is also determined by the Taxes (Interest Rate) Regulations 1989, applying regulation 3AB. The basic calculation is to take the average base lending rate determined in the same way as for interest on unpaid tax plus 1 per cent but then deduct income tax at 20 per cent, and rounding down the result to the nearest multiple of 0.25. For example, if the average base rate is 3.75 per cent this is then rounded to 4 per cent, plus 1 per cent equals 5 per cent, less 20 per cent equals 4.0 per cent, which requires no further rounding. Supplement is free of tax (s842(8) ICTA 1988).

13.4 Carry back claims

Various provisions of the Taxes Acts allow losses or payments to be carried back to an earlier year(s). The two main examples in practice are loss claims under s380 ICTA 1988 for trading losses against general income or personal pension (or retirement annuity) contributions carried back and deemed to have been paid in the earlier year. Under self-assessment, carry back claims create a practical problem because of the need to obtain finality for a year and make payments on account for the next year based on the liability for the preceding year. This would be aggravated because a claim to carry back can be made after the balancing payment for a year has been made.

The solution to this is contained in Schedule 1B TMA 1970, which also applies to averaging for farmers under s96 ICTA 1988 and certain other carry back spreading reliefs as set out in paras 5 and 6. Loss relief and pension carry backs are dealt with under paragraph 2. This makes it clear that the income tax reduction is computed by reference to the year to which it is carried back but the income tax reduction made as a result is to be given effect in the year in which the loss is incurred or payment made, as the case may be. The reduction in income tax for the year for which the relief is actually given is dealt with in that later year, by repayment or set off against other liabilities or as if it were a payment on account under s59B(1)(b) TMA 1970. Stand-alone claims can be made under Schedule 1B without having to be included in a tax return or amendment thereto (Sch 1B para 2(2) TMA 1970). Schedule 4A ICTA 1988 contains similar provisions for giving effect to creative artists' averaging claims.

One particular reason why a carry back claim may be made, rather than deducted in the actual year of loss or payment, is to obtain a higher rate of income tax relief. This might apply where an individual pays higher rates one year but only basic rate the next. In the case of pension contributions, the carry back claim may enable one extra year of unused relief to be utilised.

Example 13.2

An individual incurs a trading loss in his accounting year to 30 September 2003 of £10,000. His income in 2003/04 is only £5,000 but in the year 2002/03 his assessable income was £50,000. It is clearly in his interest to make a carry back claim under s380(1)(b) ICTA 1988, so that relief for loss can be given at 40%, rather than simply waste personal allowances in 2002/03.

In making such a claim, his self-assessment return for 2002/03 is not altered as such but the income tax reduction of £4,000 could be applied in setting against any balancing payment due on 31 January 2004 for 2002/03 or repaid. In practice, though, it is likely that the loss will not be established until a later date, in which case repayment will be the only option. No effect can be given to the repayment until the loss has been quantified and the loss relief claim made. In *Tax Bulletin* August 2001, the Revenue state that as a rule a loss claim cannot be made until the accounting period has ended. Subject to that, a best estimate claim can be made with the final figure following as soon as possible.

A repayment of tax arising from such a claim will not be made unless tax for the earlier year has been paid in full or if a liability for any year is outstanding (or will become due within 35 days of the claim). In those cases the relief is given by set off. Moreover, the payments on account for the earlier year will not be reduced unless the tax adjustment exceeds the balancing payment. Repayment supplement begins to run only from 31 January following the later year. Detailed examples are given in *Tax Bulletin* of December 1996.

One particular, and unattractive, feature of these claims is that in determining the payments on account for the next year, the tax effect of a carry back claim is not taken into account. This factor should be taken into account in the final decision on how best to deal with a loss or pension carry back claim.

The Revenue have confirmed in *Tax Bulletin* of August 2000, that the reduction in income tax resulting from a carry back claim includes all consequential matters such as becoming entitled to the age-related personal allowance.

Example 13.3

An individual's income tax liability for 2002/03 is £15,000 (after tax deducted at source) and he makes a carry back claim for pension payments made in 2003/04, reducing his income tax liability for 2002/03 by £3,000.

Effect can be given to the reduction of £3,000 by set off against any outstanding liability but the payments on account for 2003/04 will still be based on the original liability for 2002/03 of £15,000 (i.e., £7,500 on each of the two dates). Had the carry back claim not been made, relief would have been given in 2003/04, affecting the balancing payment on 31 January 2005 and also reducing the payments on account due on that date and 31 July 2005 for 2004/05.

13.5   Rates of tax deducted at source

The following is a summary of the rates at which income tax is deducted at source from various types of income:

Interest paid by:	Rate %
– Banks building societies and other deposit takers	20
– UK government and other securities	20
– National Savings first option bonds	20
– Interest distributions of authorised unit trusts	20
– Cash deposits withdrawn from PEPs	20
– Other annual interest payable net	20
– Foreign dividends and other amounts paid by paying or collecting agents	20
Purchased life annuities (income element)	20
Deductible annual payments	22
Annuities (PAYE applies to certain pension annuities)	22
Rents paid to a non-resident landlord	22
Patent royalties	22
Capital sums for patents paid to non-residents – (s524(3) ICTA 1988)	22
Copyright and design royalties (where owner abroad) – (ss536 and 537B ICTA 1988)	22
Payments to foreign entertainers and sportsmen	22
Payments to discretionary beneficiaries of trusts (under s687 ICTA 1988)	34
Sub-contractors in construction industry	18

The above rates can be reduced but not increased by the terms of a UK double taxation treaty where payments are made to a resident of the other contracting state to a treaty. Revenue approval through the Centre for Non-Residents must be obtained to deduct income tax at the lower rate specified in the treaty or make payments without deducting tax where this is permitted by the treaty.

14 Revenue enquiries and investigations

14.1 General

This chapter concentrates on the Revenue's powers to delve into a taxpayer's affairs in detail. In making the procedures statutory the Revenue's ability to delve appears to be restricted under self-assessment. However, as will be seen later, in other ways this restriction is perhaps illusory. If a taxpayer has failed culpably to disclose the correct income (or capital gains for that matter) there is really no more protection under self-assessment than previously.

The label 'enquiry' is a statutory word denoting a specified process (s9A TMA 1970). Investigation does not appear as a word in the Tax Acts as such. These two words are used here to draw a rule of thumb distinction between the Revenue raising questions regarding the tax return to satisfy themselves that the return is correct and a more detailed examination, particularly where the Revenue believe that there has been a loss of tax owing to a taxpayer's failure to comply with tax obligations. The approach to an investigation will also depend upon the particular office of the Revenue dealing with it. Most investigations are dealt with at local office level by trained inspectors. More serious cases are handled by Special Compliance Office (SCO). A practitioner without experience of investigations should not be too proud to seek advice, even to the extent of passing over the entire investigation to an experienced person.

In the case of businesses, accountancy expenses will not be deductible unless any adjustment that is made to profits is not culpable (SP 16/91 as amended). The Revenue have also confirmed, in *Tax Bulletin* of June 2003, that fees protection insurance follows the same principle where there is cover for acts of fraud or neglect.

Section 144 FA 2000 enacts a specific criminal offence directed at tax frauds committed after 31 December 2000. Provision is made for proceedings to be taken before magistrates. The Revenue have increased staff numbers in prosecution work in Special Compliance Office.

For further information on enquiries see Tax Digest 174 *Self-Assessment. The Enquiry Regime* and *Enquiries under Self-Assessment* published by ABG Professional Information.

14.2 Enquiries into a tax return

14.2.1 Correction of obvious errors and amendments by taxpayer

Section 9ZB TMA 1970 provides that a personal or trustee return may be corrected by the Revenue to correct any obvious errors or mistakes in a return within nine months of receiving it (a repair). Such a correction has no effect if rejected by the taxpayer within 30 days of the issue of the notice of correction.

The taxpayer also has the right under s9ZA to amend his self-assessment within 12 months of the due date for filing (usually before the following 31 January unless the notice to complete the return was given after 31 October).

There are similar provisions for partnership returns in s12ABA and ABB TMA 1970.

14.2.2 Conduct of an enquiry

Power to enquire into a return

Section 9A TMA 1970 for personal returns and s12AC for partnerships, give the Revenue the right to enquire into a self-assessment return, any amendment to that return or any claim or election included in the return. A small number of cases will be selected at random. A taxpayer will not be aware why he or she has been selected. A random selection requires a full enquiry, although the sifting procedure might exclude very simple cases. Paragraph 1503 of the *Enquiry Manual* makes it clear that the Revenue officer should not distinguish random enquiries from other enquiries, otherwise the choice is a matter for human judgement, but the Revenue do use computerised risk assessment. Again the taxpayer will not know the reason for selection and has no right to know.

Under the statutory rules the Revenue officer must give notice in writing to the taxpayer of his intention to make an enquiry before the end of the period of 12 months beginning with the filing date if the return was delivered or an amendment made by that date. A notice to enquire into a partnership return is deemed to be a notice given to each partner, under s12AC(6) TMA 1970. The main purpose of this is to ensure that any amendment can be made to an individual partner's return and does not necessarily mean that an individual partner's return is generally under enquiry. If the return or amendment is made after the filing date, the period is the end of the first quarter day following the first anniversary of the delivery of the return or making of the amendment. The quarter days are 31 January, 30 April, etc. This means that if an individual receives his tax return for 2002/03 in April 2003 but does not submit it until February 2004, the Revenue have until 30 April 2005 to make enquiries. In *Tax Bulletin* of April 2000 the Revenue state that although a return received after 7.30am on 1 February will not give rise to a fixed penalty, that fact nevertheless extends the enquiry period by an extra three months.

It is clear that the Revenue must themselves exercise extreme care when they issue a notice around the time of the expiry date, as a day or two may make all the difference. For example, a tax return issued in, say, April 2003 for the tax year 2002/03 must be filed by 31 January 2004. For the Revenue to give a valid enquiry notice this must be given by 31 January 2005 at the latest. The Special Commissioners' decision in *Wing Hung Lai* v *Bale* [1999] STC (SCD) 238 makes it clear that a notice is deemed to have been effected at the time at which it would have been delivered in the ordinary course of post and not, therefore, the date of actual posting by the Revenue. In that case, the Revenue sent the notice by second class post on 27 January 1999 and it was actually received by the taxpayer on 2 February 1999. For second class post, the effective date of service is treated as the fourth working day after posting. Thus, the saving of a few pence postage by the Revenue meant that they could not enquire into the taxpayer's return. Even if a notice should have been delivered by the deadline, the Special Commissioners have now held, in *Holly* v *Insp of Taxes* [2000] STC (SCD) 50, that the actual date of receipt can determine the effectiveness of an enquiry notice. In that case, a notice posted by second class post on 25 January 1999 was not actually received by the taxpayer until 3 February 1999, after the then deadline of 30 January 1999. It was vital to the taxpayer's successful argument that he could prove the time of actual receipt. In the absence of such proof, the expected date of delivery in the ordinary course of post will be the determining factor. However, as mentioned at the start of this chapter, the Revenue may have a back door way into a taxpayer's return if they miss a deadline, where they can make a valid discovery.

Section 9A(3) TMA 1970 makes it clear that a return which has been subject of one notice of enquiry may not be the subject of another, giving the Revenue one opportunity only. This is subject to an officer's right to give further notices in consequence of a taxpayer's amendment to a return. Even then, s9A(5) provides that an officer is confined to matters related to the amendment if it is no longer possible to give a notice of enquiry into the initial return or an enquiry into the return has been completed.

Until the passing of FA 2001, a personal return could not be amended by the taxpayer at a time when an enquiry was in progress. Section 9B TMA 1970 now allows an amendment during the course of an enquiry but it is specifically provided that the amendment does not restrict the scope of the enquiry or affect the amount of tax payable. In a closure notice, the officer of the Board can state that he has either taken into account the amendment or that the amendment is incorrect. If no comment is made regarding the amendment then it automatically takes effect when the closure notice is issued.

In most cases an enquiry is made simply to raise particular questions arising out of the return, and not a full investigation. An inspector might, for example, ask for an analysis of repairs. Until his enquiries are completed, he could raise further points as his only statutory obligation is to notify the taxpayer of the fact of an enquiry. The Code of Practice states that the Revenue will attempt to avoid piecemeal inquiries. However, it is quite clear from *Enquiry Manual* paragraph 1905 that an aspect enquiry can develop into a full enquiry without a need for justification, although if the taxpayer was given the short Code of Practice the full Code should be issued in its place.

Selection

Until recently, where an agent is involved, all the taxpayer saw was a brief letter stating that their return was the subject of an enquiry, but without specifying any further detail. In most cases, the questions raised were quite straightforward, to seek clarification, but the taxpayer could well imagine the worst. The Revenue now send a copy of the opening letter sent to agents to their clients. The Revenue will also make it clear in that opening letter whether, initially at least, their enquiry is a full enquiry or aspect only.

Amendment by Revenue of self-assessment

Section 28A TMA 1970 sets out the procedure that must be adopted by the Revenue where a notice of enquiry has been given under s9A(1). That enquiry is treated as completed when the officer informs the taxpayer that he has completed his enquiries and states his conclusions. That closure notice must either state that no amendment is required or make the amendment to give effect to the officer's conclusion. The *Enquiry Manual* gives detailed instructions to officers as it is important that the Revenue deal with closure notices according to statute. This should quantify the resulting tax liability, with explanations as appropriate, and make amendments in the taxpayer's favour, however small. The closure notice takes effect when it is issued. If the taxpayer believes the Revenue are dilatory in dealing with the matter, an application can be made to the Commissioners for a direction requiring the officer to issue a closure notice within a specified period. This is then treated in the same way as an appeal and the Commissioners must give the direction requested unless satisfied that there are reasonable grounds for not issuing a closure notice. Similar provisions apply to partnership returns (s28B TMA 1970) and enquiries into claims, etc., not included in returns (Schedule 1A para 7 TMA 1970). The provisions do not give the taxpayer a direct remedy if the Revenue fail to comply with the Commissioners' direction in the time stated. In particular, it is not provided that the Revenue's power to amend an assessment is foregone in the event of such failure, but they should discontinue the enquiry.

Referral of questions during enquiry

A new provision has been added by FA 2001 to allow any question arising in connection with the subject-matter of an enquiry to be referred to the Special Commissioners for their determination. The rules are contained in ss28ZA to 28ZE TMA 1970. A notice of referral must be given jointly by the taxpayer and an officer of the Board although either party can withdraw. While proceedings on a referral are in progress, no closure notice (or application by a taxpayer for such notice) may be given.

Appeal

The taxpayer and the Revenue may disagree, in which case an appeal should be made under s31 TMA 1970 against any amendment proposed by the officer's closure notice. The appeal must be made in writing within 30 days after the date of issue of the notice. Ordinarily, this will be dealt with by the General Commissioners, subject to the right of election under s31D TMA 1970 to appeal to the Special Commissioners instead. The taxpayer must specify the grounds for appeal, although at the actual hearing he may put forward any other ground if permitted by the Commissioners. The Revenue may challenge the election to bring the appeal before the Special Commissioners by referring the election to the General Commissioners under s31D(3) TMA 1970. If the General Commissioners are satisfied that the taxpayer has valid arguments, the taxpayer's right to argue the matter before the Special Commissioners must prevail.

Before the appeal is finally determined, there is no reason why the taxpayer and the Revenue should not come to an agreement under s54 TMA 1970. Even then, the taxpayer has 30 days from the date of the agreement to change his mind, in which case the dispute will continue its way to a hearing before the Commissioners.

14.2.3   Jeopardy amendments

If it is believed that a taxpayer's self-assessment is insufficient and unless the assessment is immediately amended there is likely to be a loss of tax to the Crown, an officer is empowered under s9C TMA 1970 to make an immediate amendment. Ordinarily, the officer should invite the taxpayer to make a payment on account but will use the statutory procedure if agreement is not forthcoming. Paragraph 1953 of the *Enquiry Manual* states that a jeopardy amendment could be appropriate in cases where the taxpayer intends to dispose of assets, become non-resident, apply for bankruptcy or is about to go to prison. Moreover, it could also include situations where payment of tax has been delayed for an unreasonable time owing to the default of the taxpayer.

14.3   Investigations

14.3.1   General comments

There is no reason why an inspector should not make a detailed investigation under the enquiry procedure mentioned above. This itself could be a protracted affair. In this situation the Revenue are likely to be disputing the accuracy of the taxpayer's accounts, such as an allegation that the taxpayer has diverted cash takings. An officer will not be satisfied by simply challenging the particular year but will believe that the same failures arose in earlier periods. The appropriate Code of Practice should be issued by the Revenue at the start of an investigation.

The officer's normal enquiry powers will have become time barred for those earlier years under self-assessment, in which case he will have to rely upon the discovery powers in s29 TMA 1970.

14.3.2 Discovery under s29 TMA 1970

If the Revenue believe that there has been an under-assessment, whether the omission of income, insufficient measure of income or where excessive relief has been given, an assessment may be made under s29(1) TMA 1970 to make good to the Crown the loss of tax.

Where the loss of tax is attributable to fraudulent or negligent conduct on the taxpayer's part (or a person acting on his behalf) an assessment can be made at any time, subject to the overriding time limit in s36 TMA 1970 of 20 years after 31 January next following the year of assessment. In accounts investigation work, an officer will almost certainly be arguing neglect at the least. However, even though there is an error or mistake in the return, if it is on the basis or in accordance with the practice generally prevailing at the time the return was made, the taxpayer is protected by s29(2) TMA 1970. *Tax Bulletin* of August 2001 indicates that the Revenue will seek to use the discovery assessment procedure in cases of fraud or neglect where it is quicker and easier, even though there is an open enquiry window.

If the Revenue do not allege fraud or neglect, they may nevertheless be able to make an assessment within the normal time limit under s34 TMA 1970, being five years after 31 January next following the year of assessment. Even though the time limit to make normal enquiries has expired, an assessment can be made under s29(5) TMA 1970, where an officer of the Board:

> 'could not have been reasonably expected, on the basis of the information made available to him before that time, to be aware of the situation mentioned in subsection (1) above [the loss of tax].'

Broadly, the principles in determining whether an officer can make a discovery are the same for both pre- and post-self-assessment years. For self-assessment under s29(6) TMA 1970 information is deemed to be made available to an officer if:

- it is contained in a personal return for the relevant year or in any accounts, statement or documents accompanying the return;

- it is contained in any claim made for the relevant year of assessment or in any accounts, etc., accompanying such a claim;

- it is contained in any documents, accounts or particulars which are provided to the inspector, whether under a formal notice or otherwise; and

- it is information the existence of which, and the relevance of which, to the loss of tax could reasonably be expected to be inferred by an inspector from information falling in the above categories or notified in writing by the taxpayer to the Revenue.

It is also provided, by s29(7) TMA 1970, that the inclusion of information in the return also extends to information provided under a self-assessment return for either of the two immediately preceding years of assessment or contained in a partnership return under s12AA TMA 1970. Information can be provided by a person acting on the taxpayer's behalf.

The fundamental difficulty remains, though, in determining whether or not an officer can make a discovery. The principles were established by the House of Lords in *Scorer* v *Olin Energy Systems Limited* [1985] STC 218. If the information produced by a taxpayer is sufficient to raise its significance in the mind of the ordinarily competent officer then no discovery can be made. Whether or not the officer made a mistake of law or fact is irrelevant if on proper consideration of the information provided a competent officer was given the opportunity to consider the matter and ask appropriate questions. Information contained in the accounts accompanying a return should be sufficient where an officer should be put on notice if he reads the information properly. However, a taxpayer, or his agent, cannot simply bombard the Revenue with a great deal of information where the significant part is like looking for the proverbial needle in a haystack. Neither can it be argued that the information is somewhere on the files of the Revenue. Broadly, there has to be a common-sense approach along the lines of the *Olin* principles. What is equally clear is that an officer cannot change his opinion. In practice, of course, these issues are often not clear cut.

One of the few cases so far to reach the courts on the self-assessment procedures is *Langham* v *Veltema* [2002] STC 1557. Park J took a robust approach in finding that the inspector of taxes could not make a discovery assessment in circumstances where the value of an asset transferred to a director of a company was in issue. The P11D benefit had been based on a professional valuation. There had been sufficient information available to the inspector, whether in the return or in conjunction with the P11D to raise the question of valuation in his mind but he failed to issue an enquiry notice within the time allowed. In his judgment, Park J referred to the changes made by self-assessment. The taxpayer had additional burdens imposed by self-assessment but with new protections for taxpayers who conscientiously complied with the system, including the new and tighter time limits for the Revenue to make further assessments.

In arriving at the tax owed where there is fraudulent or negligent conduct, a late claim to an appropriate relief can be made by the end of the year in which an assessment or amendment to an assessment is made. This applies where the claim could not have been made but for the assessment or amendment (see ss36(3) and 43(2) TMA 1970 as amended by FA 2003).

14.3.3   Death of taxpayer

Assessments can be made on personal representatives under s40 TMA 1970, but not later than three years from 31 January next following the year of assessment in which death occurred. Moreover, under s40(2) an assessment to make good to the Crown a loss of tax attributable to fraudulent or negligent conduct cannot be made for any period ending earlier than six years before the date of death.

14.3.4   Onus of proof

In cases other than where fraud or neglect is alleged, the onus is on the taxpayer to produce evidence as to why an amendment to a self-assessment or assessment should be reduced to nil, or at least a lower figure. This is the strict position if the appeal is heard by the Commissioners. However, where fraud or neglect is required to make a valid assessment out of time, under s29 TMA 1970, the initial onus is upon the Revenue to present some evidence demonstrating a prima facie case. Once they have done this, the burden again shifts to the taxpayer in the same way as in-time determinations or assessments. The production of capital statements by the Revenue, albeit containing necessary estimates, would normally be sufficient to establish their position, leaving it to the taxpayer to produce evidence to the contrary. A recent case illustrating this is *Hurley* v *Taylor* [1999] STC 1, in which the taxpayer failed in his argument that part of the deficiencies revealed by the capital statements represented loans from his late father. The assessments in question were all pre-1996/97, but there is no reason why the same principles should not apply to self-assessment.

14.4 Special Compliance Office (SCO) investigations

Some years ago, SCO was created out of Special Office and Enquiry Branch. Thus, part of SCO continues to deal with the more technical aspects of tax avoidance and another part continues the investigation work of what was Enquiry Branch. The approach in investigations is the same, notwithstanding the change of title.

Although the essential aim of local office and SCO investigations into accounts or tax returns generally is the same, the method of handling is likely to be quite different. SCO contains very senior and high level inspectors with an aptitude for investigation work, where fraud is alleged. Indeed, SCO deals with cases where a criminal prosecution is possible, even though in most cases a financial settlement is reached. SCO also investigates certain types of taxpayer, such as professionals or individuals in public positions. Invariably, SCO will require full capital statements for the agreed period of investigation, prepared on double entry principles. This involves a detailed examination of all bank accounts, particularly private ones excluded from business accounts, and other available records. At local level, such detailed capital statements are not likely to be required, but rather more rule of thumb capital statements based on movements in net assets from one year to another. Even there, the practitioner might have to resort to more detailed capital statements for at least one year, to prove a point. Such an investigation is time consuming and expensive to the taxpayer, not to mention the psychological impact of having such a heavy cloud over him for what will seem, or could be, a lengthy period of time. Thus, the practitioner needs not only experience of handling SCO investigations but the time to handle it in the timescale agreed at the outset with SCO.

As indicated above, there is always a fear that a criminal prosecution will result from a SCO investigation. This may be apparent from the beginning if the *Hansard* extract is not produced at the initial meeting. In that case, a taxpayer is well advised to have present at the initial meeting a solicitor with experience in criminal law. Without such advice, on the first indication that a criminal prosecution is likely, the practitioner should consider adjourning the meeting to ensure proper legal representation.

In the majority of cases, though, SCO will agree beforehand that the meeting will be conducted on the *Hansard* extract. This is based on a statement made by the then Chancellor of the Exchequer in 1990, to the effect that in most cases of serious fraud the Revenue will agree a financial settlement and not prosecute. However, it is also made clear that, by giving the extract, the Revenue are not barred from instigating criminal proceedings at a later date. This could happen if something comes out of the investigation which is unexpected or if the taxpayer makes misleading statements. The difficulty always facing the Revenue in deciding whether or not to prosecute is that the onus of proof must be such that a jury would convict, given that the jury must be satisfied that the taxpayer has committed the alleged crime beyond a reasonable doubt. Even if the Revenue do not prosecute, there is no bar to another government department commencing criminal proceedings (*R* v *W and another* [1998] STC 550). Local offices are instructed not to use the *Hansard* extract approach. FA 2003 updates the statutory support to the *Hansard* approach by amending s105(1) TMA 1970. This amendment makes it clear that statements and documents are not inadmissible in criminal etc proceedings by reason only that the Revenue may accept a money settlement if a full confession is made or that helpful and voluntary information will be taken into account in determining penalties. At the time of writing the Hansard procedure in practice has been thrown into some doubt by a recent Court of Appeal decision. The exact ramifications are still to be worked out.

At the meeting, the SCO will also ask the taxpayer five questions, which require simple yes or no answers. Effectively, the taxpayer is asked whether or not the tax returns and accounts submitted are correct and if he is prepared to submit to an examination of financial records, both business and private. It is usual for a detailed investigation report to be prepared on behalf of the taxpayer, but if he is not willing for this to be done then the Revenue will take this over. This could point, though, to lack of co-operation in determining the penalty level (see below). A timescale for production of the detailed report will be agreed either at the meeting or shortly afterwards and the SCO inspector will be in contact with the practitioner from time to time to discuss progress.

Eventually, the detailed report will be submitted to SCO, having been formally adopted by the taxpayer. The SCO may also look in detail at the business records of a taxpayer and any businesses with which he has been connected. SCO also has the services of qualified accountants employed by the Revenue. Once all matters have been considered and investigated by SCO, as appropriate, a final meeting (or meetings) will be held to agree the quantum of the irregularities, the calculation of interest and the appropriate penalty loading. Statements of personal assets and liabilities will be required and a certificate of complete disclosure. These may also be required in local office investigations to conclude the matter. These statements are vitally important because if there are omissions at that point and these are discovered by the Revenue at a later date, there is a strong possibility of a criminal prosecution.

14.5 Penalties

Before considering tax-geared penalties, it should be noted that, under s99 TMA 1970, anyone who assists in or induces the preparation of incorrect information, return, accounts or documents which are or are likely to be used for any tax purpose, is liable to a penalty of up to £3,000.

Tax-geared penalties for incorrect returns, accounts or statements are provided by s95 TMA 1970 in cases of fraud or neglect. There are corresponding provisions in relation to partnership returns or accounts under s95A TMA 1970. This ensures that any fraud or neglect on the part of the representative partner is visited on all partners, and so each partner can also be liable to a tax-geared penalty on additional partnership tax payable by reason of fraud or neglect, whether or not he has been personally culpable. Section 97A TMA 1970 provides that penalties can only be levied once with respect to the same tax, being the greater or greatest amount.

The maximum penalty for incorrect returns, etc., under s95 or s95A is 100 per cent of the additional tax payable as a result of the incorrect returns, accounts, etc. In practice, the Revenue do not argue for the maximum penalty in negotiations, otherwise the taxpayer simply appeals to the Commissioners. The Revenue approach to penalties is set out in IR 73. The starting point is 100 per cent which the Revenue then mitigate under their powers by taking account of three factors, being disclosure, co-operation, and size and gravity. Penalties will be reduced on the following lines.

Disclosure (up to 20 per cent)

If the taxpayer has made a voluntary disclosure without any prompting or pre-empting of an expected enquiry, the reduction can in fact be up to 30 per cent. Otherwise, the maximum is 20 per cent. Proper credit will be given if there is an admission of irregularities, even though the amount cannot be quantified until a later date.

Co-operation (up to 40 per cent)

Attending meetings when asked, providing a proper report and other information required by the Revenue is necessaryto provide mitigation. In investigation cases, delays will be inevitable and deadlines extended. It is important to keep the Revenue informed of progress as it should help to reduce penalties. This must not prevent the taxpayer and his agent from arguing all valid points.

Size and gravity (up to 40 per cent)

The SCO handles cases because of the size and gravity of the matter and so little or no mitigation can be expected in those instances. Higher discounts can be expected in local office cases as they are likely to be of a less serious nature. The mere fact, though, that the tax at stake is relatively low could nevertheless involve a small discount if the nature of the irregularity is regarded as heinous.

In practice, the ultimate penalty is negotiated. It is rare for cases not to be settled on this count alone. When considered in the round, the amount involved in a dispute on penalties is often relatively small compared to the actual tax involved and interest on the tax. The Revenue do have power to mitigate interest although this is quite rare. Having said that, the Revenue will often have regard to the resources available to a taxpayer in meeting the overall sum found to be due. They will agree to payment by instalments where appropriate, perhaps with an interest factor built in, or will reduce the tax owed to a lower figure than might otherwise have been argued if the taxpayer had greater resources available. It is not really in the interests of the Revenue to bankrupt a taxpayer if there is some prospect of payment over a period of years.

Finally, even if the original tax return or accounts, etc., were not produced either fraudulently or negligently, but the taxpayer becomes aware that the returns are incorrect, this should be remedied without unreasonable delay. If the Revenue are not notified, by an amendment of self-assessment where appropriate, the returns are deemed by s97 TMA 1970 to have been made negligently. This brings with it the right of the Revenue to assess under s29 TMA 1970.

14.6 Powers of Revenue to obtain information

The TMA 1970 confers considerable powers on the Revenue to obtain information, either from the taxpayer or another person. In practice, the exercise of the statutory powers is rare, as a simple request produces the information required. A time limit is usually placed on the request. In the background the taxpayer or his agent will be aware that the formal powers could be invoked. Resistance to providing information could, no doubt, count against the taxpayer in the determination of penalties, showing a lack of co-operation. An officer may request a meeting or suggest that the records are inspected at the business premises. The *Enquiry Manual* at paragraph 1861 recognises that there is no statutory power to back either of these suggestions, although in practice it may be the best way to help move the investigation forward.

In summary, the main statutory powers of the Revenue are as follows.

(a) Section 19A TMA 1970 supplements the Revenue's power to enquire into the return under s9A(1) or s12AC(1) TMA 1970. A formal notice in writing can be given to the taxpayer to provide documents in the taxpayer's possession or power, accounts or particulars within a time limit of not less than 30 days. This means 30 days after receipt by the taxpayer according to the Special Commissioner in *Self-assessed* v *Inspector of Taxes* [1999] STC (SCD) 253. The documents or information requested must be reasonably required for the purposes of the enquiry. Copies may be given provided the original can be inspected by the Revenue if required. The taxpayer cannot be obliged to produce anything relating to the conduct of any pending appeal. Failure to comply renders the taxpayer liable to penalties under s97AA TMA 1970. In *Accountant* v *Inspector of Taxes* [2000] STC (SCD) 522 the Special Commissioners held that a s19A notice can include a reasonable request for a balance sheet, even though not prepared at the date of the notice.

(b) At any time, s20 TMA 1970 gives an inspector the right to require a taxpayer in writing to produce documents in his possession or power which are relevant to his tax liability, or furnish particulars that the inspector may reasonably require for that purpose. There is also power to obtain information and documents from any other person. However, an inspector can only give notice, whether to a taxpayer or another person, if authorised by the Board of Inland Revenue and with the consent of a General or Special Commissioner. The Board is also empowered to require information to be provided by the taxpayer to a named officer, but only if the Board has reasonable grounds for believing that there may have been a failure to meet tax obligations and the failure is likely to lead to serious prejudice to the proper assessment or collection of tax. Notices can also be given to other persons without naming the taxpayer, under s20(8) TMA 1970, which is likely to be appropriate where a tax avoidance scheme has been marketed. The Revenue cannot require the production of documents which are personal records or journalistic material, as set out in s20(8C).

(c) Under s20A TMA 1970 documents relating to a client's tax liability can be obtained from a tax accountant who has been convicted of an offence in relation to tax or on whom a penalty has been imposed under s99 TMA 1970 for assisting in the preparation of incorrect information for tax purposes. Consent of a circuit judge or equivalent is a pre-requisite to serving a notice under this section.

Restrictions on the powers in the above provisions are contained in s20B TMA 1970 so that:

- a lawyer is protected where he can claim professional privilege;

- an auditor's working papers, etc., cannot be required if they were produced in performing his statutory functions. However, link documents, which have assisted in the preparation of accounts, may be required under a notice, although the protected part can be covered up. The *Enquiry Manual* at paragraph 2572 instructs officers not to ask to see the working papers of an accountant although access to specific link papers may be required where these are effectively part of the accounting record;

- a tax adviser cannot be required to make available documents which are his property and consist of communications between that adviser and his client or another adviser for the purpose of giving or obtaining advice on that client's tax affairs;

- where there is a pending appeal relating to tax, documents or particulars relating to the conduct of such an appeal cannot be required, except where given by the Board under s20(2) TMA 1970; and

- before giving a notice under s20 or s20A TMA 1970 an inspector must give the person a reasonable opportunity to provide the information or documents in question.

Intentionally falsifying, concealing, destroying or otherwise disposing of a document which has been required by a notice is an offence under s20BB TMA 1970, unless permitted under subsection (2). This is clearly a serious matter and if a person is indicted, he runs the risk of imprisonment for up to two years (as well as a fine).

Lastly and hopefully of total academic interest for any reader, is s20C TMA 1970, which contains the Revenue's power, under warrant, to enter premises to obtain documents if the procedure in s20BA TMA 1970, mentioned below, might seriously prejudice the investigation. This is reserved for the very serious cases and so is rarely exercised. A warrant can only be issued if a circuit judge (or equivalent in Scotland and Northern Ireland) is satisfied (on oath given by an officer of the Board) that there is reasonable ground for suspecting a serious fraud and that evidence may be found on the premises. The Revenue's powers in suspected cases of serious fraud are improved by a new s20BA TMA 1970, added by s149 FA 2000 to require the production of documents within 10 working days, if ordered by the appropriate judicial authority.

14.7 Preventing an enquiry

In simple cases, an explanation with the self-assessment return in the white space additional explanation box (or schedule referred to) may pre-empt a Revenue enquiry, which might otherwise lead to a more detailed investigation. An obvious example is disclosing the source of new monies received by a taxpayer, such as a large inheritance. Otherwise, an increase in investment income received by a taxpayer could raise suspicions. It might also be appropriate to comment on particular features of accounts information, such as a low gross profit rate. There may be a simple explanation, which will make sense to an inspector reviewing a return. It has to be acknowledged, though, that providing information might just prompt an enquiry, especially if the details provided are not explained sufficiently well or accurately.

Even more important, perhaps, is to ensure that the return itself, and particularly accounts, have been properly prepared. In the perfect world, there will be detailed reviews of every aspect of a client's business to ensure that the accounts are correct. In the real world, though, this is at a cost, which the client is unlikely to be willing to pay. Nevertheless, a few simple procedures might either eliminate the enquiry or at least defend it if an investigation does result. Thus, just thinking about matters such as the following in discussion with a client will at least produce a file note that can be used at a later date, or be the basis of realising that the draft accounts prepared may not show the full picture:

- gross profit rate;

- source of capital introduced;

- level of drawings based on the taxpayer's circumstances and known style of living; and

- private adjustments such as own consumption, motor expenses and business use of home. Insufficient care on a matter as simple as private motoring could lead to a long investigation on other matters as well, and in itself produce a large liability in settlement as a lump sum.

Moreover, although this may sound obvious, an appreciation of a client's business is essential. It is perhaps not unknown for the individual preparing accounts, even an auditor, to complete the work required without really understanding even the nature of the business. This is particularly relevant in determining when profit should be recognised for accounting purposes. Cut-off procedures around the end of an accounting date are vitally important. For example, cash received after the year-end from the sale of goods or services might properly be recognised in the year-just ended, even though invoiced shortly after the year end. If the services have been completed by the year-end, the income should have been recognised in that year. Awareness of these matters will lead to a better understanding of a client's business, not only ensuring that the taxation liability is correctly stated, but also in providing a better overall service.

The Revenue can, if reasonably required, ask for the production of private bank accounts. Paragraphs 2220 to 2223 of the new *Enquiry Manual* indicate the Revenue's practice in this. In particular, the Manual indicates that non-business bank details should not be requested in the opening letter unless there is a valid reason for such a request. However, failure to meet an informal request when production of private account details is reasonable can be backed up by the statutory powers in s19A TMA 1970.

If money has been banked and which cannot be identified, the usual approach of the Revenue is to argue that it is from a taxable source.

This line of argument is considerably enhanced if they can identify at least one example of omission of taxable receipts from a tax return or accounts. It is usually not cost efficient for a practitioner to review private accounts, but if nothing else he should warn his client to keep records of bankings. An appropriate paragraph in a letter of engagement might well save the practitioner from, at the very least, an argument with his client at a later date.

Statistical information on a particular business might be an appropriate source of information to compare with the results shown by draft accounts. This might be a confidential comparison with similar businesses of clients of the practitioner or from general sources. The Revenue have considerable information available to them, some of which is published in their Business Economic Notes (BENs). The published notes do not contain all of the information available to an inspector but at least will give some guidance. Currently, BENs are available for the following businesses:

BEN 1 – Travel agents
BEN 2 – Road haulage
BEN 3 – Lodging industry
BEN 4 – Hairdressers
BEN 5 – Waste materials reclamation and disposal
BEN 6 – Funeral directors
BEN 7 – Dentists
BEN 8 – Florists
BEN 9 – Licensed victuallers
BEN 10 – The jewellery trade
BEN 11 – Electrical retailers
BEN 12 – Antiques and fine art dealers
BEN 13 – Fish and chip shops
BEN 14 – The pet industry
BEN 15 – Veterinary surgeons
BEN 16 – Catering – general
BEN 17 – Catering – restaurants
BEN 18 – Catering – fast foods, cafes and snack bars
BEN 19 – Farming – stock valuation for income tax purposes
BEN 20 – Insurance brokers and agents
BEN 21 – Residential rest and nursing homes
BEN 22 – Dispensing chemists
BEN 23 – Driving instructors
BEN 24 – Independent fishmongers
BEN 25 – Taxi cabs and private hire vehicles
BEN 26 – Confectioners, tobacconists and newsagents

Index

References are to paragraph numbers